WOF MANUAL

for

850 COMMANDO ELECTRIC START

MARK 3
motorcycles

	FROM 1975
MODELS 850:	INTERSTATE
	ROADSTER
	HI-RIDER (USA. and Canada only)
	INTERPOL

Commencing at Engine No. 325001 — Frame No. F125001

NORTON TRIUMPH INTERNATIONAL LIMITED

KITTS GREEN - BIRMINGHAM B33. 0LF - ENGLAND

TELEPHONE: BIRMINGHAM 021-784-5151 · TELEX: 339478   Publication No. 00-4224

ACKNOWLEDGEMENT

We would like to take the opportunity to extend our appreciation to Norton Motorcycle Company for the publications included in this compilation. It is important to remember that the company was founded in 1898 and helped pave the way for the motorcycles we enjoy today. We are pleased to offer this reprint as a service to all Norton motorcycle owners and collectors worldwide, and we extend our thanks to the Norton Motorcycle Company for their contribution to the British motorcycle industry.

INTRODUCTION

Welcome to the world of digital publishing ~ the book you now hold in your hand was printed using the latest state of the art digital technology. The advent of print-on-demand has forever changed the publishing process, never has information been so accessible and it is our hope that this book serves your informational needs for years to come. If this is your first exposure to digital publishing, we hope that you are pleased with the results. Many more titles of interest to the classic automobile and motorcycle enthusiast, collector and restorer are available via our website at www.VelocePress.com. We hope that you find this title as interesting as we do.

NOTE FROM THE PUBLISHER

The information presented is true and complete to the best of our knowledge. All recommendations are made without any guarantees on the part of the author or the publisher, who also disclaim all liability incurred with the use of this information.

TRADEMARKS

INFORMATION ON THE USE OF THIS PUBLICATION

This manual is an invaluable resource for those interested in performing their own maintenance. However, in today's information age we are constantly subject to changes in common practice, new technology, availability of improved materials and increased awareness of chemical toxicity. As such, it is advised that the user consult with an experienced professional prior to undertaking any procedure described herein. While every care has been taken to ensure correctness of information, it is obviously not possible to guarantee complete freedom from errors or omissions or to accept liability arising from such errors or omissions. Therefore, any individual that uses the information contained within, or elects to perform or participate in do-it-yourself repairs or modifications acknowledges that there is a risk factor involved and that the publisher or its associates cannot be held responsible for personal injury or property damage resulting from the use of the information or the outcome of such procedures.

WARNING!

One final word of advice, this publication is intended to be used as a reference guide, and when in doubt the reader should consult with a qualified technician.

FOREWORD

The purpose of this manual is to provide the necessary technical instructions to enable distributor and dealer staff, and also enthusiastic private owners, to carry out all routine maintenance, running repairs and major overhaul operations.

To provide the clearest possible technical information, and in view of the major improvements and mandatory design changes introduced on the latest 850 Commando, it has been decided to omit all earlier versions and devote this manual solely to the Electric-Start, Left-foot-shift 1975 Mark III model.

Mark III Commencing Engine No. 325001.
Frame No. F. 125001.
For earlier models refer to previous publications issued.
From 1970   Part No. 065146.

Separate sections of the manual cover major areas and, where necessary, cross references are used to facilitate step by step dismantling and re-assembly. The manual is well provided with line illustrations for clarity and care has been taken to ensure that each illustration fulfils a useful purpose rather than merely increasing manual content.

Where special service tools are necessary, they are referred to by part number in the text. An illustrated service tools catalogue is available covering special tools common to previous 850 models. New tools will be catalogued as soon as possible, and page size and piercing will be as before, allowing inclusion in the master binder in due course.

A fully illustrated parts list and Rider's Manual are available, and will further assist service operations. Publication Numbers 00-5756 and 066240 respectively

To ensure repair to the same standards as used for a new Commando, it is essential to use only genuine Norton spares available through the normal spares supply system. The main distributors for the various markets of the world are given below:

EUROPE: Norton Triumph Europe Limited,
North Way,
Walworth, Andover,
Hampshire.
Telephone: Andover (0264) 61414

U.S.A.

West of Mississippi River:
Norton Triumph Corporation,
6765 Paramount Boulevard,
North Long Beach,
California 90805.
Telephone : (213) 531-7138.

East of Mississippi River:
Berliner Motor Corporation,
Railroad Street and Plant Road
Hasbrouck Heights,
New Jersey 07604.
Telephone : (201) 288–9696.

CANADA:

CANADA
Norton Triumph Canada Limited.,
9001 Salley Street,
La Salle,
Province of Quebec.
Telephone : (514) 363–7066.

AUSTRALASIA,
NEW ZEALAND,
FAR EAST:

Norton Triumph Motorcycles Pty. Ltd.,
25 Moxon Road,
Punchbowl,
New South Wales, 2196.
Telephone : Punchbowl 02–700731.

SOUTH AFRICA:

Jack's Motors (Pty.) Ltd.
115 Main Street,
Johannesburg.
Telephone : Johannesburg 217.021.

CONTENTS

Each section is laid out generally in order of disassembly and assembly; however, use the following index to locate any particular subject.

ENGINE

BRAKES WHEELS AND TIRES

ELECTRICAL

ROUTINE MAINTENANCE

GLOSSARY OF PART NAMES AND ALTERNATIVES

ENGINE

Gudgeon Pin	Piston pin. Small-end pin. Wrist pin.
Inlet Valve	Intake valve.
Piston Oil Control Ring	Piston scraper ring.
Induction Manifold	Inlet manifold. Intake manifold.
Oil Sump	Oil pan. Oil reservoir. Sump tray.
Muffler	Silencer. Expansion box.
Gasket	Joint. Sealing washer.
Engine	Motor.
Banjo Bolt	Pipe union bolt.
Crankcase Drain Plug	Sump plug.
Garter Type Seal	Spring pressure seal.
Mute	Sound deadener.
Oil Filter Gauze	Gauze strainer.

CLUTCH

Clutch Lining	Friction plate.
Primary Chaincase	Oil bath. Transmission case.
Clutch Operating Arm	Clutch thrust mechanism.
Clutch Sprocket	Clutch drum. Clutch housing.

GEARBOX

Gearbox	Transmission.
Gear Lever	Change speed lever. Gearshift lever.
Selector Fork	Change speed fork. Shift fork.
Countershaft	High sleeve gear. Output gear.
Countershaft Sprocket	Final drive sprocket. Gearbox sprocket.
Kickstarter	Starter pedal.

FRAME

Frame Rails	Frame tubes.
Oil Tank	Oil reservoir.
Battery Tray	Battery carrier.
Crankcase Shield	Sump shield. Skid plate. Bash plate. Rock guard.
Accessory Cover	L.H. side cover.
Grab Rail	Sissy bar. Passenger handhold.
Footrest	Footpeg.
Passenger Footrest	Pillion footrest. Buddy peg.
Prop. Stand	Side stand. Jiffy stand.
Frame	Chassis.
Swinging Arm	Swinging fork. Pivoting fork.
Suspension Unit	Rear shock absorber. Shock.

FORK

Front Fork	Telescopic fork. "Roadholder" fork. Front suspension.
Main Tube	Stanchion.
Fork Slider	Bottom member. Sliding member.

FUEL

Throttle Stop Adjuster Screw	Idle speed adjuster
Pilot Air Screw	Idling screw. Volume control screw. Idle mixture screw.
Pilot Jet	Slow running jet. Idling jet.
Fuel Line	Petrol pipe. Gas line.
Fuel Tap	Petrol tap. Gas cock. Petcock.
Air Cleaner	Air filter. Air box. Air silencer.
Fuel Tank	Petrol tank. Gas tank.
Petrol	Gasoline.
Paraffin	Kerosene.

ELECTRICAL

A.C. Generator	Alternator.
Alternator	Rotor and stator.
Capacitor	Condenser.
Lens	Glass.
Direction Indicators	Flashing indicators. Turn signals. Flashers
Rear Lamp	Tail lamp. Stop/tail lamp.
Headlamp Rim	Headlamp bezel. Headlamp surround.
H.T. Lead	High tension lead. Plug lead.
Assimilator	Simulator, Actuator. Control unit.
Contact Breaker	Points. Breaker.

WHEELS AND BRAKES

Axle	Spindle.
Security Bolt	Tire lock.
Brake Expander	Brake cam.
Master Cylinder	Main cylinder. Reservoir.
Brake Lining	Brake facing.

INSTRUMENTS

Odometer	Mileage recorder.
Speedometer Gearbox	Speedometer drive box.
Tachometer	Rev. counter. Engine speed indicator.

Technical Data

Technical Data

SECTION A

TECHNICAL DATA

FRAME, ENGINE MOUNTINGS AND REAR SUSPENSION UNITS

Steering head bearing type: Single-row ball: Double sealed.
Front and Rear engine mountings.

Adjustable Isolastic: Adjuster on Right-hand side Front.
Adjuster on Left-hand side Rear.

Ideal Free Play 0·005"/0·006" equivalent to "1½ holes" turn on adjuster, Front and Rear.

ISOLASTIC MOUNTINGS ADJUSTMENT: METHOD

Engineering Instruction No. 19 refers as follows:–

1. Loosen the nut on the ½" diameter (¾" A/F) through bolt at least two turns.
2. Slide the clip away from the 8 holes in the adjuster (chaincase side on the rear, timing side on the front).
3. Turn the adjuster clockwise, as tightly as possible with tool 06-6532. Do not use extra leverage.
4. Back the adjuster off 1/5 turn (1½ holes).
5. Tighten nut on through bolt (torque wrench setting 30 lbs./ft. 4·15 Kg/m).
6. Replace clip to cover holes in adjuster.

Rear suspension units

Type – Girling : Spring/oil damped
Total length 13 inches between centres.
Spring fitted length : 8·4 in. (213·36 mm)
Spring colour code : Red/Yellow/Red (chrome spring)
Spring rate : 126 lb. per inch
Sping free length : 8·75 in. (222·25 mm)

SPEEDOMETER GEARING

Using Dunlop 4·10 in. x 19 in. rear tyre
Rolling radius : 12·57 in. (319·3 mm)
Revs./mile : 806
Gearbox ratio : 15/12   1 : 1·25

Technical Data

WHEELS AND BRAKES

Front wheel

    Rim size : WM2 – 19

    Spokes – Disc brake wheel: Inner L.H. – 90° head 9 SWG 0·270 (6·9 mm) head dia.

                                             Outer L.H. – 90° head 9 SWG 0·270 (6·9 mm) head (80° bend)

                                             Right hand – 90° head 8 SWG 0·290 (7·35 mm) head dia.

    Wheel bearing L.H. : 17 mm x 40 mm x 12 mm

    Wheel bearing R.H. : NM 17721 : 17 mm x 40 mm x 16 mm (Double row).

    Bearing housing I.D. : 1·5732 in./1·5740 in. (39·96 mm/39·98 mm)

    Spindle (bearing/dia.) : 0·6671/0·6670 in. (16·945/16·942 mm)

    Tire size : 4·10X19

    Tire pressure : 26 lbs./psi (1·83 kg/sq. cm.). Refer "Tire Pressures" section for permissible
                variation

    Tire diameter (Dunlop) : 26·46 in. (672 mm)

    Sectional width (Dunlop) : 4 in. (101·6 mm)

Front brake (disc) & Rear brake (disc) using common components.

    Type : Disc – hydraulically operated

    Pad type : Steel backed, moulded and bonded friction material

    Pad friction area diam. : 1·65 in. (41·9 mm)

    Pad new thickness (Pad and backing together) : ·38/·37 in. (9·652/9·398 mm)

    Pad minimum thickness 0·0625 in. (1·5875 mm)

    Disc diameter : 10·70 in. (271·7 mm)

    Disc width at friction area : 0·260/0·250 in. (6·604/6·35 mm)

    Brake fluid type : Lockheed series 329 Hydraulic Fluid for disc brakes.
                (Complies with U.S. Safety Standard 116).

Rear wheel

    Rim size : WM2 – 19

    Rear Spokes: { L.H.Outer   6·155″ (153·8 mm) x 9 SWG Acute Angle Head
                        L.H. Inner 6·140″ (155·9 mm) x 9 SWG Obtuse Angle Head
                        Right hand 8·075″ (205·1 mm) x 9 SWG (Fitted in Hub Cone).

    Wheel bearing L.H. : 17 mm x 40 mm x 12 mm (Single sided rubber seal).

    Wheel bearings: Ball Journal: L.H. 17 mm x 40 mm x 12 mm/R.H. 20 mm x 47 mm x 14 mm.

    Sprocket bearing: NM.17721: Double Row: 17 mm x 40 mm x 16 mm.

    Tire size : 4·10 x 19 in. (104·14 x 482·60)

    Tire pressure : 26 lbs./psi (1·83 kg/sq. cm.). Refer "Tire Pressure" section for permissible
                variation

    Tire diameter (Dunlop) : 26·46 in. (672·084 mm)

    Tire sectional width (Dunlop) : 4 in. (101·6 mm)

Technical Data

Front forks

    Type : Telescopic, hydraulically damped, internal springs

    Main tube O.D.: 1·3589/1·3574 in. (34·518 mm/34·480 mm)

    Top bush fitted I.D.: 1·3595/1·3604 in. (34·531/34·556 mm)

    Bottom bush O.D.: 1·4979/1·4990 in. (38·049 mm/38·075 mm)

    Fork slider I.D.: 1·4995/1·5010 in. (38·087/38·125 mm)

    Spring – No. of coils: $75\frac{1}{2}$ approx.

           Free length : 18·687 in. (474·65 mm)

           Rate : 36·5 lb./in. (6·52 kg/cm) Red paint marked

    Steering crown lug and stem

        Stem diam. at bearing areas: 0·9840/0·9836 in. (24·97/24·96 mm)

        Fork tube top nut hexagon size: 1·3125/1·3005 in. (33·33/33·03 mm)

        Head bearing spacer length: 5·06 in. (128·524 mm)

    Fork leg capacity : 150 cc (5 fl. oz.) each leg

    Total fork movement : 6 in. (15·24 cm)

ELECTRICAL

    System voltage : 12 volt – Positive earth

    Alternator type: RM23: 180 watts.

    Rectifier type: 2DV. 406.

    Zener diode type: Z D 715. 2 OFF.

    Battery type: Norton Villiers 066515; Yuasa YB.14.L or B.64.12. 12 volt.

    Battery rating: 13AH at 10 hour rate.

    Coil type: 17M6 – 2 OFF.

    Ballast resistor type: 3 BR.

    Contact breaker type: 10CA.

    Warning light assimilator type: 066393 standard / 066392 Canada

    Fuse rating : 35 amp ($17\frac{1}{2}$ amp continuous rated)

    Direction indicator flasher unit type : 8 FL.

    Capacitor: Lucas 2MC.

    Starter Motor: Prestolite MGD.4111.

    Solenoid for Starter: Prestolite SAZ 42OIN.

    Brake light switch: 2SH. 2 OFF.

    Condenser Pack: Lucas 2CP.

    Reflector: Lucas RER14.

    Horn: Lucas 9H.

    Master Switch: Lucas 149SA. standard: Lucas 30825(Canada only)

    Lock Master Switch: Wilmot Breedon 1/6545.

    Bulbs:

           Headlight: STD Type 370 – 12 volt – 45/40 watt. Continental Type 410 – 12 volt –
           45/40 watt. France Type 411 – 12 volt – 45/40 watt.

           Quartz Halogen

           Headlamp Bulb: STD Type 463 – 12 volt – 60/55 watt. Continental Type 472 –
           12 volt – 60/55 watt.

           Tail light/stop light : Type 380 – 12 volt – 21/6 watt, transverse offset pin

           Parking light : Type 989 – 12 volt – 5 watt, coil, miniature bayonet cap

           Direction indicator lights : Type 382 - 12 volt - 21 watt

           Warning lights type : Type 281 – 12 volt – 1·2 watt, coil, sub-miniature

    Warning Lights:

    Maker: Pistor & Kronert.

    Complete Replacement Unit.

        Amber: 06·5734 ⎫

        Green: 06·5735 ⎬ Type P & K

        Blue: 06·5736 ⎰ 1208/6CR A1/1N.

        Red: 06·5737 ⎭

           Speedo Tacho Bulbs: Type 643 – 12 volt – 2·2 watt.

Technical Data

ENGINE

Specification:
- Capacity: 828 cc (50·5 cu. in.)
- Bore: 3·030 in. (77 mm)
- Stroke: 3·503 in. (89 mm)
- Max. Torque: 56 lb./ft. at 5000 r.p.m.
  Peak Power - 5,800 r.p.m.
- Compression Ratio: 8½ : 1

Crankshaft
- Material: EN16
- Big end journal diameter: 1·7509/1·7504 in. (44·472/44·460 mm)
- Crankcheek bolts: EN 16 S
- Balance factor: 63% Dry, 52% Wet. 23·55 oz (667·6 gms) on each journal
- Permissible end Float: 0·010"/0·024" (0·254 mm/0·610 mm)

Main bearings:
- Drive side and Timing side: 30 mm x 72 mm x 19 mm Special Roller (Single Lipped)

Connecting rods
- Material: Aluminium alloy BS.L83 or 2L65 or L77
- Length between centres: 5·877/5·873 in. (129·276/129·274 mm)
- Big end eye I.D.: (Less shells cap bolted on) 1·8950/1·8955 in. (48·133/48·145 mm)
- Width at big end eye: 1·010/1·008 in. (25·65/25·60 mm)
- Rod side clearance: 0·013 – 0·016 (0·330/0·406 mm)
- Rod end clearance: Less than 0·001 (0·0254 mm)

Pistons
- Material: BS.1490 – LM..13WP
- Wrist pin boss I.D.: 0·6869/0·6867 in. (17·447/17·442 mm)
- Diameter: bottom of Skirt 3·028/3·0271 in. (76·888/76·913 mm) std. bore

Piston rings
- Type: Top chrome compression. Second compression.
  Taper. "S.E." oil control.
- Top ring fitted gap: 0·010 – 0·012 in. (0·254/0·305 mm)
- Middle ring (taper) fitted gap: 0·008 – 0·012 in. (0·203/0·305 mm)

Wrist pins (Gudgeon pins)
- Length: 2·559/2·544 in. (65 mm/64·619 mm)
- Diameter: 0·6869/0·6867 in. (17·447 mm/17·442 mm)

Technical Data

Cylinder block

    Material : Cast iron
    Finished size : Grade A 3·0315/3·0320 in.
                 Grade B 3·0320/3·0325 in.

Cylinder head

Material :	RR 53 B
Valve seat angle :	45°
Inlet port nominal dia. :	1⅛ in. (28·573 mm)
Ex. port nominal dia. :	1¼ in. (31·75 mm)
Ex. ring thread size :	1·997 in. x 14 T.P.I. (50·93 mm)

Camshaft

Material :	EN 32 B
Maximum lift – inlet	0·332 in. (8·432 mm)
exhaust :	0·322 in. (8·178 mm)
Base circle dia. :	0·885 in. (22·479 mm)
Bearing journal dia. :	0·8735 in. (22·187 mm)

Camshaft bushes

Fitted I.D. (Left bush) :	0·8750 in. (22·225 mm)
Fitted I.D. (Right bushes) :	0·8750 in. (22·225 mm)

Tappets

    Material : Cast iron Grade 14 – stellite tipped

Push rods

    Material : Heat treated Dural tube "B" or "S"
    Inlet – assembled length : 8·166/8·130 in. (207·416/206·466 mm)
    Exhaust-assembled length : 7·321/7·285 in. (186·053/185·039 mm)

Rockers

    Material : EN33
    Rocker ratio – inlet : 1·13 :1
    Rocker ratio – exhaust : 1·13 :1
    Bore diameter : 0·4998/0·5003 in. (12·694/12·708 mm)
    Adjuster thread size : 9·39 mm x 26 TPI. Whit Form

Technical Data

Rocker shaft
    Diameter : ·4988/·4985 in. (12·669/12·661 mm)

Valve (tappet) Clearances (engine cold)
    Inlet : ·006 in. (0·15 mm)
    Exhaust : ·008 in. (0,2 mm)

Valve Lift
    Inlet & Exhaust 0·375 in. (9·525 mm)

Valve duration : (excluding ramps)
    152°

Valves
    Material : Inlet – EN52 – Chrome plated stem
              Ex. – KE965 – Chrome plated stem
    Inlet – head dia. : 1·490 in. (37·846 mm)
        stem dia. (plated area) : 0·3115/0·3105 in. (7·912/7·886)
    Exhaust – head dia. : 1·302 in (33·0708 mm)
           stem dia. : 0·3115/0·3105 in. (7·912/7·886 mm)

Valve guides
    Inside dia. : 0·3145/0·3135 in. (7·988/7·962 mm)
    Outside dia. : 0·6265/0·6260 in. (15·913/15·900 mm)
    Heat resisting washer material : Tuffnol grade ASP
    Heat resisting washer thickness : 0·062 in. (1·574 mm)

	Inlet	Exhaust
Valve springs		
Inner – free length : 1·482 in. (37·642 mm)	1·197 in.	1·222 in.
Fitted length	(30·40 mm)	(31·04 mm)
Outer – free length : 1·618 in. (41·097 mm)	1·259 in.	1·284 in.
Fitted length	(31·98 mm)	(32·61 mm)

Valve Spring Collapse
    Minimum acceptable free lengh :   Outer 1·500 in (38·100 mm)
                                  Inuer 1·375 in (34·925 mm)

Valve timing (measured at ·013 in. (·3302 mm)
    cam lift

Inlet opens BTDC	50°
Inlet closes ABDC	74°
Exhaust opens BBDC	82°
Exhaust closes ATDC	42°

Intermediate timing gear
    Bush material : Phosphor bronze
    Bush finished dia. : 0·5627/0·5620 in. (14·292/14·274 mm)

Intermediate gear shaft dia. : 0·5615/0·5610 in. (14·262/14·249 mm)

GENERAL GUIDANCE TABLE – TORQUE RECOMMENDATIONS

BOLTS & NUTS – TIGHTENING TORQUES: LBF/FT.
(From G.K.N. – Davis & Timmins Ltd.).

N.B. These figures are for "raw material" fasteners (viz. unplated). Lubrication, plating, and hardened mating faces make bolts easier to turn and therefore lower torques should be used.

Recommended Torque for UNF-S. cond.

Plated Bolts	*Condition	UNC A & B	UNC S	UNC V	UNF A & B	UNF S	UNF V	BSW A & B	BSW S	BSW V	BSF A & B	BSF S	BSF V
lbs./ft.	$\frac{3}{16}$							2	4		2½	5	
	No. 10	2	4½										
	2 BA										2½	5	
8	$\frac{1}{4}$	4	9	12	4	11	14	4	8	12	4	9	14
15	$\frac{5}{16}$	7	20	25	8	22	28	7	17	25	8	18	27
25	$\frac{3}{8}$	13	35	45	14	40	50	13	30	45	14	32	49
40	$\frac{7}{16}$	21	56	73	22	62	81	21	47	72	22	51	78
60	$\frac{1}{2}$	31	85	111	36	96	125	31	70	107	34	77	118
80	$\frac{9}{16}$	46	123	160	51	137	180	46	105	160	50	112	173
	$\frac{5}{8}$	64	170	212	72	192	238	63	145	210	68	155	224
	$\frac{3}{4}$	113	300	393	126	335	435	113	255	390	118	268	410
	$\frac{7}{8}$	182	485	632	200	535	695	182	410	628	191	432	660
	1	274	730	950	297	795	1000	272	620	945	288	650	995
	$1\frac{1}{8}$	388	1035	1345	433	1160	1500	388	875	1330	410	930	1420

(Left margin note, vertical text: "Use these torque figures for UNF-S. cond. Plated bolts except when there is good reason to change them. If using higher torques, check quality of nuts.")

Bright mild steel: En 1A is in Condition B (28 tonf/in²) Brass has tensile strength 25 tonf/in².

B.S. 1768

	BOLTS		NUTS		
*Condition	Min. Tensile Strength Ton. Sq. in.		Grade	Brinell Hardness	Suitable for Bolts
A & B	28		0	120/235	A, B, P
P	35		1	163/240	S
S	50		3	183/300	T
T	55		5	270/335	V, X
V	65				
X	75				

Controlling British Standards employed in manufacture }
Dimensions of Bolts and Nuts: BS 1768
Screw Threads (UN): BS 1580
Plating (0·06 to 0·75 dia): BS 3382   (over 0·75) BS 1706

Technical Data

Camshaft chain
    Size: 0·375 in. x 0·225. Single row (Endless)
    No. of links: 38
    Ideal adjustment: $\frac{3}{16}$ in. (4·8 mm) up and down on top run of chain

Ignition timing
    Fully advanced position: 28° BTDC

Contact breaker
    Points gap: 0·014/0·016 in. (0·35/0·40 mm)
    Centre bolt thread size: $\frac{1}{4}$ in. x 26 T.P.I.

Spark plug
    Type: Champion N7Y (was N6Y)
    Gap: 0·023/0·028 in. (0·59/0·72 mm)

Carburetor
    Type: Twin concentric float Amal 932 32 mm
    Main jet: 230
    Needle jet: 0·106
    Needle position: Top (Weakest notch).
    Throttle valve: $3\frac{1}{2}$
    Needle: 928/104
    Choke (spray) tube: 928/107

Air filter
    Element type: Oil Impregnated Foam.

TORQUE SETTINGS

    Cylinder head nuts and bolts ($\frac{3}{8}$ in.) : 30 lbs./ft. (4·15 Kg/m)
    Cylinder head bolts ($\frac{5}{16}$ in.) : 20 lbs./ft. (2·75 Kg/m)
    Cylinder base nuts ($\frac{3}{8}$ in.) : 25 lbs./ft. (3·45 Kg/m)
    Cylinder base nuts ($\frac{5}{16}$ in.) : 20 lbs./ft. (2·75 Kg/m)
    Cylinder through bolt: 30 lbs./ft. (4·15 Kg/m)
    Connecting rod nuts. : 25 lbs./ft. (3·45 Kg/m)
    Rocker spindle cover plate bolt: 8 lbs./ft. (1·11 Kg/m)
    Crankshaft Flywheel nuts: 30 lbs./ft. (4·15 Kg/m)
    Cam chain tensioner nuts : 15 lbs./ft. (2·07 Kg/m)
    Oil pump stud nuts : 15 lbs./ft. (2·07 Kg/m)
    Rocker feed banjo bolts : 15 lbs./ft. (2·07 Kg/m)

Technical Data

Engine mount bolts : 25 lbs./ft. (3·45 Kg/m)
Rotor nut Crankshaft: 70 lb./ft. (9·68 Kg/m)
Alternator mounting stud nuts: lbs./15 ft. (2·07 Kg/m)
Clutch-to-mainshaft nut: 70 lbs./ft. (9·68 Kg/m)
Mainshaft nut : 40/50 lbs./ft. (5·50 Kg/m)
Countershaft sprocket nut : 80 lbs/ft.. (11·06 Kg/m)
Gearbox inner cover nuts : 12 lbs./ft. (1·66 Kg/m)
Top gearbox fixing bolts : 55 lbs./ft. (7·60 Kg/m)
Oil pressure release valve : 25 lbs./ft. (3·46 Kg/m)

The part numbers referred to, are taken from the "850 Commando Parts List", Publication No.065034.
The references following the part numbers, refer back to the parts list, as indicated below:-
The initial number refers to the group, while the number after the decimal point indicates the plate
number.

NM 25087	Speedo cable to speedo G.B: 15 lbs./ft. (2·07 Kg/m)
060361 (18·2)	Front wheel spindle nut: 60 lbs./ft. (8·30 Kg/m)
27815 (17·57)	Front fork pinch bolt nut: 15 lbs./ft. (2·07 Kg/m)
060599 (9·27)	Kickstart pinch bolt: 25 lbf.ft. 3·46 Kgm
060348 (12·4)	Carburettor stud nut and screws (12·6): 8 lbf.ft. 1·10 Kgm
NM 19437 (13·2)	Engine steady to head screw: 12 lbs./ft. (1·66 Kg/m)
060348 (13·9)	Engine steady stud nut: 12 lbs./ft. (1·66 Kg/m)
063245 (1·13)	Engine front plate nut: 25 lbs./ft. (3·46 Kg/m)
063598 (13·16)	Front engine mounting nut. 30 lbs./ft. (4·15 Kg/m)
063024 (13·31)	Rear engine plate nut: 30 lbs./ft. (4·15 Kg/m)
063246 (13·34)	Rear engine plate nut: 20 lbs./ft. (2·76 Kg/m)
061702 (13·52)	Centre stand nut: 45 lbs./ft. (6·21 Kg/m)
060651 (14·20)	Rear wheel adjuster nut: 8 lbs./ft. (1·10 Kg/m)
060327 (14·22)	Swinging arm pivot pin bolt: 10 lbs./ft. (1·38 Kg/m)
060029 (14·35)	Suspension unit nuts: 25 lbs./ft. (3·46 Kg/m)
063089 (14·43)	Prop stand nut: 60 lbs./ft. (8·30 Kg/m)
033057 (14·51)	Chain guard nut. 8 lbs./ft. (1·10 Kg/m)
060029 (15·6)	Rear side plate mounting nut: 25 lbs./ft. (3·46 Kg/m)
063598 (15·9)	Main isolastic nut: 30 lbs./ft. (4·15 Kg/m)
20948 (15·13)	Footpeg nut: 40 lbs./ft. (5·53 Kg/m)
060348 (15·17)	Footrest mounting flange nut: 8 lbs./ft. (1·10 Kg/m)
061246 (15·18)	Footrest mounting bolt: 15 lbs./ft. (2·07 Kg/m)
062240 (23·16)	Nut (exhaust balance pipe clamp bolt): 7 lbs./ft. (0·97 Kg/m)
060652 (16·6)	Bolt. Oil Tank mounting: 4 lbs./ft. (0·553 Kg/m)
030448 (16·20)	Oil junction block bolt. 8 lbs./ft. (1·10 Kg/m)
060359 (17·18)	Fork-Damper tube anchor bolt: 10 lbs./ft. (1·38 Kg/m)
060345 (17·33)	Stanchion top chrome nuts: 30 lbs./ft. (4·15 Kg/m)
060355 (17·37)	Nut mudguard bridge stud: 8 lbs./ft. (1·10 Kg/m)
0700101 (17·43)	Steering stem nut: 30 lbs./ft. (4·15 Kg/m)
061911 (17·44)	Socket pinch screw – lower yoke: 25 lbs./ft. (3·46 Kg/m)
27815 (17·57)	Front spindle – Pinch bolt nut: 10 lbs./ft. (1·38 Kg/m)
060361 (18·2)	Front spindle nut: 60 lbs./ft. (8·30 Kg/m)
060348 (18·24)	Disc to hub nuts: 20 lbs./ft. (2·76 Kg/m)
0700291 (18·34)	Caliper to fork bolts: 30 lbs./ft. (4·15 Kg/m)
	Caliper end plug: 25 lbs./ft. (3·46 Kg/m)
060292 (20·3)	Rear wheel nut (dummy spindle): 80 lbs./ft. (11·06 Kg/m)
060289 (20·2)	Rear wheel spindle: 80 lbs./ft. (11·06 Kg/m)
062240 (22·22)	Front brake lever pivot bolt nut: 25 lbs./ft. inches (0·29 Kg/m)
26078 (22·28)	Front hydraulic hose nut: 15 lbs./ft. (2·07 Kg/m)
062240 (23·16)	Nut (balance pipe clamp bolt): 7 lbs./ft. (0·97 Kg/m)
060029 (23·21)	Silencer clip clamp-bolt nut: 9 lbs./ft. (1·24 Kg/m)
060618 (23·22)	Bolt pillion footrest-plate: 25 lbs./ft. (3·46 Kg/m)
060348 (23·29)	Nut footrest-plate: 10 lbs./ft. (1·10 Kg/m)
0700267 (23·37)	Nut pillion footrest pivot bolt nut: 8 lbs./ft. (1·10 Kg/m)
060678 (26·6)	Mudguard stay nut: 4 lbs./ft. (0·553 Kg/m)

Technical Data

060357 (26·7)	Front mudguard stay bolt: 10 lbs./ft.	(1·38 Kg/m)
060029 (27·5)	Rear mudguard nut: 8 lbs./ft.	(1·10 Kg/m)
060348 (27·9)	Rear mudguard nut. $\frac{5}{16}$: 15 lbs./ft.	(2·07 Kg/m)
062240 (27·10)	Rear mudguard nut. $\frac{1}{4}$: 8 lbs./ft.	(1·10 Kg/m)
062921 (27·14)	Tail lamp-pillar nut: 2 lbs./ft.	(2·77 Kg/m)
060348 (27·21)	Lift handle-clip nut. $\frac{1}{4}$: 8 lbs./ft.	(1·10 Kg/m)
25607 (29·5)	H.T. and Coil clip bolts: 10 lbs./inches	(0·12 Kg/m)
062348 (29·6)	Spark plug: 15 lbs./ft.	(2·07 Kg/m)
M1002/15E (29·12)	Reflector nut: 20 lbs./inches	(0·27 Kg/m)
060865 (29·14)	Coil mounting bracket bolts: 8 lbs./ft.	(1·10 Kg/m)
033057 (29·33)	Rectifier nut: 3 lbs./ft.	(0·42 Kg/m)
25607 (29·41)	Screw (condenser pack): 2 lbs./ft.	(0·27 Kg/m)
22061 (29·43)	Nut (condenser pack): 2 lbs./ft.	(0·27 Kg/m)
033057 (29·46)	Zener diode nut: 24 lbs./inches	(0·27 Kg/m)
033057 (29·49)	Horn nut: 8 lbs./ft.	(1·10 Kg/m)
062321 (30·34)	Headlamp bolt: 15 lbs./ft.	(2·07 Kg/m)

GEARBOX

Ball journal bearings:
  Mainshaft (Clutch end) Ball journal $1\frac{1}{4}$ in. x $2\frac{1}{2}$ in. x $\frac{5}{8}$ in.
  Mainshaft (K/S end): Ball journal $\frac{5}{8}$ in. x $1\frac{9}{16}$ x $\frac{7}{16}$ in.
  Layshaft (Clutch end): Ball journal 17 mm x 40 mm x 12 mm

Reductions
  4th (HIGH): 1:1
  3rd: 1·21:1
  2nd: 1·70:1
  1st (LOW): 2·56:1

No. of teeth on pinions
  Layshaft: 4th 18t
  Layshaft: 3rd 20t
  Layshaft: 2nd 24t
  Layshaft: 1st 28t
  Mainshaft: 4th 23t
  Mainshaft: 3rd 21t
  Mainshaft: 2nd 18t
  Mainshaft: 1st 14t

Theoretical road speeds using various countershaft (gearbox) sprockets
  Table assumes standard sprockets: Engine 26T ⎫
  Clutch 57T ⎬ Primary drive ratio 2·192:1
  Rear 42 T ⎭

	Sprocket Teeth	19	20	21	22	23
	Overall Gear Ratio	4·84	4·60	4·38	4·18	3·99
Engine RPM	6000	92	97	102	106	112
	6500	99	105	110	115	121
	7000	107	113	119	124	130

Technical Data

Overall Ratios	With 19T Gearbox Sprocket	1975 Mark III USA/Canada With 20T Gearbox Sprocket	With 21T Gearbox Sprocket	1975 Mark III Except USA/Canada With 22T Gearbox Sprocket
4th (HIGH):	4·84 :1	4·60 :1	4·38	4·18 :1
3rd:	5·90 :1	5·57 :1	5·30 :1	5·10 :1
2nd:	8·25 :1	7·83 :1	7·45 :1	6·84 :1
1st (Low):	12·40 :1	11·79 :1	11·20 :1	10·71: 1

Gearbox

    High gear bush O.D.: 0·9060/0·9053 in. (23·012/22·995 mm)
    High gear bush I.D.: 0·8145/0·8140 in. (20·688/20·675 mm)
    High gear bush fitted I.D.: 0·8133/·8120 in. (20·657/20·625 mm)
    K/S spindle bush fitted I.D.: 1·126 in./1·124 in. (28·60/28·549 mm)
    Mainshaft second gear bush fitted I.D.: 0·8125/0·8115 in. (20·637/20·612 mm)
    Layshaft third gear bush fitted I.D.: 0·8125/0·81 in. (20·637/20·574 mm)
    Layshaft first gear bush fitted I.D.: 0·6885/0·6875 in. (17·488/17·462 mm)
    Footchange spindle bush, K/S case fitted I.D.: 0·6290/0·6285 in. (15·976/15·964 mm)
    Camplate/Quadrant bush fitted I.D.: 0·5005/0·4995 in. (12·713/12·687 mm)
    Layshaft bush I.D.: 0·675/0·673 in. (17·145/17·094 mm)
    Gearbox sprocket: 20T or 22T Standard (Alternative sprockets available – see table above)

Camplate plunger spring

    Free length: 1·500 in. (38·1 mm)
    Spring rate: 21 lbs./in. (3·74 kg/mm)

    Selector spindle diameter: 0·3740/0·3735 in. (9·499/9·486 mm)
    Selector fork bore: 0·3755/0·3745 in. (8·537/9·525 mm)

Primary Transmission and Rear Chain

    Engine sprocket no. of teeth: 26
    Primary chain details 92 pitches: 0·375 in. x 0·250 in. Triple row
    Rear chain details 100 pitches: 0·400 in. x 0·380 in. simple type (99 pitches with 20T gearbox sprocket).
    Clutch chainwheel no. of teeth: 57
    Clutch pushrod – length: 9·813/9·803 in. (244·250/243·996 mm)
    Clutch pushrod – diameter: 0·237/0·232 in. (6·019/5·892 mm)
    Clutch operating ball diameter: ½ in. (12·70 mm)
    Clutch operating body lock ring thread size: 41·4 mm x 20 TPI
    Clutch type: Multi plate, diaphragm spring
    Clutch friction plate no. off: 5
    Clutch friction plate thickness: 0·148/0·142 in. (3·759/3·607 mm)
    Clutch friction plate material: Sintered bronze
    Clutch centre bearing specification: Deep grove ball bearing – one dot
                                OD 62 mm, ID 35 mm, Width 14 mm
                                 Corner rad 1·5 mm
    Clutch adjuster dia. and thread: ½ in. x 20 UNF 2A
    Clutch adjuster length: 0·904 in. x 0·894 in. (22·962/22·708 mm)

Technical Data

CAPACITIES

(All tanks of steel construction from 1975)
Fastback fuel tank capacity: 3¼ Imp. galls (15 litres) 3·9 U.S. galls
L.R. Fastback fuel tank capacity: 4 galls. (18 litres) 4·8 U.S. galls
Roadster fuel tank capacity: 2·7 Imp. galls
(12 litres) 3·2 U.S. galls.
S.S. Hi-rider fuel tank capacity: 2 Imp. galls (9 litres) 2·4 U.S. galls
Interstate fuel tank capacity: 5·5 Imp. galls
(25 litres) 6·6 U.S. galls.
Interpol fuel tank capacity: No radio: 4 Imp. galls. (18 litres) 4·8 U.S. galls.
　　　　　　　　　　　　　　Radio insert: 3½ Imp. galls. (16 litres) 4·2 U.S. galls.
Oil tank: 5 Imp./6 U.S. pints, 2·8 litres
Gearbox: 0·75 Imp./0·9 U.S. pints, 0·42 litres
Front forks: 150 cc (5 fl. oz.) each leg
Primary chaincase: 200 cc (7 fl. oz.)

MISCELLANEOUS DATA

Height – 40·75 in. (103·5 cm)
　　　　　Hi-Rider only – 50¼ in. (127·6 cm)
Length: 87·5 in. (222 cm)
Wheelbase: 56·75 in. (144 cm)
Dry Weight includes battery, but not petrol, oil and tools
Roadster 465 lb. (211 kg)　　　　　Interstate 475 lb. (215 kg)
(For motorcycle equipped with 4·10 in. x 19 in. tyres front and rear)
Weights rounded to nearest 5 lbs to allow for variations in materials of construction;
castings, forgings, tubes, etc. ranging 5%
Ground clearance: 6 in. (15 cm)
Width: 26 in. (66 cm)
Overall length of exhaust system (from flange at exhaust port end of pipe to tip of
muffler: 65 in. (165·1 cm)
Exhaust system maximum diameter: 3·5 in. (8·92 cm)
Maximum theoretical road speed 122 m.p.h. (196·336 K.p.h.)
Road speed at 1000 r.p.m. in gears (20T sprocket)
　　　　Bottom:　6·61 m.p.h. = (10·64 K.p.h.)
　　　　Second:　9·96 m.p.h. = (16·03 K.p.h.)
　　　　Third:　13·86 m.p.h. = (22·30 K.p.h.)
　　　　Top:　　16·92 m.p.h. = (27·22 K.p.h.)
Total movement of front forks: 6 in. (15·2 cm)
Turning circle (full circle): 17 ft. 10 in. (518·16 cm)
Gross vehicle rating: 880 lb. (399·16 Kg)
Centre of gravity: 19¾ in. (501·65 mm) above ground unladen
Seat height (nominal): 33 – 34 in. (838·2 – 863·6 mm) dependent on model

Technical Data

SPECIAL WORKSHOP TOOLS

060941   Engine sprocket (clutch hub and cam sprocket) puller (with longer studs: Mark III)

060949   Auto advance unit lock washer (for static timing)

060999   Clutch diaphragm spring tool

061015   Clutch lock tool (locks clutch body with plates removed)

064298   Rocker spindle and auto advance slide hammer

ET2003   Crankshaft timing pinion extractor

063964   Valve guide screw-type extractor and inserter

063965   Peg spanner (wrench) for wheel bearings and disc caliper

064292   Contact breaker seal and crankshaft-to-timing cover seal drift set

063968   Exhaust lockring "C" spanner

063969   Valve seat cutting tool complete

063970   Roller bearing race extractor (with longer studs for Mark III)

060942   Steering head adjustment spanner (Pre 1971)

061359   Contact breaker oil seal guide

NM12093 $\frac{7}{8}$ in. box spanner

064622   Strap wrench

Note: A separate illustrated tool list part no. 604621 is available for 1973 models. This will be up-
dated as soon as possible to include Mark III special service tools.

Conversion Tables

Conversion Tables

U.N.E.F.

Dia.	No of thds.
1/4 in.	32
5/16 in.	32
3/8 in.	32
7/16 in.	28
1/2 in.	28
9/16 in.	24
5/8 in.	24
11/16 in.	24
3/4 in.	20
13/16 in.	20
7/8 in.	20
15/16 in.	20
1 in.	20
1-1/16 in.	18
1-1/8 in.	18
1-3/16 in.	18
1-1/4 in.	18
1-5/16 in.	18
1-3/8 in.	18
1-7/16 in.	18
1-1/2 in.	18
1-9/16 ins.	18
1-5/8 in.	18
1-11/16 in.	18

U.N.F.

Dia.	No. of thds.
1/4 in.	28
5/16 in.	24
3/8 in.	24
7/16 in.	20
1/2 in.	20
9/16 in.	18
5/8 in.	18
3/4 in.	16
7/8 in.	14
1 in.	12
1-1/8 in.	12
1-1/4 in.	12
1-3/8 in.	12
1-1/2 in.	12

U.N.C.

Dia.	No. of thds.
1/4 in.	20
5/16 in.	18
3/8 in.	16
7/16 in.	14
1/2 in.	13
9/16 in.	12
5/8 in.	11
3/4 in.	10
7/8 in.	9
1 in.	8
1-1/8 in.	7
1-1/4 in.	7
1-3/3 in.	6
1-1/2 in.	6
1-3/4 in.	5
2 in.	4-1/2

B.A.

No.	Dia. of bolt	Thds. per inch
0	·2362	25·4
1	·2087	28·2
2	·1850	31·4
3	·1614	34·8
4	·1417	38·5
5	·1260	43·0
6	·1102	47·9
7	·0984	52·9
8	·0866	59·1
9	·0748	65·1
10	·0669	72·6
11	·0591	81·9
12	·0511	90·9
13	·0472	102·0
14	·0394	109·9
15	·0354	120·5
16	·0311	133·3

B.S.W.

Dia. of bolt (inch)	Threads per inch
1/4	20
5/16	18
3/8	16
7/16	14
1/2	12
9/16	12
5/8	11
11/16	11
3/4	10
13/16	10
7/8	9
15/16	9
1	8

B.S.F.

Dia. of bolt (inch)	Threads per inch
7/32	28
1/4	26
9/32	26
5/16	22
3/8	20
7/16	18
1/2	16
9/16	16
5/8	14
11/16	14
3/4	12
13/16	12
7/8	11
1	10
1-1/8	9
1-1/4	9
1-3/8	8
1-1/2	8
1-5/8	8

Conversion Tables   **B**

WIRE GAUGES

No. of Gauge	Imperial Standard Wire Gauge	
	Inches	Millimetres
1	·300	7·620
2	·276	7·010
3	·252	6·400
4	·232	5·892
5	·212	5·384
6	·192	4·676
7	·176	4·470
8	·160	4·064
9	·144	3·657
10	·128	3·251
11	·116	2·946
12	·104	2·641
13	·092	2·336
14	·080	2·032
15	·072	1·828
16	·064	1·625
17	·056	1·422
18	·048	1·219
19	·040	1·016
20	·036	·914
21	·032	·812
22	·028	·711
23	·024	·609
24	·022	·558
25	·020	·508
26	·018	·457
27	·0164	·416
28	·0148	·375
29	·0136	·345
30	·0124	·314

No. of Gauge	Brown and Sharpe's American Wire Gauge	
	Inches	Millimetres
1	·289	7·348
2	·258	6·543
3	·229	5·827
4	·204	5·189
5	·182	4·621
6	·162	4·115
7	·144	3·664
8	·128	3·263
9	·114	2·906
10	·102	2·588
11	·091	2·304
12	·081	2·052
13	·072	1·827
14	·064	1·627
15	·057	1·449
16	·051	1·290
17	·045	1·149
18	·040	1·009
19	·035	·911
20	·032	·811
21	·028	·722
22	·025	·643
23	·023	·573
24	·020	·511
25	·018	·454
26	·016	·404
27	·014	·360
28	·012	·321
29	·011	·235
30	·010	·254

DRILL SIZES (INCHES)

Number	Size		Number	Size		Letter	Size
1	·2280		27	·1440		A	·234
2	·2210		28	·1405		B	·238
3	·2130		29	·1360		C	·242
4	·2090		30	·1285		D	·246
5	·2055		31	·1200		E	·250
6	·2040		32	·1160		F	·257
7	·2010		33	·1130		G	·261
8	·1990		34	·1110		H	·266
9	·1960		35	·1100		I	·272
10	·1935		36	·1065		J	·277
11	·1910		37	·1040		K	·281
12	·1890		38	·1015		L	·290
13	·1850		39	·0995		M	·295
14	·1820		40	·0980		N	·302
15	·1800		41	·0960		O	·316
16	·1770		42	·0935		P	·323
17	·1730		43	·0890		Q	·332
18	·1695		44	·0860		R	·339
19	·1660		45	·0820		S	·348
20	·1610		46	·0810		T	·358
21	·1590		47	·0785		U	·368
22	·1570		48	·0760		V	·377
23	·1540		49	·0730		W	·386
24	·1520		50	·0700		X	·397
25	·1495		51	·0670		Y	·404
26	·1470		52	·0635		Z	·413

GALLONS

Gallons (Imperial)   Gallons (U.S.)

Imperial Gallons	U.S. Gallons		U.S. Gallons	Imperial Gallons
1	1·2		1	0·83
2	2·4		2	1·66
3	3·6		3	2·50
4	4·8		4	3·33
5	6·0		5	4·16
6	7·2		6	5·00
7	8·4		7	5·83
8	9·6		8	6·66
9	10·8		9	7·49
10	12·0		10	8·30

50 miles per U.S. gallon
is equivalent to
60 miles per Imperial gallon.

NOTE: 1 British Gallon = 1.2 U.S. Gallons

Conversion Tables

B

PINTS (IMPERIAL) TO LITRES

	0	1	2	3	4	5	6	7	8
—	—	·568	1·136	1·705	2·273	2·841	3·841	3·978	4·546
¼	·142	·710	1·279	1·846	2·415	2·983	3·552	4·120	4·688
½	·284	·852	1·420	1·989	2·557	3·125	3·125	4·262	4·830
¾	·426	·994	1·563	2·131	2·699	3·267	3·836	4·404	4·972

GALLONS (IMPERIAL) TO LITRES

	0	1	2	3	4	5	6	7	8	9	
—		4·546	9·092	13·638	18·184	22·730	27·276	31·822	36·368	40·914	—
10	45·460	50·005	54·551	59·097	63·643	63·189	72·735	77·281	81·827	86·373	10
20	90·919	95·465	100·011	104·557	109·103	113·649	118·195	122·741	127·287	131·833	20
30	136·379	140·924	145·470	150·016	154·562	159·108	163·645	168·200	172·746	177·292	30
40	181·838	186·384	190·930	195·476	200·022	204·568	209·114	213·660	218·206	222·752	40
50	227·298	231·843	236·389	240·935	245·481	250·027	254·473	259·119	263·605	268·211	50
60	272·757	277·303	281·849	286·395	290·941	295·487	300·033	304·579	309·125	313·671	60
70	318·217	322·762	327·308	331·854	336·400	340·946	345·492	350·038	354·584	359·130	70
80	363·676	368·222	372·768	377·314	381·860	386·406	390·952	395·498	400·044	404·590	80
90	409·136	413·681	418·227	422·773	427·319	431·865	436·411	440·957	445·503	450·049	90

MILES TO KILOMETRES

	0	1	2	3	4	5	6	7	8	9	
—		1·609	3·219	4·828	6·437	8·047	9·656	11·265	12·875	14·484	—
10	16·093	17·703	19·312	20·922	22·531	24·140	25·750	27·359	28·968	30·578	10
20	32·187	33·796	35·406	37·015	38·624	40·234	41·843	43·452	45·062	46·671	20
30	48·280	49·890	51·499	53·108	54·718	56·327	57·936	59·546	61·155	62·765	30
40	64·374	65·983	67·593	69·202	70·811	72·421	74·030	75·639	77·249	78·858	40
50	80·467	82·077	83·686	85·295	86·905	88·514	90·123	91·733	93·342	94·951	50
60	96·561	98·170	99·780	101·389	102·998	104·608	106·217	107·826	109·436	111·045	60
70	112·654	114·264	115·873	117·482	119·092	120·701	122·310	123·920	125·529	127·138	70
80	128·748	130·357	131·967	133·576	135·185	136·795	138·404	140·013	141·623	143·232	80
90	144·841	146·451	148·060	149·669	151·279	152·888	154·497	156·107	157·716	159·325	90

MILES PER GALLON (IMPERIAL) TO LITRES PER 100 KILOMETRES

10	28·25	15	18·83	20	14·12	25	11·30	30	9·42	35	8·07	40	7·06	50	5·65	60	4·71	70	4·04
10½	26·90	15½	18·22	20½	13·78	25½	11·08	30½	9·26	35½	7·96	41	6·89	51	5·54	61	4·63	71	3·98
11	25·68	16	17·66	21	13·45	26	10·87	31	9·11	36	7·85	42	6·73	52	5·43	62	4·55	72	3·92
11½	24·56	16½	17·12	21½	13·14	26½	10·66	31½	8·97	36½	7·74	43	6·57	53	5·33	63	4·48	73	3·87
12	23·54	17	16·61	22	12·84	27	10·46	32	8·83	37	7·63	44	6·42	54	5·23	64	4·41	74	3·82
12½	22·60	17½	16·14	22½	12·55	27½	10·27	32½	8·69	37½	7·53	45	6·28	55	5·13	65	4·35	75	3·77
13	21·73	18	15·69	23	12·28	28	10·09	33	8·56	38	7·43	46	6·14	56	5·04	66	4·28	76	3·72
13½	20·92	18½	15·27	23½	12·02	28½	9·91	33½	8·43	38½	7·34	47	6·01	57	4·96	67	4·22	77	3·67
14	20·18	19	14·87	24	11·77	29	9·74	34	8·31	39	7·24	48	5·89	58	4·87	68	4·16	78	3·62
14½	19·48	19½	14·49	24½	11·53	29½	9·58	34½	8·19	39½	7·15	49	5·77	59	4·79	69	4·10	79	3·57

Conversion Tables

POUNDS PER SQUARE INCH TO KILOGRAMS PER SQUARE CENTIMETRE

	0	1	2	3	4	5	6	7	8	9	
—		0·070	0·141	0·211	0·281	0·352	0·422	0·492	0·562	0·633	—
10	0·703	0·773	0·844	0·914	0·984	1·055	1·125	1·195	1·266	1·336	10
20	1·406	1·476	1·547	1·617	1·687	1·758	1·828	1·898	1·969	2·039	20
30	2·109	2·179	2·250	2·320	2·390	2·461	2·531	2·601	2·672	2·742	30
40	2·812	2·883	2·953	3·023	3·093	3·164	3·234	3·304	3·375	3·445	40
50	3·515	3·586	3·656	3·726	3·797	3·867	3·937	4·007	4·078	4·148	50
60	4·218	4·289	4·359	4·429	4·500	4·570	4·640	4·711	4·781	4·851	60
70	4·921	4·992	5·062	5·132	5·203	5·273	5·343	5·414	5·484	5·554	70
80	5·624	5·695	5·765	5·835	5·906	5·976	6·046	6·117	6·187	6·257	80
90	6·328	6·398	6·468	6·538	6·609	6·679	6·749	6·820	6·890	6·960	90

POUNDS TO KILOGRAMS

	0	1	2	3	4	5	6	7	8	9	
—		0·454	0·907	1·361	1·814	2·268	2·722	3·175	3·629	4·082	—
10	4·536	4·990	5·443	5·987	6·350	6·804	7·257	7·711	8·165	8·618	10
20	9·072	9·525	9·079	10·433	10·886	11·340	11·793	12·247	12·701	13·154	20
30	13·608	14·061	14·515	14·968	15·422	15·876	16·329	16·783	17·237	17·690	30
40	18·144	18·597	19·051	19·504	19·953	20·412	20·865	21·319	21·772	22·226	40
50	22·680	23·133	23·587	24·040	24·494	24·948	25·401	25·855	26·308	26·762	50
60	27·216	27·669	28·123	28·576	29·030	29·484	29·937	30·391	30·844	31·298	60
70	31·751	32·205	32·659	33·112	33·566	34·019	34·473	34·927	35·380	35·834	70
80	36·287	36·741	37·195	37·648	38·102	38·855	39·009	39·463	39·916	40·370	80
90	40·823	41·277	41·731	42·184	42·638	43·091	43·545	43·998	44·452	44·906	90

FOOT POUNDS TO KILOGRAMETRES

	0	1	2	3	4	5	6	7	8	9	
—		0·138	0·277	0·415	0·553	0·691	0·830	0·968	1·106	1·244	—
10	1·383	1·521	1·659	1·797	1·936	2·074	2·212	2·350	2·489	2·627	10
20	2·765	2·903	3·042	3·180	3·318	3·456	3·595	3·733	3·871	4·009	20
30	4·148	4·286	4·424	4·562	4·701	4·839	4·977	5·116	5·254	5·392	30
40	5·530	5·668	5·807	5·945	6·083	6·221	6·360	6·498	6·636	6·774	40
50	6·913	7·051	7·189	7·328	7·466	7·604	7·742	7·881	8·019	8·157	50
60	8·295	8·434	8·572	8·710	8·848	8·987	9·125	9·263	9·401	9·540	60
70	9·678	9·816	9·954	10·093	10·231	10·369	10·507	10·646	10·784	10·922	70
80	11·060	11·199	11·337	11·475	11·613	11·752	11·890	12·028	12·166	12·305	80
90	12·443	12·581	12·719	12·858	12·996	13·134	13·272	13·411	13·549	13·687	90

Conversion Tables

B

MILLIMETRES TO INCHES

mm.	0	10	20	30	40	50	60	70	80	90
0		·39370	·78740	1·18110	1·57480	1·96851	2·36221	2·75591	3·14961	3·5433
1	·03937	·43307	·82677	1·22047	1·61417	2·00788	2·40158	2·79528	3·18891	3·5826
2	·07874	·47244	·86614	1·25984	1·65354	2·04725	2·44095	2·83465	3·22835	3·6220
3	·11811	·51181	·90551	1·29921	1·69291	2·08662	2·48032	2·87402	3·26772	3·6614
4	·15748	·55118	·94488	1·33858	1·73228	2·12599	2·51969	2·91339	3·30709	3·7007
5	·19685	·59055	·98425	1·37795	1·77165	2·16536	2·55906	2·95276	3·34646	3·7401
6	·23622	·62992	1·02362	1·41732	1·81103	2·20473	2·59843	2·99213	3·38583	3·7795
7	·27559	·66929	1·06299	1·45669	1·85040	2·24410	2·63780	3·03150	3·42520	3·8189
8	·31496	·70866	1·10236	1·49606	1·88977	2·28347	2·67717	3·07087	3·46457	3·8582
9	·35433	·74803	1·14173	1·53543	1·92914	2·32284	2·71654	3·11024	3·50394	3·8976

MILLIMETRES TO INCHES (DECIMALS OF)

1/1000			1/100			1/10	
mm.	inches		mm.	inches		mm.	inches
0·001	·000039		0·01	·00039		0·1	·00394
0·002	·000079		0·02	·00079		0·2	·00787
0·003	·000118		0·03	·00118		0·3	·01181
0·004	·000157		0·04	·00157		0·4	·01575
0·005	·000197		0·05	·00197		0·5	·01969
0·006	·000236		0·06	·00236		0·6	·02362
0·007	·000276		0·07	·00276		0·7	·02756
0·008	·000315		0·08	·00315		0·8	·03150
0·009	·000354		0·09	·00354		0·9	·03543

INCHES TO MILLIMETRES (DECIMALS OF)

Inches	0	10	20	30	40
0		254·0	508·0	762·0	1016·0
1	25·4	279·4	533·4	787·4	1041·4
2	50·8	304·8	558·8	812·8	1066·8
3	76·2	330·2	584·2	838·2	1092·2
4	101·6	355·6	609·6	863·6	1117·6
5	127·0	381·0	635·0	889·0	1143·0
6	152·4	406·4	660·4	914·4	1168·4
7	177·3	431·8	685·8	939·8	1193·8
8	203·2	457·2	711·2	965·2	1219·2
9	228·6	482·6	736·6	990·6	1244·6

1/1000		1/100		1/10	
inches	mm.	inches	mm.	inches	mm.
·001	·0254	·01	·254	·1	2·54
·002	·0508	·02	·508	·2	5·08
·003	·0762	·03	·762	·3	7·62
·004	·1016	·04	1·016	·4	10·16
·005	·1270	·05	1·270	·5	12·70
·006	·1524	·06	1·524	·6	15·24
·007	·1778	·07	1·778	·7	17·79
·008	·2032	·08	2·032	·8	20·32
·009	·2286	·09	2·286	·9	22·86

FRACTIONS TO DECIMALS — DECIMALS OF INCH TO MILLIMETRE

Fractions			Decimals	mm.
		1/64	·015625	·3969
	1/32		·03125	·7937
		3/64	·046875	1·1906
1/16			·0625	1·5875
		5/64	·078125	1·9844
	3/32		·09375	2·3812
		7/64	·109375	2·7781
1/8			·125	3·1750
		9/64	·140625	3·5719
	5/32		·15625	3·9687
		11/64	·171875	4·3656
3/16			·1875	4·7625
		13/64	·203125	5·1594
	7/32		·21875	5·5562
		15/64	·234375	5·9531
1/4			·25	6·3500
		17/64	·265625	6·7469
	9/32		·28125	7·1437
		19/64	·296875	7·5406
5/16			·3125	7·9375
		21/64	·328125	8·3344
	11/32		·34375	8·7312
		23/64	·359375	9·1281
3/8			·375	9·5250
		25/64	·390625	9·9219
	13/32		·40625	10·3187
		27/64	·421875	10·7156
7/16			·4375	11·1125
		29/64	·453125	11·5094
	15/32		·46875	11·9062
		31/64	·484375	12·3031
1/2			·5	12·700

Fractions			Decimals	mm.
		33/64	·515625	13·0969
	17/32		·53125	13·4937
		35/64	·546675	13·8906
9/16			·5625	14·2875
		37/64	·578125	14·6844
	19/32		·59375	15·0812
		39/64	·609375	15·4781
5/8			·625	15·875
		41/64	·640625	16·2719
	21/32		·65685	16·6687
		43/64	·671875	17·0656
11/16			·6375	17·4625
		45/64	·703125	17·8594
	23/32		·71875	18·2562
		47/64	·734375	18·6531
3/4			·75	19·05
		49/64	·765625	19·4469
	25/32		·78125	19·8437
		51/64	·796875	20·2406
13/16			·8125	20·6375
		53/64	·828125	21·0344
	27/32		·84375	21·4312
		55/64	·859375	21·8281
7/8			·875	22·225
		57/64	·890625	22·6219
	29·32		·90625	23·0187
		59/64	·921875	23·4156
15/16			·9375	23·8125
		61/64	·953125	24·2094
	31/32		·96875	24·6062
		63/64	·984375	25·0031
1				25·4

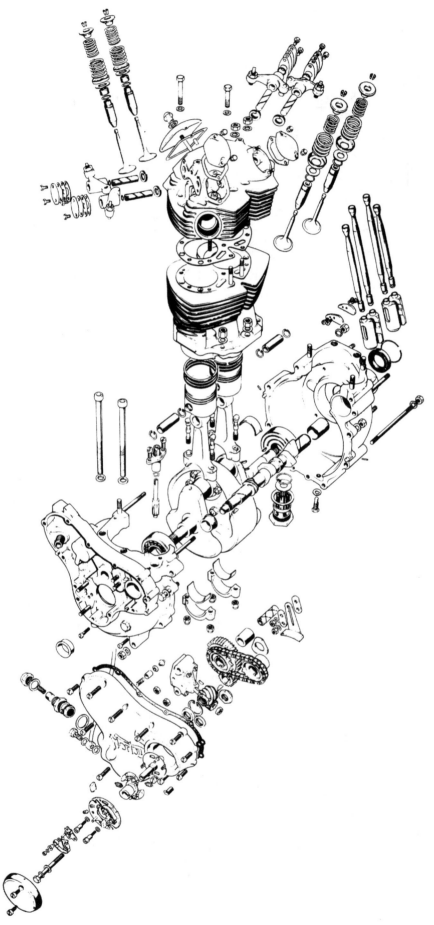

Engine

and

Primary

Transmission

Engine/Primary Transmission C

ENGINE/PRIMARY DRIVE

SECTION C

The engine/gearbox/primary transmission can be removed from the main frame as an assembly, bolted up in the engine plates as in Section F1. Alternately, either the engine or gearbox can be removed from the frame as complete assemblies after dismantling the primary transmission. For engine removal see Section C15 and for gearbox removal see Section D7. Unless it is specifically required to remove the engine complete, the simplest method is to dismantle to crankcase level for removal as in Section C11.

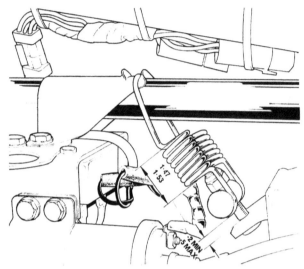

Fig. Cl(a)   Suspensory Spring Device

SECTION C1

REMOVING CYLINDER HEAD

Commence dismantling by removing surrounding parts as follows:

1   Lift twin seat clear by slackening R.H. large knurled knob and rotating lock-key forward to release catch, or if preferred, remove seat completely by releasing hinge at four posidrive screws.
Remove fuse from battery negative lead.

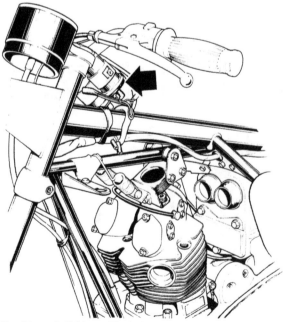

Fig. C1   Coil Cluster lifted clear of cylinder head

2   Remove the fuel tank (see Section F9).

3   Remove the exhaust system (see Section F19).

4   Disconnect the oil separator tube from the tee-piece at the balance pipe and remove the Carburetors with spacers.

5   Dismantle the Head-Steady, removing the frame nuts first, otherwise they will tend to revolve in the frame.

6   Remove the three $\frac{7}{32}$" internal flat socket-headed screws securing the head-steady to the cylinder

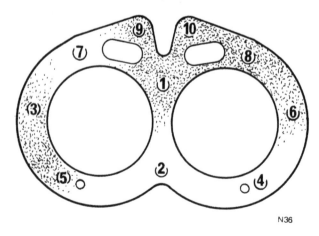

N36

TIGHTENING SEQUENCE

Fig. C2   Cylinder head; order of slackening and tightening

Engine/Primary Transmission C

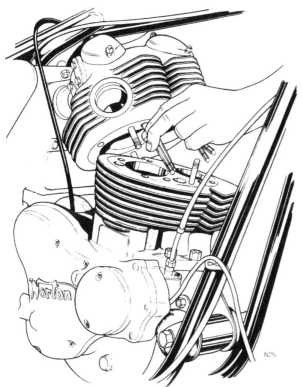

Fig. C3   Tilting cylinder head with pushrods held into cylinder head.

head. This releases the tension on the auxiliary suspensory spring device which is preferably removed intact, leaving the factory-set adjustment *undisturbed*. This device is new on the Mark III model and provides a pre-set bias which supports the engine unit, complementing the isolastic mounting, minimising oscillation at low speeds and gives smoother running generally.

If the adjustment is disturbed during dismantling, the trunnion should be rebuilt to the dimensions given in diagram C1 (a) and the tensioning nut (x) adjusted say, six flats per time between test runs until the optimum smoothness is restored.

7   Detach the suspensory spring stirrup from the coil-bracket, noting which notch locates the loop of the spring (usually this is on the forward notch) lift off spark plug caps, then remove the coil cluster complete from the frame.

    To keep it clear for work on the cylinder head, we recommend it is tied up to the handlebar at this stage.

It is not necessary to remove the rocker covers at this stage since they may be removed with the cylinder head. During removal of the head securing bolts and nuts,

leave the front centre bolt (shown in *Fig.* C2) till last.

8   Remove the rocker feed pipe banjo unions from both sides of the rocker boxes and collect the copper washers from both sides of the banjos. Leave the rocker feed pipe connected to the timing case.

9   Remove both sparking plugs.

10 Remove the cylinder head securing bolts and nuts (excepting the front centre bolt), in opposite order as shown in Fig. C2.

11 To achieve the minimum valve lift position and allow maximum space for removing the cylinder head, turn the engine by revolving the rear wheel with top gear engaged until the pistons are as near as possible to top dead centre. The Mk III engine incorporates an inspection plug in the crankcase bowl for locating T.D.C. See fig. C3.

12 Remove the cylinder head front centre bolt and the head should lift slightly against valve spring pressure.

Technique at this stage is to lift the cylinder head and recess the pushrods into the head as far as possible so that the head can be slid out between the cylinder barrel and frame tubes. Do this as follows:

13 Lift the cylinder head from either side of the motorcycle, support with one hand and slide the pushrods as far as possible into the cylinder head. *Fig. C3* shows the cylinder head tilted to the rear to facilitate the operation.

14 Withdraw the cylinder head.

The cylinder head gasket may adhere either to the cylinder or cylinder head. The gasket should be removed and protected from damage since, if remaining in undamaged condition, it may be put into further service.

SECTION C2

REMOVAL OF ROCKERS

In order to gain access to the inlet valve guides, the inlet rockers and spindles may have to be removed as follows:

1   Remove the two set screws retaining each rocker spindle cover plate (see *Fig.* C4).

2　Collect the cover plate, retaining plate and gaskets as a set. In all probability these items will adhere to one another and need not be disturbed.

3　Use service tool 064298 to extract the rocker spindles as shown in *Fig.* C5. Heat the cylinder head gently to ease removal and avoid damage to head or spindles. Ensure the shaft of the slide hammer is threaded well into the rocker spindles then slide the weight back against the nut sharply several times and the spindle will be drawn out.

4　Lift out the rockers and collect the plain and double spring thrust washers. On each rocker the plain thrust washer is outboard of the rocker and the double spring washer inboard (see *Fig.* C4).

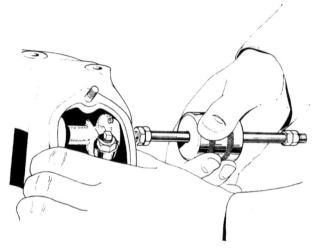

Fig. C5　*Extracting rocker spindles using slide hammer 064298*

SECTION C3

VALVE REMOVAL AND REASSEMBLY

The valves need to be removed during decarbonising (as described in Section C4) or when changing valve springs or inlet guide to stem seals. Removal of the cylinder head (Section C1) and inlet rocker cover stud is necessary to gain access to the valves.

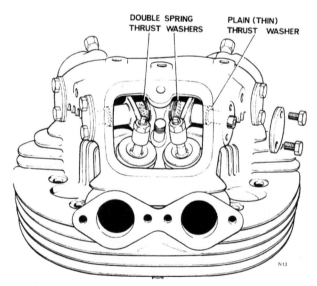

Fig. C4　*Rocker thrust washers and securing plates.*

Proceed as follows:

1　Using a suitable overhead valve spring compressor, (proprietary spring compressors are readily available) place the fixed jaw against the valve head and the movable jaw against the valve collar. Tighten down the movable jaw to compress the valve spring and remove the split collets. Collet removal may be facilitated by the use of a small screwdriver or long nose pliers.

2　Release the pressure from the compressor and collect the valve, springs, collars and where necessary, the inlet guide seals.

3　As each valve is removed, mark it in some way so that it can be replaced in its original location.

4　Examine the valves for burning or damage and grind in the cleaned up or new valves as described in Section C7. The seats should not need to be recut unless new valve guides have been fitted.

5　Check the valve springs for collapse. This can most easily be done by comparison with new springs or by checking free length to the dimension given in Technical Data.

6　Clean all parts very thoroughly in gasoline (petrol) and allow to dry.

7　Ensure that heat insulators are fitted between the exhaust valve spring seat and cylinder head.

Engine/Primary Transmission C

8 With the valve spring seat in position, loose assemble the valve (with lightly lubricated stem) inner and outer valve spring and top valve collar.

9 Using the valve spring compressor, compress the collar and springs and insert the split valve cotters.

10 When the collets are firmly in position in the valve stem groove, remove the compressor. The cylinder head is now ready to refit.

SECTION C4

DECARBONISING

After the motorcycle has been in use for some time, carbon deposits accumulate within the combustion chamber and exhaust ports and also the valves cease to seal completely due to wear and a certain amount of burning on the valve seatings. These conditions result in a lack of compression and an increase in the compression ratio, giving symptoms of a gradual loss of power, poor compression and difficult starting. To remedy these conditions, it is necessary to remove the carbon deposits and grind the valves to their seatings to obtain a gas-tight seal. To do so, remove the cylinder head (Section C1) and remove the valves (Section C3).

Unless a carbon dispersant vat is available, the carbon must be scraped from the combustion chambers, exhaust ports and piston crowns. Since the cylinder head and pistons are produced from an aluminium alloy material which is scratched easily, the carbon must only be removed by a soft metal or hard wood scraper which will not damage the surface. A steel scraper or screwdriver blade must not be used. *DO NOT* remove the

thin ring of carbon round the top of each cylinder bore and leave also a ring of carbon around the edge of each piston crown. Removal of this carbon will tend to increase the oil consumption.

The valve stems and heads should be scraped clear of carbon but take care not to scratch the facings. Examine the facings for deep pitting which would render the valves unfit for re-use.

When all parts are perfectly clean and in good condition grind in the valves and reassemble.

SECTION C5

VALVE GUIDE RENEWAL

The cast iron valve guides are a tight interference fit in the cylinder head and can be removed and refitted only after heating the cylinder head to a temperature of 150° to 200°C. A special Service Tool 063964 is available for removing and refitting the valve guides. Proceed as follows:

1 Place the tool adaptor marked "Remover" hollow end down over the valve guide.

2 Place the cranked and threaded stem through the valve guide from the hemisphere.

3 Hold the cranked stem to prevent it turning and screw on the handle (see *Fig.* C6). As the handle is tightened the guide and cranked stem will be pulled through into the remover body.

Caution: If guides seem difficult to remove, ensure head is heated evenly. Do not force guides in or out of their bores.

33

Engine/Primary Transmission C

New valve guides are available in oversizes : +0·002 in. and +0·010 in. for the 850 engine. The valve guide to cylinder head interference should be ·0015 in. — ·0025 in. and if there is ovality and oversize guides are to be fitted the valve guide bores in the head must be reamed to suit. As a matter of course use the improved inlet guides with valve guide-to-stem seals during re-assembly.

Fit new valve guides as follows :

4   Place the new guide in line with the bore in the cylinder and place the adaptor marked "Replacer" from Service Tool 063964 over the guide.

5   Place the replacer stem through the cylinder head and bore of the valve guide and locate the abutment to the valve seat.

6   Fit the handle and turn to pull the guide fully home into the head. If necessary the abutment can be prevented from turning by the use of a suitable key in the socket provided. Be careful not to crush circlips on guides, just pull down tightly enough to seat.

7   Recut the valve seats at the points where new guides have been fitted. This operation is described in Section C6.

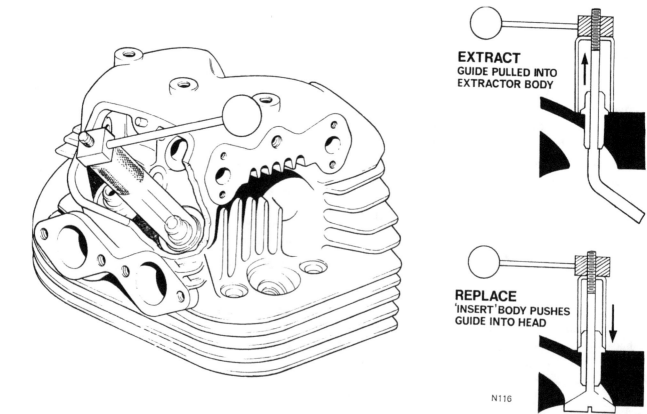

EXTRACT
GUIDE PULLED INTO
EXTRACTOR BODY

REPLACE
'INSERT' BODY PUSHES
GUIDE INTO HEAD

N116

Fig. C6   Using valve guide tool 063964 to remove a valve guide

SECTION C6

RESEATING THE VALVES

After renewal of valve guides (as in Section C5) or where the valve seats are in badly pitted condition, it is necessary to recut the valve seats. During decarbonising or after recutting the valve seats, the valves must be reground.

Cutting the valve seats – Valve seat cutters, a suitable arbor and pilot are available under the following Part Number: 063969

    Arbor and pilot.
    Valve seat cutter (45°).
    Blending cutter .

Before commencing to cut the seats we stress that the essence of cutting valve seats satisfactorily is to remove the minimum of metal and to use the cutters in such a way as to prevent possible "chatter" in the cutting pattern. Proceed as follows:

1 Assemble the cutter and pilot to the arbor.

2 Enter the pilot into the valve guide from inside the combustion chamber hemisphere.

3 Applying sufficient pressure on the arbor to give a clean cut without "chatter", take the first 120° cut.

4 Repeat the operation, 120° at a time until the seats are cleaned up free of any pitting.

5 Wash with gasoline (petrol) and blow clear any displaced material.

6 Cut the other valve seats which are affected by pitting.

7 Use a good quality fine grade grinding compound and smear a little compound all round the valve facing.

8 Drop the valve into position and using a backward and forwards rotary motion by holding either the valve head or valve stem with a suitable grinding tool, lap the valve facing to the seat.

9 Lift the valve off the seat and rotate the head 180°.

10 Repeat the lapping and rotating operations until there is a uniform dull grey bedding-in pattern on both surfaces.

11 Wash the affected areas free of grinding compound, then assemble the valves and springs to the head as in Section C3.

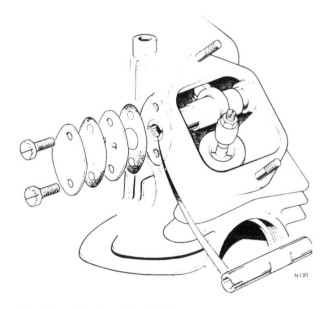

Fig. C7   Aligning rocker spindle

SECTION C7

Grinding-in the valves – Examine the valve heads for cleanliness and the valve stems for cleanliness, excessive wear or pronounced scuffing. Excessive wear or scuffing would necessitate renewal of a valve. If the valve head facings are pitted, they can be cleaned up on a valve facing machine though excessive removal of material is not recommended since it would affect the performance of the valve.
Grind the valve facings to the seats as follows:

12 Test the seating of the valves by supporting the cylinder head with valves assembled, hemispheres upwards. Pour gasoline or kerosene (petrol or paraffin) into each inlet port and allow 20 seconds to elapse. If the liquid has not passed the seatings into the combustion chambers in this time, the lapping operation has been successful. Repeat the operation at the exhaust valves.

Engine/Primary Transmission C

SECTION C8

REFITTING ROCKERS

The rocker spindles must be positioned correctly to allow satisfactory lubrication. It is recommended that the cylinder head be heated to 150°–200°C. prior to offering the rocker spindles, to facilitate entry and alignment. Assembly is as follows:

1   Heat the cylinder head gently.

2   Engage a rocker spindle into the cylinder head with flat facing rearwards on the inlet side and forwards on the exhaust and tap it through very gently with a soft drift until it protudes approximately $\frac{1}{16}$ in. (1·59 mm) through the outer boss into the rocker cavity.

3   Fit the plain washer then the rocker in position.

4   Drive the rocker spindle part way through the rocker and fit the double spring washer between the other end of the rocker and the boss in the rocker box.

5   Centralise the spring washer and drive the spindle through until it protrudes no more than $\frac{3}{8}$ in. (9·52 mm).

6   Align the rocker spindle as shown in *Fig. C7*.

   Note: Flat on spindle faces away from centre of head, towards rocker cover.

7   Drive the spindle home taking care that the rocker spindle does not turn during this operation. The spindle should be flush or fractionally below the joint facing on the rocker box.

SECTION C9

REFITTING CYLINDER HEAD

The cylinder head should be cleaned, inspected and overhauled as described in previous sections, and the valves and rockers assembled. As with dismantling, the cylinder head and pushrods should be offered as a set. The operation is described fully below:

1   Place the cylinder head gasket in position on top of the cylinder.

2   Turn the engine until the pistons are at top dead centre so that there is minimum valve lift and on assembly one pair of pushrods is fractionally higher than the other.

3   Place the pushrods in the pushrod tunnels in the cylinder head with the inlet pushrods (that is the longer pair) inboard and the shorter exhaust ones, outboard.
The cupped end of each pushrod is uppermost.

4   Take the cylinder head firmly in one hand and feed the pushrods as far into the cylinder head as possible, holding them with the other hand. See *Fig. C3*.

5   Place the cylinder head over the cylinder, forward end downwards and allow the pushrods to drop down the cylinder barrel pushrod tunnels.
Note that the pushrods cannot do other than locate on the cam followers at the lower end.

6   Starting with the pair of pushrods which are slightly higher, engage the tops of the pushrods to the rocker ball ends as the cylinder head is lowered. Use an implement such as a thin screwdriver through the exhaust rocker box to guide the pushrods into position as shown in *Fig. C8*. Having engaged the first pair of pushrods engage the second pair in a similar manner.

The cylinder head is ready to be secured. The tightening sequence is shown in *Fig. C2*.

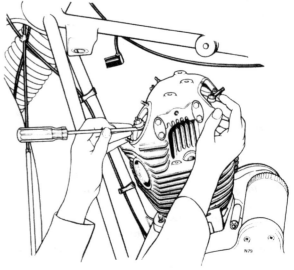

Fig. C8   Guiding pushrods into engagement with the rockers

Engine/Primary Transmission C

7 Fit and tighten down the short cylinder head bolt with its washer – this bolt should be inserted down through the cylinder head fins to the centre front position. The cylinder head should be pulled down to the gasket against valve spring pressure using this bolt.

8 Check that all four pushrods are correctly engaged to the ball ends of the rocker arms.

9 If pushrod engagement is correct, fit the four bolts with washers on either side of the sparking plugs, followed by a long sleeve nut under each exhaust port and a short nut under the inlet ports, (these are without washers) and 2 $\frac{5}{16}$ in. nuts and washers on the studs (no's 9 and 10 in *Fig.* C2) which seal the joint by the pushrod tunnel. There are no washers on the nuts fitted from beneath the cylinder head.

10 Finally tighten the cylinder head bolts and nuts in the order shown in *Fig.* C2. The torque settings are :
Cylinder head bolts and nuts $\frac{3}{8}$ in: 30 lbs./ft. (3·68 Kg/m).
Cylinder head bolts $\frac{5}{16}$ in. : 20 lbs./ft. (2·75 Kg/m)

11 Adjust the rocker clearances as described in Section C10.

12 Using new sealing gaskets only if the originals are unfit for further use, refit the inlet and exhaust rocker covers and secure with the blind nuts. There is a washer only at the inlet rocker cover nut.

13 Refit the carburettors with spacers as described in Section E5, and refit the sparking plugs to avoid washers being dropped into the engine during the next operation.

14 Refit the suspensory spring stirrup and coil cluster to the frame bracket.
Refit the cylinder head steady as a reversal of the dismantling procedure, the tension on the spring should be unaltered, providing the trunnion nut has not moved and the loop is notched as before on the stirrup.

IMPORTANT NOTE
Assembly line drill should be followed when replacing the head-steady.
To ensure that engine mountings are in repose and avoid bias or pre-load on the head-steady rubbers,

arrange a support off the frame cradle, or have the machine on its wheels. **Never** tighten up the torque stay with the machine on its centre stand.

15 Reconnect the rocker feed pipe banjos at the cylinder head using copper washers at each side of the banjos. Take care that the plastic part of the rocker pipe is clear of the rocker boxes, cylinder head and head steady.

16 Connect the spark plug caps.

17 Reconnect the low tension leads from the contact breaker to the main harness. These leads are coloured white/black and yellow/black and should be connected colour to colour. The standard assembly procedure is white/black to right cylinder and yellow/black to left cylinder.

18 Refit the exhaust system (Section F19).

19 Refit the fuel tank (Section F9) and connect the fuel lines.

20 Refit the fuse.

21 Refit the seat and secure with the knurled side nut and lock.

SECTION C10

ROCKER CLEARANCES

It is essential for the correct valve to rocker clearances to be maintained to prevent excessively noisy operation and subsequent wear or conversely to prevent insufficient clearances, a loss of compression and burning of the valves and seats. After checking clearances at the time of the first free service, the clearances should be checked and corrected as necessary at 2500 mile (4000 Km) intervals. To provide sufficient room at the rocker boxes for satisfactory checking, the fuel tank should be removed as in Section F9.
The correct rocker clearances are as below, checked with the engine cold :

Inlet   0·006 in. (0·15 mm)
Exhaust   0·008 in. (0·2 mm)

Engine/Primary Transmission C

Proceed to check rocker clearances as below:

1 Remove the two exhaust and one inlet rocker covers.

2 To facilitate rotating the engine, remove both sparking plugs.

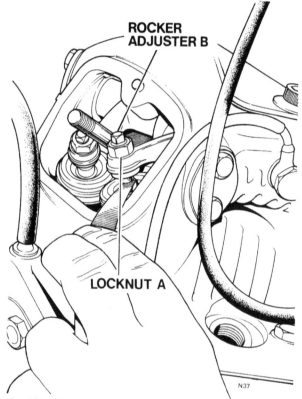

ROCKER ADJUSTER B

LOCKNUT A

Fig. C9 Checking valve clearances

3 Rotate the engine, either by the kickstart or by turning the rear wheel forwards with fourth gear engaged, until the left side inlet valve is fully open.

4 Using the correct feeler gauge (see table above for thickness) check the rocker clearance of the right side inlet valve. *Fig.* C9 shows the point where the feeler gauge is inserted.

5 If the clearance is correct i.e. the feeler gauge *just* nips, proceed to check the next valve as in (7). If gauge will not enter or if it does not nip, adjust as in (6).

6 Referring to *Fig.* C9, slacken the adjuster locknut (A) and screw out the adjuster (B) two turns. Place the feeler gauge between the adjuster and end of the valve stem and screw the adjuster in until it *just* nips the feeler gauge. Tighten the lock-

nut and withdraw the gauge which should not be gripped tightly but should slide relatively easily from the gap. This clearance is now correct.

7 Rotate the engine until the right side inlet valve is fully open and adjust the left side inlet valve in a similar manner.

8 Adjust the right side and left side exhaust valves in the same sequence but using a feeler gauge in accordance with the table of clearances.

SECTION C11

REMOVING CYLINDER AND PISTONS
Remove the cylinder head as detailed in Section C1. The cylinder is then removed as follows:

1 Remove the four through-bolts and release the five cylinder base nuts. It will be necessary to raise the cylinder so that the nuts will clear the fins. All nuts have washers except the front centre one. Be very careful that all nuts and washers are removed before the cylinder is lifted off.

At this stage the engine may be decarbonized as in Section C4 or the cylinder, pistons and piston rings given attention.

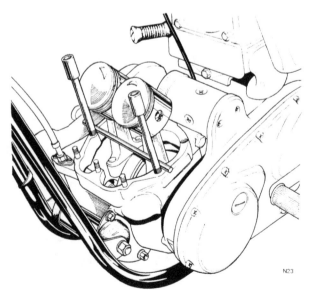

Fig. C10 Support connecting rods to prevent damage against crankcases

Engine/Primary Transmission **C**

2 Commence lifting the cylinder off the base studs and prepare to support the connecting rods as the cylinder is lifted clear of the pistons. In *Fig.* C10 a suitable implement has been inserted between the refitted cylinder through bolts to prevent the connecting rods and pistons falling against the crankcase mouth. Any damage to the connecting rods could result in failure of the rods at a later stage of use.

3 Place a piece of clean non-fluffy cloth over the crankcase mouth to prevent foreign matter entering the crankcase mouth.

4 Remove one circlip from each wrist pin (gudgeon pin).

5 Before removing the piston, support the body (*Fig.* C11) shows the piston body being supported by a second operative) and push out the first wrist (gudgeon) pin, then the second, using a suitable sized implement such as an aluminium drift.

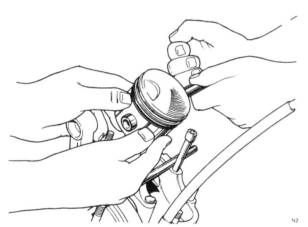

Fig. C11   Supporting piston body whilst pushing out gudgeon pin

SECTION C12

CYLINDER REBORING AND OVERSIZE PISTONS

After considerable mileages, or on engines where air filtering has been inefficient or oil changes neglected, wear may be expected on the cylinder bores or pistons. The maximum degree of wear may be expected to occur at the top front and rear areas of the cylinder bores.

Similarly, the maximum wear will take place on the front and rear faces of the pistons. Measure the cylinder bore diameter front and rear within ½ in. (12·70 mm) of the top of each bore and again front and rear at a point in the bore below the piston ring swept area. If the bores are in acceptable condition, the difference between the measurements should not exceed 0·005 in. (·1270 mm).

An alternative (but less accurate) method of measurement is to place one compression ring in the bore, approximately ½ in. (12·70 mm) from the top and measure the ring gap with feeler gauges. Place the ring lower in the bore below the piston ring swept area and again measure the gap. Subtract the second reading from the first and divide by three to arrive at the diameter wear. The amount of wear should not exceed 0·005 in. (·1270 mm).

Excessive wear will necessitate reboring and the fitting of oversize pistons which are available in oversizes of + 0·010 in. and + 0·020 in. Bore measurements are listed below:

STANDARD:	3·032 in. (77·013 mm)
+·010 in. oversize	3·042 in. (77·267 mm)
+·020 in. oversize	3·052 in. (77·521 mm)

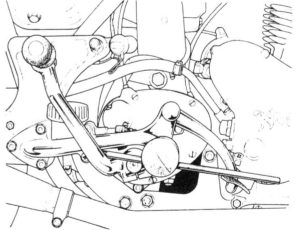

Fig. C12   Wedging of rear brake

SECTION C13

REMOVING PRIMARY CHAINCASE

To remove the engine or gearbox from the mounting plates or from the frame it is necessary to dismantle the

Engine/Primary Transmission C

primary transmission completely but the engine/gearbox transmission assembly can be removed from the frame as a single unit.

Dismantle the outer primary chaincase as follows:

1 Depress the gear-shift pedal and engage low gear and disconnect the electric starter terminal.

2 Wedge a large screw-driver, rod or similar over the brake pedal pad, under the footrest rubber and hook the end under the kick-start pedal to 'lock-on' the rear brake and prevent the transmission turning, as shown in Fig. C12.

3 Remove the two $\frac{1}{2}$" A/F nuts and bolt from the L.H. footrest mounting flange noting the rear bolt also locates the red earth-wire terminal from the zener-diode.

4 Place a large drain-tray under the primary cover, preferably long enough to extend the full length. Remove drain plug below alternator bulge in cover and allow oil to drain.

5 Remove the eleven posidrive screws securing the chaincase and noting the one long screw which passes through the inner cover and locates the electric starter. The joint may need a few gentle blows with a hide or rubber mallet to break the seal on the paper washer and dowels. As the seal breaks watch out for residual oil which will now fall into your tray if the cover was not fully drained. The outer cover now lifts clear complete with foot-shift pedal which disengages from the cross-shaft pinion, leaving the machine in low gear in readiness for onward dismantling.

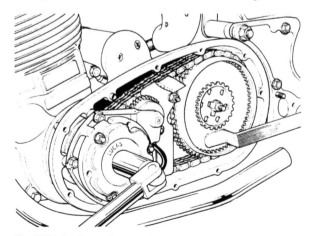

Fig. C12(a) Removing rotor nut whilst applying rear brake to prevent movement

6 Withdraw the gear-shift cross-shaft from its splined connector with rubber sleeve on the opposite side of the machine leaving the pinion and circlips in situ on the shaft.

SECTION C14

DISMANTLING PRIMARY TRANSMISSION AND CLUTCH

With the rear brake pedal wedged on as C13 (2) Proceed as follows:

1 Using a suitable sized socket wrench $\frac{1}{2}$ in. Whit. on the alternator rotor nut, remove the rotor nut as shown in *Fig.* C12.(a)

2 As the rotor nut is removed, collect the fan disc washer from behind.

3 Remove the alternator stator. This is secured by three nuts and plain washers. As the stator is removed, it may be left hanging on the stator lead whilst the two snap connector terminals are disconnected beneath the air box.

4 At this stage remove the alternator rotor which is keyed to the engine crankshaft. If the rotor should prove to be extremely tight on the engine crankshaft, slight pressure may be applied from behind equally, using two flat section tyre levers. Remove the rotor key packing collar and shims from the engine shaft.

5 Bend back the locking tabs on the four $\frac{1}{2}$" A/F nuts securing the alternator outrigger plate and remove nuts and washers. The mounting will now lift off, revealing the large dia. reduction gear which engages in the sprag mechanism (housed in the engine sprocket), and runs on its own needle bearing which is mounted on a hardened sleeve pinched between the rotor spacer and backing washer in the sprocket recess. Lift off the gear, withdrawing sprag roller-cage complete; the hardened sleeve and the backing washer, revealing the two tappings provided for the sprocket-extractor, as on previous models. (N.B. Longer extractor screws are necessary with the Mk III mainshafts).

6 Remove the starter-intermediate gear shaft complete with back-fire "overload" device, withdrawing its shaft spline from engagement in the large gear at the back of the inner-cover. The over-load clutch mechanism remains undisturbed as set at the factory and should require no attention. Its 3 disc-springs will hold the driving balls in their detents for starting, but allow slip under shock-load in the unlikely event of a backfire.

7 Remove the small nut in the Primary Chain Tensioner followed by the two $\frac{1}{2}$" A/F nuts releasing the steel outer-plate and allowing the tensioner assembly to lift off its studs. To avoid interchanging plungers in opposite bores the assembly relationship should be marked e.g. with indelible pencil or similar, and the plungers taped or wired in position to obviate mixing the fits, avoiding the need for re-priming the dashpot on re-assembly. Cleanliness is essential for efficient operation and on no account must the nuts be over tightened on re-assembly. The tensioner is fully automatic, the oil dashpot taking up adjustment as required. This refinement permits a rigidly mounted gearbox and allows the gearshift to be transferred to the left hand side of the machine on the Mk III model. with a minimum of complication.

8 Slacken the clutch push rod adjuster nut and remove the adjuster and nut together.

9 In order to dismantle the clutch, a compressor tool part number 060999 is needed for the diaphragm spring of the clutch. The tool is shown in use in *Fig.* C13. Note that the tool has been screwed into the adjuster hole in the spring centre. The centre bolt must be lightly tightened and must be at least $\frac{1}{4}$ in. engaged into the diaphragm spring centre. Now place a spanner on the withdrawal nut as shown in *Fig.* C13. Turning clockwise will tighten the withdrawal nut until pressure has been released from the diaphragm spring and the spring completely free to rotate

10 When the spring is compressed and free to rotate and using a screwdriver blade as shown in *Fig.* C14, lift the first end of the diaphragm spring clear of the circlip groove in the housing and commence to peel the circlip away from the groove.

11 The compressor tool and diaphragm spring should now be lifted clear as a pair.

It is not necessary to remove the tool from the diaphragm spring. If it is desired to remove the tool from the

diaphragm spring, support the centre bolt to prevent it turning and slacken off the withdrawal nut to relieve all spring pressure. If this is not done there is a grave risk of the spring being released suddenly from the tool with possible injury.

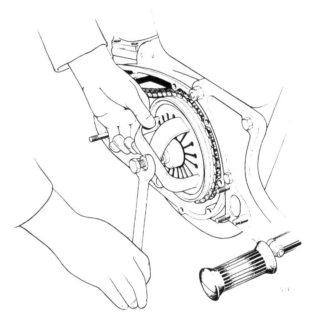

Fig. C13   Diaphragm spring compressor tool 060999 in use

12 Fit clutch tool 061015 over hub and remove the clutch centre nut and tab washer. Alternatively the clutch can be held by wedging the rear brake (as C13.2) while the nut is slackened.

13 Prepare to remove the engine sprocket, primary chain and remainder of the clutch as a set. This necessitates the use of engine sprocket puller part number 064297 assembled to the sprocket and engine crankshaft as shown in *Fig.* C15. It is essential that the side bolts are screwed into the sprocket at least $\frac{1}{2}$ in. prior to tightening of the centre bolt for extraction purposes for otherwise the thread may be stripped. Now tighten the centre bolt of the puller against the crankshaft and shock the side of the sprocket using a soft metal drift and hammer, whereupon the taper joint between the sprocket and shaft should be broken.

14 For convenience, remove the engine sprocket puller from the sprocket and lift away the remainder of the clutch, the engine sprocket and primary chain as a set as shown in *Fig.* C16, feeding the stator between the runs of the primary chain.

15 It will be noted that clutch and engine sprocket alignment has been ensured by the use of a collar

Engine/Primary Transmission C

and spacers over the gearbox mainshaft and these items should be collected and stored carefully for use during re-assembly. Note that if the crankshaft, engine sprocket, mainshaft or clutch have been renewed, re-alignment may be necessary.

16 The inner primary cover can now be removed as follows: First ensure the clutch adjustment circlip is removed from the gearbox mainshaft and

the internal fixing nut detached from the central boss.

The inner cover can now be lifted off its studs with or without the stator which is merely retained by its cable passing through the grommet.

The electric starter may remain attached if desired.

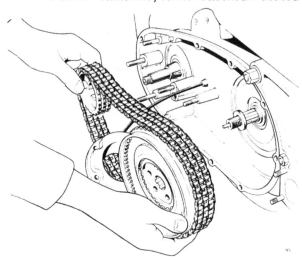

Fig. C16   Removing engine sprocket clutch and primary chain as a set

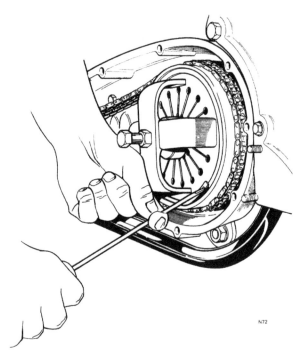

Fig. C14   Using a screwdriver blade to peel circlip away from housing

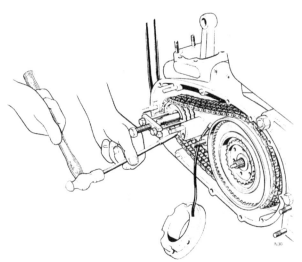

Fig. C15   Use of engine sprocket puller 064297

SECTION C15

REMOVING CRANKCASE ASSEMBLY FROM FRAME

Removal of the crankcase assembly from the frame is most easily achieved by removing the remaining ancillary equipment then taking out the front mounting complete and draining all remaining oil from the crankcase.

The full routine is as follows :

1 Disconnect the tachometer cable at the front of crankcase.

2 Remove the rocker feed pipe from the back of the crankcases and collect the copper washers.

3 Remove the gear indicator warning light wire at snap connector.

4 Slacken jubilee clip and detach breather pipe at timing cover.

5 Place a large capacity drain tray beneath the crankcases.

6   Remove the oil pipe junction block from the rear of the crankcase.

7   Slacken the large hexagon sump filter on the bottom of the crankcases. This filter requires the use of a $\frac{7}{8}$ in. Whit. (or $1\frac{1}{2}$ in. AF) spanner. Service tool NM 12093 is suitable.

8   Remove the large diameter centre bolt of the front mounting from the timing side. This will necessitate aligning the flats on the bolt head to clear the timing case. The Mark III isolastic mountings are now adjustable and the new design permits dismantling in one piece, with end caps in position. Remove the two nuts from the timing side of the engine mounting studs, then pull out the studs complete with remaining nuts from the drive side. The front mounting can then be pulled free away from the crankcases.

9   Remove the bottom rear crankcase-to-engine-plate bolt and the bottom centre stud. Extract the bottom stud by lifting the crankcase assembly slightly so that the stud clears the frame rails.

10 The sump filter can now be removed completely and the engine lifted vertically to enable the crankcase to be drained. *Fig.* C17 shows the crankcases supported by a bar from below whilst the sump filter is removed with the fingers after slackening at an earlier stage.

11 Remove the top rear engine to engine plate nut, supporting the weight of the crankcase as the stud is pulled out.

12 The crankcase assembly is now free to be removed from the mounting plates as shown in *Fig.* C18. Further dismantling of the engine can proceed more conveniently on the bench after removal.

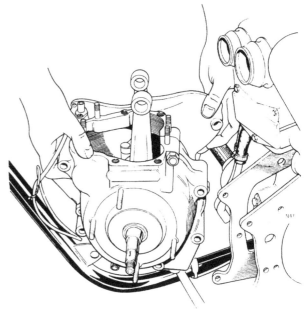

Fig. C18   *Removal of the crankcase assembly from mounting plates*

SECTION C16

DISMANTLING THE CRANKCASES

The majority of the work on the crankcases can be carried out best with the crankcase mounted in a plain jaw vice as shown in *Fig.* C19.

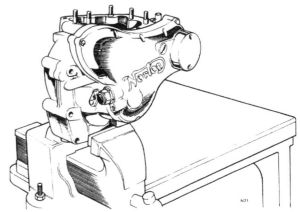

Fig. C17   *Showing crankcases supported by a bar to remove sump filter*

Fig. C19   *Showing crankcases mounted in a plain jaw vice for ease of handling*

Engine/Primary Transmission **C**

The basic order of dismantling is to remove the timing cover and dismantle the camshaft chain and sprockets, then the oil pump. At this stage the crankcases should be removed from the vice to be parted for removal of the crankshaft. The full routine is described below:

1 If the remaining crankcase bottom bolt is still fitted, this should be removed to allow the crankcase to be mounted securely in a vice.

2 Remove the two contact breaker cover screws and lift away the C.B. cover.

3 Remove the contact breaker cam centre bolt, serrated washer and plain washer.

4 Using service tool 064298 as shown in *Fig. C20*, screw the shaft into the contact breaker cam then slide the weight back sharply several times until the cam is lifted off the camshaft taper. It is unnecessary to remove the contact breaker plate from the timing cover at this stage unless so desired.

5 Remove the timing cover screws and part the joint between the timing cover and crankcase by a careful tap from behind the pressure release valve body using a hide hammer.

6 Lift the timing cover away, withdrawing the contact breaker lead from the timing case. It may be necessary to turn one of the snap connector bullets backwards so that the lead feeds through the case, one snap connector bullet at a time.

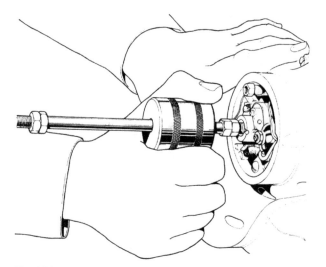

Fig. C20 Removing contact breaker cam using slide hammer 064298.

As the timing cover leaves the pump the new plunger at the conical rubber seal should be collected with its spring. This device is new on the Mark III and is designed to cut-off the flow of oil when the engine stops, preventing seepage past the pump and the possibility of oil building up in the crankcase during storage. (See *Fig.* C30 for illustration).

The inclusion of this anti-leak valve has introduced an important requirement on *INITIAL RUNS* of *the Mark III model.*

It is essential to prime the oil pump, and oil feed pipe before running the engine. See section C.30 for method. See *Fig.* C30 for illustration of valve.

7 Remove the two nuts securing the oil pump. The oil pump may be quite tight on its studs and in these circumstances it is advantageous to turn the oil pump drive wheel nut so that the oil pump will pull itself away along the worm drive. This operation is shown in *Fig. C21*.

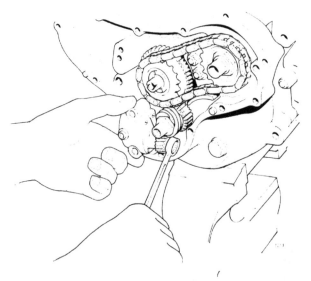

Fig. C21 Using a spanner to turn the oil pump drive wheel nut and remove the pump

8 Remove the oil pump driving worm from the crankshaft with its integral left hand threaded nut. To achieve this it is necessary to stop the crankshaft turning in the cases either by passing a round bar through the small ends and supporting on clean wooden blocks across the crankcase mouth or by placing a suitable bar into the deepest balance hole and allowing the bar to abut against the crankcase mouth in a similar manner to that shown in *Fig.* C22.

Engine/Primary Transmission C

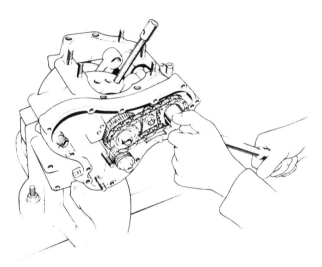

Fig. C22   Preventing flywheel turning by use of a bar lodged in a flywheel balance hole

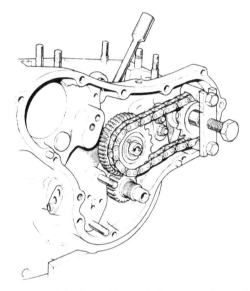

Fig. C23   Releasing a tight camshaft using sprocket service tool 064297

9   With the flywheel still prevented from turning, remove the nut securing the camshaft sprocket. Under no circumstances must anything but firm steady pressure be applied to unscrew the camshaft sprocket nut – normal right hand thread – unless a dummy cut away timing cover is fitted and secured with screws at extreme front rear and bottom. If a hammer or mallet is used without such a cover to support the end of the intermediate gear spindle, there is risk of the latter being pulled out of the crankcase.
The size of the sprocket nut is $\frac{9}{16}$ in. Whitworth.

10   Lift the sprocket, idler gear, and timing chain away as a set. If the camshaft sprocket should prove to be tight on the camshaft, it may be removed by using the special jaws supplied with the 064297 engine sprocket extractor.

Do not remove camshaft key from camshaft except for replacement.

11   Providing the timing cover joint gasket is not damaged during dismantling, there is no reason why it should be removed from the crankcase facing as it will be perfectly suitable for re-use.

12   Using Service Tool ET.2003 as shown in Fig. C24, extract the crankshaft pinion. It should be noted that the jaws of the service tool locate to the spaces provided in the pinion backing washer.

13   Lift away the pinion key which is of the Woodruff type. Remove also the backing washer.

14   Remove the oil sealing disc which is lipped. This disc tends to cling to the main bearing due to the presence of oil and the use of two small magnets or some other means is recommended to lift the disc clear.

15   If desired, the timing chain tensioner, clamping plates, nuts and fan disc washers can be removed from the crankcase at this stage.

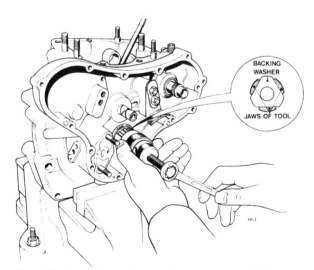

Fig. C24   Extracting crankshaft pinion using tool ET 2003

16 Dismount the crankcases from the vice so that they may be parted and the crankshaft assembly extracted.

17 Remove the two studs, one bolt and two set screws, holding the crankcases together. Unless the additional bottom stud has been removed to mount the crankcases in a vice, the stud should be removed at this stage.

18 Part the crankcases, releasing the crankcase joint by the use of bar of wood against the drive side crankcase as shown in *Fig. C25*.

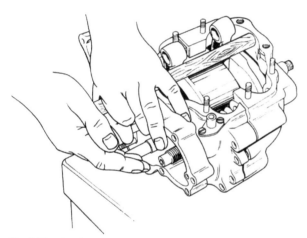

Fig. C25 Parting the crankcases using a wood block against the inner drive side

19 Withdraw the camshaft from the timing crankcase and collect the chamfered thrust washer.

20 The Mark III is equipped with two roller bearings and the timing side crankcase should now lift off without difficulty.

SECTION C17

CRANKCASE OVERHAUL

The following text covers the renewal of main bearings only. In our experience the camshaft bushes have an extremely long life and renewal cannot be accomplished without extensive machining facilities. To remove the main bearings, it is necessary to heat the area surrounding each main bearing with a soft flame such as a gasoline or kerosene (petrol or paraffin) blow lamp or butane or propane. Concentrate the heat in the area of the crankcase surrounding the main bearing and by bumping the joint facing of the crankcase hard against a flat wooden surface, the main bearing outer

race should be dislodged. In the case of drive side heated, in the case of a timing side crankcase equipped with the ball type of main bearing, use a suitable soft drift against the inner race of the main bearing and the bearing can be drifted out. In the case of a timing side crankcase equipped with the roller type of main bearing, heat the area of the crankcase surrounding the main bearing and by bumping the joint facing of the cankcase hard against a flat wooden surface, the main bearing outer race should be dislodged. In the case of drive side crankcases, the complete crankcase will need to be appreciably hotter since the only method of removing the main bearing outer race will be to bump the crankcase sharply against a flat wooden surface.

To refit the main bearings, the cases must be similarly heated and the main bearings, whether of the ball or roller variety should drop, completely freely, into their housings. The main bearings must be fully home into the housings both at the drive side and timing side cases.

SECTION C18

REMOVING CONNECTING RODS

Remove the connecting rods by releasing the two self locking nuts when it should be possible to pull the connecting rod away from the cap by hand pressure. The bearing shells remain in position at this stage but if they are to be re-used, they must be protected from dirt and possible damage. It is vitally important that at no stage are the connecting rod end caps interchanged between rods and it is equally important that the end caps should not be reversed on their own connecting rods.

A scribe marking is used on the connecting rod and end cap to show the correct direction of fitting. The locating tabs on both of the bearing shells fit to the same side of each connecting rod.

SECTION C19

DISMANTLING THE CRANKSHAFT

The Mark III crankshaft is of stiffer construction than previous assemblies, the webs are thicker and the main bearings have been spread to accommodate the wider cheeks. The drive side oil-seal is also retained by a circlip on the new engine. The drive side mainshaft is extended to accommodate the electric starter mechanism.

Engine/Primary Transmission C

The flywheel clamping studs have been increased from $\frac{5}{16}$" to $\frac{3}{8}$" dia. and on early despatches the alignment was dowelled by one $\frac{7}{16}$"/$\frac{3}{8}$" dia. *shouldered* stud on the crank centre line and one each $\frac{3}{8}$" dia. fitted stud at 11 o'clock and 1 o'clock respectively. The remaining four studs were a clearance fit.

On final production the arrangement has been rationalised to use a common stud. The shouldered stud has been replaced by a further $\frac{3}{8}$" dia. stud in common with the fitted studs at 11 o'clock and 1 o'clock. The remaining four studs are clearance. The fit is obtained by varying the hole sizes only. See section C27 illustration C33.

It is to be expected that the crankshait assembly which is now to be stripped will contain approximately one teacup full of oil and provision should be made for collecting this oil in a suitable receptacle.

Before parting the crank cheeks from the flywheel, it is recommended that the flywheel be marked e.g. "T.S." for timing side so that it is not reversed during re-assembly. Proceed as follows:

1 Slacken the fixed nuts on the timing side securing the crank cheek to the flywheel, noting that the nuts have been 'loctited' during assembly and may be expected to be extremely tight.

2 Jar the crank cheeks free from the flywheel using a hammer and soft drift. The drive side crankshaft will come away.

Dependent upon mileage there is likely to be a considerable build up of sludge and foreign matter in both the crank cheeks and the recess in the flywheel. This foreign matter must be cleaned out most thoroughly.

Tool No. 063970 is available to remove roller bearing races from the crankshaft, as shown in *Fig.* C28.

SECTION C20

CRANKSHAFT INSPECTION AND REGRINDING

Wash each crank cheek in clean petrol and blow dry with an air line. Examine the big end journals for scoring and remove light score marks by the use of smooth emery tape. If there is excessive scoring or ovality and it exceeds 0·0015 in. (·0381 mm) on the big end journals, regrinding is necessary.

The regrind sizes are shown overleaf. The revised big end journal sizes necessitate the use of connecting rod shell bearings of the correct undersize. The steel backed big end shells are finished to provide the correct diametrical clearance and must not, under any circumstances, be scraped. Shell bearings are available

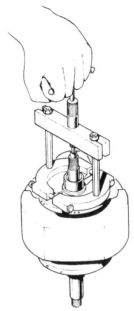

Fig. C28   Removing roller bearing inner race using extractor 063970.

in undersizes of minus 0·010 in., minus 0·020 in., minus 0·030 in. and minus 0·040 in.

SECTION C21

ENGINE LUBRICATION SYSTEM

The Commando lubrication system as shown in *Fig.* C29 is of the dry sump type, oil contained in the separate oil tank being fed through a wire strainer by gravity and by suction through the feed side of the gear type oil pump to the crankshaft. The oil pump delivers lubricant under pressure to the oil pressure relief valve and a bleed off the main feed supplies lubricant to the rocker gear. The main oil supply is delivered through the end of the crankshaft, (which is sealed by a garter type seal in the timing cover) to both big ends and escapes between the big end shells and crank journals to lubricate the cylinder walls, main bearings, camshaft and cam followers by splash. Oil collects in the crankcase sump, the inlet rocker box draining through a drill way in the cylinder barrel, and the exhaust rocker box draining through a drill way into the push rod tunnel and providing additional lubrication whilst returning to the crankcase between the cam followers to the camshaft.

The return side of the oil pump draws oil from the sump via the collecting area in the crankcase and returns it to the oil tank.

N.B. The chain oiler previously used is now discontinued. On the Mark III an aerosel can of chain-spray is provided in the tool kit.

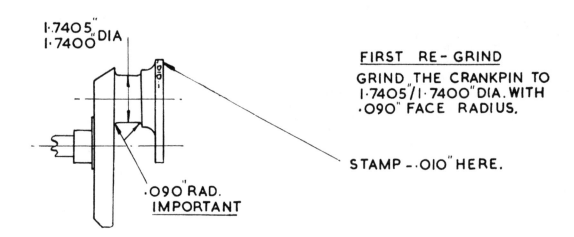

FIRST RE-GRIND

GRIND THE CRANKPIN TO
1·7405"/1·7400"DIA. WITH
·090" FACE RADIUS.

STAMP -·010" HERE.

1·7405"
1·7400" DIA

·090" RAD.
IMPORTANT

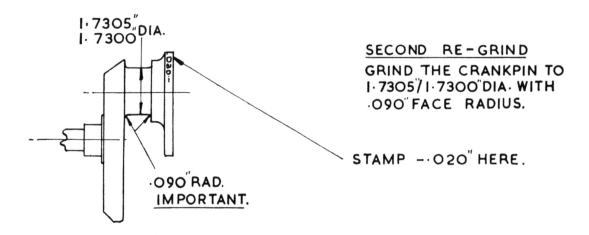

SECOND RE-GRIND

GRIND THE CRANKPIN TO
1·7305"/1·7300"DIA. WITH
·090" FACE RADIUS.

STAMP -·020" HERE.

1·7305"
1·7300" DIA.

·090" RAD.
IMPORTANT.

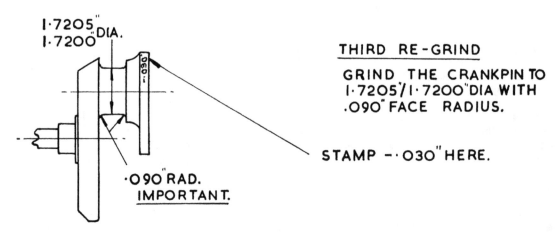

THIRD RE-GRIND

GRIND THE CRANKPIN TO
1·7205"/1·7200"DIA WITH
·090" FACE RADIUS.

STAMP -·030" HERE.

1·7205"
1·7200" DIA.

·090" RAD.
IMPORTANT.

N106

Fig. C26   *Crankshaft big-end journal regrind particulars*   (Note: **Fig. C27** *intentionally omitted*)

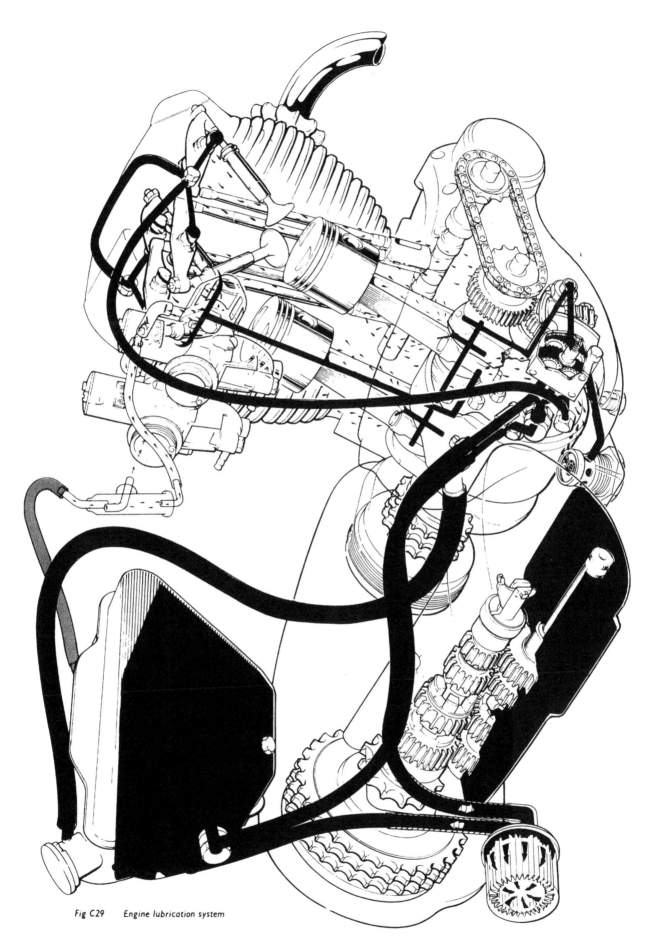

Fig C29   Engine lubrication system

Engine/Primary Transmission C

SECTION C22

OIL PRESSURE RELIEF VALVE

The relief valve is fitted to prevent oil pressure rising above 45/55 lbs. sq. inch. It is fitted to the rear of the timing cover below the rocker oil feed pipe banjo. The valve consists of a spring loaded steel sleeve pre-set at the factory using shims to regulate the blow off pressure and the valve requires no attention. Oil escaping from the valve returns to the feed side of the pump. The Mark III design has been modified to improve flow, reduce aeration and increase pressure at high temperature.

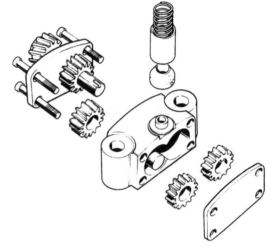

Fig. C30   Comprising parts of oil pump

SECTION C23

CRANKCASE BREATHER

The Mark III engine has a breather located at the top rear of the timing chest. As with earlier models, the breather is vented through the oil tank to the air filter, but the new model has an additional oil separator which traps oil passing beyond the breather before it enters the air-box.

Oil collected in the separator will be sucked into the engine via the intake balance pipe which now has a tee-piece junction to accommodate the oil pipe.

SECTION C24

OIL PUMP

The oil pump is of the gear type and is shown in detail in *Fig.* C30. The return side of the pump, which is of twice the capacity of the feed side to provide sufficient capacity to keep the crankcases clear of surplus oil, is identified by the wider gears. The oil pump is sealed to the timing cover bore with a conical rubber oil seal located on the pump body by a steel ferrule and compressed by the timing cover. An additional cut-off valve is now a standard feature on the Mark III, see C16 paragraph 6. Removal of the oil pump is included

in Section C16 and the servicing routine covered in Section C25.

SECTION C25

SERVICING THE OIL PUMP

Removal of the oil pump is described in Section *C16*. The criterion of oil pump condition is the degree of end float on the oil pump pinions, most easily felt by movement of the oil pump driving gear relative to the pump body. After some period of use, the tendency is for the pinions to wear into the pump end covers and such wear can only be removed by taking off the covers and flattening down the actual pump body.

1   Detach the pump top covers and drive gear with drive spindle by tapping the spindles through the keyed pinion with a pin point drift. The remaining parts can be lifted from the pump body at this stage.

2   Wash all the components thoroughly in clean gasoline (petrol) and allow to dry.

It is most important to correct end float on the feed gears (the narrow ones) first.

Engine/Primary Transmission C

3 Remove the feed gears and rub down the back plate end of the pump body surface against a high grade quality emery cloth on a perfectly flat surface such as a small surface plate. Flattening of the surface should continue a little at a time until the stage is reached where, on re-assembly of the oil pump, there is barely discernible stiffness on the oil pump driving spindle. This barely discernible stiffness will indicate that there is just sufficient freedom of movement and that there is no excess clearance between the feed gears and housing.

4 Remove the feed gears and repeat the flattening down process on the return side of the pump body until with the return gears only in the pump body and the screws tight there is similar slight stiffness.

5 Strip the pump body again and wash with very great care. Reassemble the pump and tighten the screws completely. At this stage there should be some degree of stiffness in the complete pump.

6 Introduce oil into the feed hole then, holding the oil pump with one hand, place a ring spanner over the driving spindle nut, and revolve the oil pump a number of times to allow oil to circulate completely. The oil pump should now have freed off considerably. Slight stiffness remaining should decrease, if not disappear completely.

SECTION C26

TIMING COVER

There are two garter type seals in the timing cover, one at the contact breaker housing and one to seal the crankshaft to the cover.

Contact Breaker Seal – Failure of this seal is indicated by the presence of oil in the contact breaker housing. To remove the old seal it is necessary to prise out with a screwdriver or similar implement thus rendering the seal scrap. A new seal should be fitted, pressure side, that is spring side, towards the engine and the seal should be tapped fully home into the housing using Service Tool 064292.

Crankshaft Seal – This seal is retained in the housing with a circlip. After removing the circlip, the seal can be prised out of its housing but will be damaged beyond further use. Care must be taken to avoid damage to the housing. Fit the new seal pressure side towards the timing cover and drive fully home using Service Tool 064292. Refit the circlip "sharp" side towards the crankcase and make sure that it is fully seated all-round.

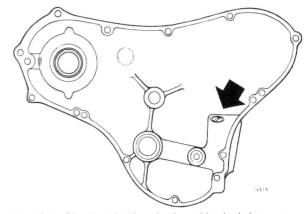

Fig. C31 Showing blanking plug in position in timing cover

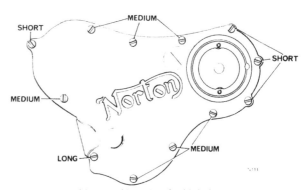

Fig. C32 Positions and lengths of odd timing cover screws

Where a new timing cover is being prepared for fitting, check that the blanking plug shown in *Fig.* C31 is in position. The timing cover odd screw lengths are shown in *Fig. C32*.

Engine/Primary Transmission C

SECTION C27

RE-ASSEMBLY OF THE CRANKSHAFT

Prior to assembly, it is vital to polish the crank journals using a fine grade emery tape then make absolutely sure that all parts are washed very thoroughly in gasoline (petrol) until clean. Ensure also that the oil ways are clean and blown through with an air line. Re-assembly proceeds as below:

1 Fit the drive side crank cheek to the flywheel, mating the markings previously made.

2 Fit the central dowel stud through from drive side to timing side, check alignment of crank cheeks, and assemble remaining two dowel studs at 11 o'clock and 1 o'clock respectively.

3 Assemble the timing side crank cheek over the three studs noting that all three studs are a good fit in the crank cheeks and will probably need tapping home with a drift.

4 Assemble the four remaining studs, driving side to timing side, these are a clearance fit and should assemble without difficulty.

5 Apply loctite LT. 241 or similar thread locking compound to all studs and assemble nuts, tightening progressively and diagonally to 30 lbs./ft. torque (4·15 Kgm).

6 Ensure that the oil way blanking plug is fitted in the timing side crank cheek, particularly if a new timing side crank cheek is in use.

ALL NUTS NOW $\frac{3}{8} = 14$ OFF

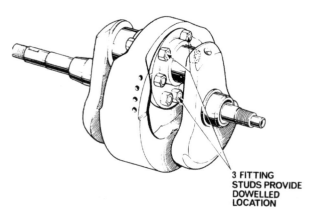

3 FITTING STUDS PROVIDE DOWELLED LOCATION

Fig. C33   Showing crankcheek to flywheel securing hardware

SECTION C28

RE-ASSEMBLING CONNECTING RODS TO CRANKSHAFT

As a matter of practice always use new bearing shells and at the time of fitting the shells, smear them with clean engine oil. Proceed as follows:

1 Press the drilled shell into the connecting rod big end eye and rotate into position, locating with the tab.

2 Fit the plain shell into the connecting rod cap and again locate the tab. The tab positions are shown in *Fig.* C34.

3 Fit the connecting rods but before doing so, note that it is unnecessary to renew the connecting rod bolts though new nuts should always be used. The connecting rods must be fitted with the oil holes from the big end eye outwards in each case. Fit the end caps with shells, ensuring that the mating marks align, and tighten the nuts evenly by hand.

4 Tighten the connecting rod nuts to a torque reading of 25 lbs./ft. (3·456 Kg/m).

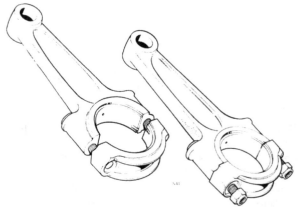

Fig. C34   *Connecting rods showing both sides of big end eye and bearing shell tab locations - Mark III now shot-peened for greater fatigue life.*

Engine/Primary Transmission **C**

SECTION C29

RE-ASSEMBLING CRANKSHAFT
TO CRANKCASES

1   Push the timing side crankcase over the crankshaft which must be supported upright on the bench. See *Fig.* C35. At this time check that the connecting rods clear the crankcase mouth of the crankshaft end of the bearing. If the bearing is too tight to push home over the crank, place a scrap main bearing inner race and a large washer over the crankshaft, outboard of the timing side crankcase then, using the oil pump driving worm on the crankshaft, pull it home through the bearing.

2   Position the camshaft thrust washer over the timing side camshaft bush and locate this, flat side towards the crankcase and bush, locating with a blob of grease.

3   Smear the timing side crankcase joint facing with a non-setting sealing compound. A little may be applied to the timing side case facing where there is no spigot.

4   Offer the drive side crankcase to the timing side after oiling the camshaft bearing area and the drive side roller main bearing. The operation of mating the crankcases is shown in *Fig.* C36. It is most important that the drive side connecting rod does not come into contact with the crankcase mouth and at the final stage of mating the crankcases, it may well be necessary to turn the tachometer drive to locate into the camshaft worm drive.

5   Now tap the crankcases together with a hide hammer until the joint faces meet all-round.

6   Before tightening the crankcase securing nuts, ensure that there is end float on the camshaft, indicating its freedom.

7   Fit the crankcase front and rear screws, studs, nuts and washers.

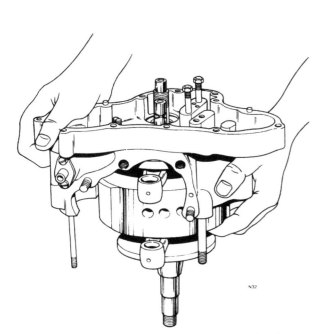

Fig. C35   Pushing timing side crankcase over crankshaft

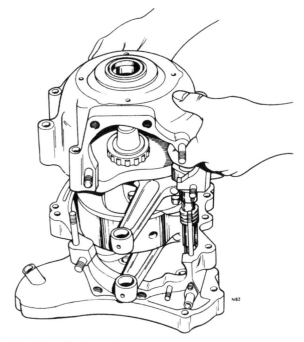

Fig. C36   Mating crankcases.

Engine/Primary Transmission C

8 Fit the short front crankcase mating bolt from drive side to timing side then fit the front bottom stud unless the crankcase is to be mounted in the vice in which case this front bottom stud should be omitted until a later stage.

9 Fit the two slot headed set screws from the timing side.

10 Tighten the mating nuts and screws evenly in rotation and wipe away surplus jointing compound remaining on the outside of the crankcase joint facing.

SECTION C30

ASSEMBLING RIGHT (TIMING SIDE) OF ENGINE

Having assembled the crankcases as detailed in Section C29, mount the crankcases in a plain jaw vice to facilitate handling. Re-assembly of the cam chain, sprockets and oil pump may now be undertaken as follows:

1 Fit the oil sealing disc over the timing side crankshaft, lip outwards.

2 Fit the cut-away backing washer.

3 Fit the woodruff key into the crankshaft then place on the crankshaft pinion, chamfered teeth and timing mark outwards. It may be necessary to tap the pinion fully home using a suitable tube as a drift.

4 Turn the crankshaft to top dead centre so that the timing pinion marking is uppermost.

5 Take the intermediate gear sprocket, the camshaft sprocket and cam chain, assembling as shown in *Fig.* C37. For correct timing the timing marks must be 10 rollers apart on the chain as shown in the illustration.

6 Locate the camshaft sprocket and intermediate gear and sprocket in position, mating up the marked space between the teeth on the inter-

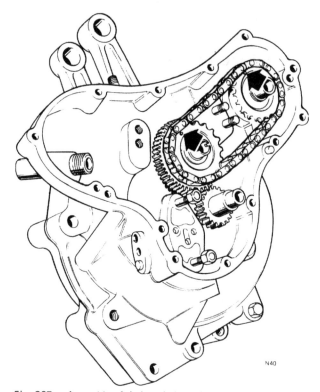

Fig. C37   Assembly of timing chain and sprockets. Note arrows

mediate gear with the marked tooth on the timing pinion. On all engines it will be found that there is a paint marking to illustrate more clearly the timing position on the intermediate timing gear.

7 Assemble the chain tensioner as shown in *Fig.* C38, The Mark III tensioner blade now has a neoprene covering and the clamp plates (which previously differed) are common and interchangeable.

8 Fit the chain tensioner, fan disc washers and nuts moving the tensioner blade up to give a maximum $\frac{3}{16}$ in. (4·8 m m) up and down movement at the tightest point of the chain and nip up the tensioner securing nut. Before finally locking up these nuts, rotate the crankshaft a little at a time, checking at each stage the chain tension lest there should be a tight spot on some point of the chain. When chain tension is correct, finally lock up the tensioner securing nuts.

9 The Mark III model has an inspection plug in the timing cover for checking tension easily in service without disturbing the cover.

Engine/Primary Transmission C

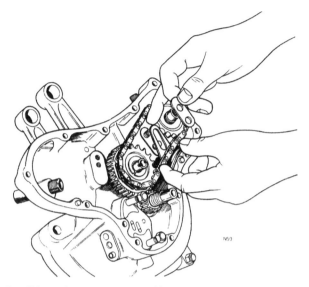

Fig. C38   *Chain tensioner - assembly*

10   Fit the oil pump driving worm which is left hand threaded.

11   Fit the camshaft sprocket nut which is normal right hand threaded.

12   In order to tighten both the oil pump driving worm nut and camshaft sprocket nut securely it is necessary to sprag the crankshaft with a suitable bar placed in the deepest of the flywheel balance holes as shown earlier in *Fig. C22*.
      Under no circumstances tighten the camshaft sprocket nut by shocking using a box spanner, tommy bar and hammer since an even pressure is required specifically for tightening this nut. Tighten securely the timing pinion nut.

Prior to fitting the oil pump it is desirable, if the pump has been stripped or parts renewed, to prime this. The pump should be turned by hand and oil fed into the gears by the use of an oil gun.

13   Fit the oil pump and secure with two nuts without washers. A torque figure of 10/12 ft. lbs. (1·383 to 1·659 Kg/m) is required.

14   Fit a new conical rubber oil seal part number NMT272 on the oil pump outlet stub.

15   After the oil pump is secured, recheck the security of the driving gear nut.

SECTION C31

REFITTING THE TIMING COVER

The timing cover should be prepared by washing very thoroughly in clean gasoline (petrol) and if necessary by renewing the oil seals as described in Section *C26*. If a new timing cover is to be fitted, check that the blanking plug is fitted into the boss for the pressure relief valve. This feature is shown in *Fig. C31*.

1   Fit the contact breaker oil seal protection tool 061359 into the camshaft and tighten. This will allow the contact breaker seal to pass over the camshaft without damage as the timing cover is placed in position. Lightly oil the tapered surface of this tool.

2   Pass the contact breaker lead through the hole in the timing case, then locate the cover in position, making sure the cut-off valve plunger and spring are fitted and the plunger is seating on the conical rubber. See C16 paragraph 6.

3   Fit the timing cover screws. The odd screw lengths are shown in *Fig. C32* but the remaining screws are all of the same length. Secure the set of screws.

4   Remove the contact breaker seal tool 061359.

5   Prepare the auto advance mechanism by cleaning very thoroughly and lubricating sparingly with clean engine oil. Ensure that the taper for the auto advance cam is clean and dry then offer the auto advance unit loosely into position.

6   Fit the contact breaker plate, yellow lead rearwards and secure with the pillar studs central in the adjustment slots. For ease of handling at a later stage, centralise both contact breaker plate adjusters. These are indicated in *Fig. C54*.

SECTION C32

RE-ASSEMBLY OF CRANKCASE ASSEMBLY TO FRAME

Re-assembly of the crankcase into the frame is virtually a reversal of the dismantling procedure though the

Engine/Primary Transmission C

operation of fitting the front mounting is given complete as below:

1 With the crankcase attached to the rear engine mounting plates, lift the crankcase assembly and gearbox, pivoting on the rear mounting to insert the bottom studs.

It is necessary to fit the front mounting at this stage before final tightening of all the engine plate to crankcase bolts and before fitting the inner chaincase. Adjustment of the front mounting has already been carried out on the bench as in Section F15.

The Mark III isolastic mountings have been re-designed with one fixed end-cap and one adjustable cap which is threaded to the central hollow spindle creating an integral assembly with no loose fittings and allowing easy adjustment and simple assembly as one unit.

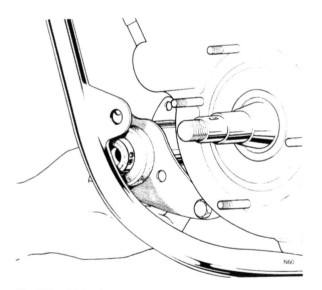

Fig. C39   Lifting front mounting into position using bottom bolt as pivot

2 Take the front mounting and slide the bottom mounting to crankcase stud into position.

3 Using the bottom stud as the pivot, lift the mounting into position on the crankcase bosses as in *Fig.* C39.

4 Grease both end cap faces to facilitate insertion between the mounting ears on the frame.

5 Lifting the crankcase a little as required to align the hollow spindle with the frame ears, insert the centre bolt from the timing side through to the left hand side, easing the threads carefully past the ear, avoiding damage to the threads, and slide fully home.

6 Ensure that gaiters are not disarranged, revolving a little to facilitate the operation.

7 Fit and secure the centre bolt nut and washer and tighten to 25 lbs./ft. (3·456 Kg/m).

8 The remaining items of the engine plates which have been assembled as a reversal of the dismantling procedure should now be tightened to the recommended torque settings. The $\frac{3}{8}$ in. diameter engine to frame stud nuts require a torque figure of 30 lbs./ft. (4·148 Kg/m) and the $\frac{5}{16}$ in. nuts to 20 lbs./ft. (2·765 Kg/m).

9 As previously mentioned in C16 paragraph 6, the Mark III engine is equipped with a new anti-leak valve between the pump and timing cover oil-way. This makes it essential to prime the pump and feed-pipe before running the engine — although the pump unit has been primed before installation. The recommended procedure (ref. Engineering instruction No. 18).

1 Fill oil tank.

2 Slacken junction block screw.

3 When oil escapes from junction block/crankcase joint retighten junction block screw to 8 lbs./ft. (1·10 Kg/m).

The oil pump and feed pipe are now primed.

Engine/Primary Transmission C

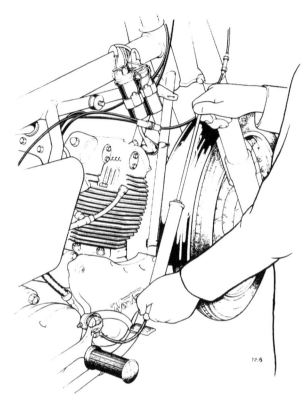

Fig. C41   Priming crankshaft with oil

Also prior to fitting the bottom connection for the rocker feed pipe it is most desirable to prime the crankshaft with approximately a teacup full of oil. This is most easily achieved by the use of an oil syringe, short length of flexible pipe, and a spare rocker feed pipe banjo which can be connected at the rear of the timing case The priming operation is shown in *Fig.* C41.

SECTION C33

REFITTING PISTONS AND CYLINDER

Throughout the fitting of the pistons and cylinder, take care to protect the connecting rods and pistons from damage caused by these parts coming into contact with the crankcase mouth or cylinder base studs. Proceed as follows:

1   Grease the crankcase studs lightly and apply a coat of Loctite "plastic gasket" material to cylinder base flange.

2   Fit one circlip to each piston, sharp edge outwards.

3   Heat the pistons in hot water to ease entry of the wrist pins (gudgeon pins).

5   Oil the small end eye and wrist pin bosses and push each wrist pin home by hand.

6   As each piston is fitted, fit the second circlip sharp end outwards.

7   Turn the engine crankshaft backwards to lower the pistons, then support the pistons as in *Fig.* C42 on two suitable bars which must not overlap the timing case.

8   Position the piston rings with the top compression ring gap central at the front of the piston body and the second taper ring gap central at the rear of the piston body.

9   Position the scraper ring expander to the side of the piston body with the rail gap 1 in. to the left and right of the expander gap to prevent the rail ends spragging in the connecting rod clearance cutaways in the cylinders.

10   Smear both piston bodies with clean engine oil. Fit piston ring clamps (also shown in *Fig.* C42) to keep the piston rings closed. Do not overtighten the ring clamps which would tend to prevent the ring clamps sliding as the cylinder is offered.

Engine/Primary Transmission C

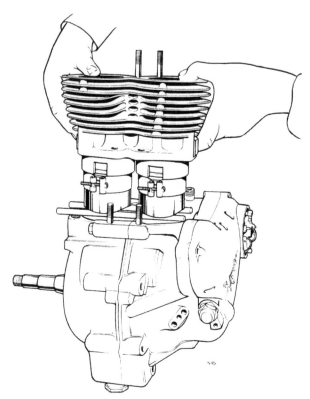

Fig. C42   Fitting cylinder over pistons. Note piston supporting bars and ring clamps in use

◕ 240 in lb/20 ft lb (2·75 Kg/m)
◔ 360 in lb/30 ft lb (4·15 Kg/m)
● 300 in lb/25 ft lb (3·75 Kg/m)

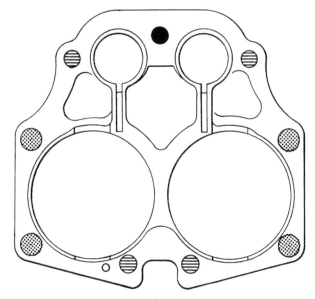

Fig. C43   Cylinder base securing torques.

11   Offer the cylinder over the pistons as shown in *Fig.* C42, pushing the cylinder down to slide the ring clamps down quickly. The pistons are now entered in the cylinder bores.

12   Remove the support bars and both rings clamps.

13   Partially lower the cylinder but start cylinder base nuts before lowering the barrel completely. Only the large centre nut lacks a washer. The outside socket head screws all have washers.

14   Tighten the cylinder fixings in diagonal sequence working to torque settings as shown in *Fig.* C43.

SECTION C34

ASSEMBLING PRIMARY TRANSMISSION

The primary transmission is assembled in the order: inner primary chaincase, engine sprocket, clutch and primary chain, rotor and stator and finally the outer primary chaincase. The full routine is detailed below:

1   Check that the engine sprocket key will pass freely through the keyway in the sprocket and if necessary relieve any roughness.

2   Fit the engine sprocket key into the crankshaft.

3   Fit the inner chaincase to crankcase gasket, holding in position with grease or a non-setting jointing compound.

4   Check that the plain washer is on the chaincase support stud.

5   Ensure that the inner and outer joint faces of the inner chaincase are clean.

6   Fit the inner chaincase, ensuring that the gearbox mainshaft seal passes over the mainshaft without damage (covering the splines with plastic tape will help) and that the chaincase forward end is

fully home on the four long studs which extend through for the new outrigger mounting plate supporting the alternator.

Make sure the central adjustable support stud is fitted behind the cover with the abutment nut slackened off, in readiness for adjustment after the outrigger nuts are tightened. (See Fig. C45)

The electric starter may still be attached by its two upper fixing screws also the small intermediate gear which assembles from the back.

7   At this point it is most important to observe a fundamental difference between the Mark III and previous Commando models: namely the *rigidly mounted gearbox.* (See note 7 Section C14).

It is important that the gearbox sprocket sleeve runs truly concentrically within the chaincase oil-seal, which is located inboard at the back of the cover, behind the clutch. The seal will cope with moderate misalignment but its function and life will benefit from extra care in ensuring that the sprocket sleeve is coaxial with the seal before clamping up the gearbox mountings. A guide tool No. ST4928D is recommended to prevent damage to the seal as it passes over the clutch circlip and sharp edge of the sleeve. Dimensions and partic-ulars are illustrated on Fig. C45.

Providing the seal is coaxial, Clamp up the gearbox mountings and proceed.

8   Assemble the clutch location circlip and spacer, recessed portion towards the gearbox, followed by the spacing washer. The purpose of the spacing washers is to align accurately the clutch sprocket with the engine sprocket.

It is always desirable to check chain alignment in case a collar is forgotten or something has been changed: Push engine sprocket full home on its taper over the woodruff key and push the clutch sprocket firmly over the splines to its abutment-collar. Check alignment with a steel rule or similar straight-edge laid along the teeth of both sprockets. *See illustration C.46:* Providing nothing has been replaced the alignment should be correct and chain fitting can proceed. (Misalign-ment will need correcting with suitable spacing washers behind the clutch).

9   Assemble the engine sprocket and clutch sprocket to the triple row chain ready for fitting.

10 With the large starter gear located in the machined recess behind the top run of the primary chain – offer the engine sprocket, clutch sprocket and primary chain as a set, feeding the stator through between the chain runs. The stator is still attached to the inner chaincase by the lead passing through the chaincase grommet.

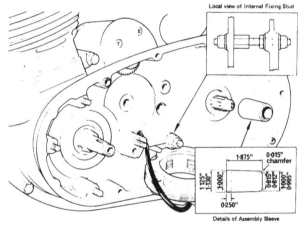

Fig. C45   Installation of inner primary cover

11 At this stage push the engine sprocket fully home over the woodruff key, if necessary using a tubular drift to push the sprocket fully home. At the same time the clutch will need to be pushed home firmly over the splines of the mainshaft.

12 Fit the clutch centre securing nut and tab washer engaging the ends in the 2 holes in the clutch centre.

13 Wedge-on the rear brake as described in Section C.13 paragraph 2 to lock transmission and tighten the clutch centre nut. 061015: workshop tool for clutch lock is available providing the best method of assembling the clutch centre. See service tool catalogue for illustration and partic-ulars. The correct torque for the clutch centre nut is 70 lbs./ft. (9·678 Kg/m). Squeeze the centre portion of the tab washer to 2 flats on the nut. Proceed to assemble the clutch.

14 If for any reason the clutch plates have been removed from the housing, re-assemble these, an inner splined friction plate first into the housing, followed by a plain steel alternately, finishing with the robust iron pressure plate next to the diaphragm spring.

Engine/Primary Transmission C

15   The clutch diaphragm spring should be assembled to the spring tool and tensioned as shown earlier in *Fig. C13* until the diaphragm spring is flat.

16   Offer the diaphragm spring on the tool to the clutch housing and push home as far as possible.

17   Enter one end of the clutch spring circlip and continue to wind the remainder of the spring into the housing.

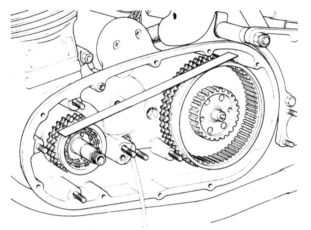

Fig. C46   Primary chain alignment check

18   When the spring circlip is well bedded into the housing all-round, remove the spring tool by slackening the centre bolt.

19   Fit the clutch push rod adjuster screw and lock nut.

20   Adjust the clutch push rod with the handlebar adjustment slackened off completely. Screw in the adjuster until there is just perceptible lift on the diaphragm spring and slacken back one full turn, holding in this position whilst the lock nut is tightened completely.

It is possible for the clutch operating lever in the kickstart case to have dropped down between the thrust ball and roller against which the lever lifts and if this has occurred, it will be found that the clutch is inoperative, and it will be necessary to remove the inspection cover which is secured by two screws to the gearbox outer cover, slacken back fully the push rod adjuster and lift the lever back into position before adjusting.

21   Proceed to assemble the starter drive mechanism as follows:

22   Replace thrust-collar in sprocket recess – this must be fitted with small dia. facing outwards.

23   Fit hardened sleeve on engine mainshaft (this is likely to be a good fit).

24   Assemble starter free-wheel sprag into sprocket recess. It is important to fit this the correct way to take the starter drive. See *illustration Fig. C48.*

The drive sprag is designed to fling clear as the engine revs increase, releasing the drive automatically as the motor starts up.

25   Fit the large starter gear with its needle roller bearing over the hardened sleeve and enter it into the roller-sprag. Revolve the gear to check that the sprag is driving the right way to start the engine.

26   Assemble the primary chain Tensioner, (previously taped or wired to prevent the skate plungers from springing out of their respective cylinders), replacing the body over its three studs and with the outer plate located in position assemble the two $\frac{5}{16}$ in. nuts and single $\frac{1}{4}$ in. nut using Loctite or a thread locking compound such as LT 241 on threads, torquing to 12 lbs./ft. on the former and *4–5 lbs./ft. only* on the small nut. These torque figures are critical.

The tightening procedure is most important and on no account should the nuts be over tightened as distortion can occur and jamming may result.

Although priming of the dash-pot should be unnecessary if the plungers were left in position, it is desirable to apply a small amount of engine oil into the catchment and squeeze the plungers to suck oil into the dash-pot. This will operate automatically in use. (See Fig. C47).

27   The over-load backfire device can now be engaged into the spline of the large gear at the back of the cover and its outer gear meshed with the sprag-gear in the engine sprocket. The starter reduction gear train is now complete. (See Fig. C48).

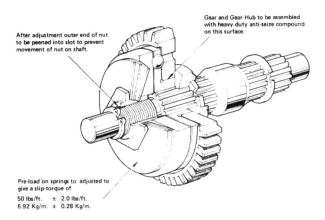

Gear and Gear-Hub to be assembled with heavy duty anti-seize compound on this surface.

After adjustment outer end of nut to be peened into slot to prevent movement of nut on shaft.

Pre-load on springs to adjusted to give a slip-torque of
50 lbs/ft. ± 2.0 lbs/ft.
6.92 Kg/m. ± 0.28 Kg/m.

Fig. C47(a)   Overload 'backfire' device: Electric starter Mark III Commando.

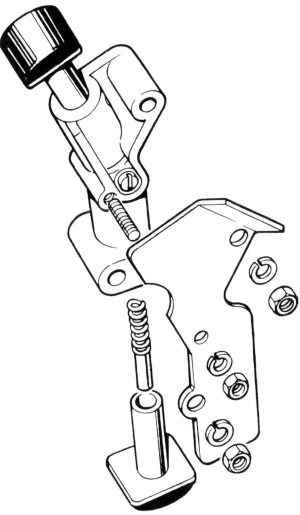

Fig. C47   Primary chain automatic tensioner; Exploded arrangement

28 Assemble the outrigger plate over its four studs engaging the backfire device intermediate-shaft in the bearing provided. The mounting stud tab washers will previously have been bent over the plate – torque up $\frac{1}{2}$ in. A/F nuts to 15 lbs./ft. (2·074 kg/m) and locate tab washers on flats in the usual manner.

With the outrigger nuts now tight, the inside central mounting can be set and tightened up.

First slack off the inner nut behind the cover boss and bring the nut up to the boss face, pinching the boss with the outer nut, carefully avoiding any stress in the cover.

Tighten to 15 lbs./ft. (210·74 Kg./m.) using LOCKTITE 241 or similar thread locking compound

29 Fit the large thrust plate over the mainshaft butting up to the starter gear.

30 Fit the rotor key.

31 Ensure that the rotor is free of any magnetic particles it may have attracted whilst dismantled and fit the rotor to the shaft and key, name and timing marks outboard.

32 Assemble the rotor nut and fan disc washer and with top gear engaged and the rear brake applied fully, as recommended in C13,2, tighten the rotor nut fully to 70 lbs./ft. (9·678 Kg/m).

33 Fit the stator on the three $\frac{5}{16}$ in. studs in the outrigger plate with the lead at the 5 o'clock position facing outboard.

34 Assemble the plain washers and stator securing nuts using Loctite LT 241 and tighten to a torque setting of 15 lbs./ft. (2·074 Kg/m). Check the gap between the stator and rotor whcih must give a minimum air gap of 0·008 in. to 0·010 in. (0·2032 to 0·254 mm). Any misalignment of the stator mounting studs would account for reduced air gap at any one given point and can only be corrected by very careful slight re-alignment of the studs.

Engine/Primary Transmission C

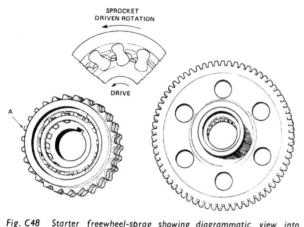

Fig. C48 *Starter freewheel-sprag showing diagrammatic view into sprocket at 'A' with sprags leaning at correct angle for drive.*

35 Replace the gearshift cross-shaft through its oil-seal in the inner cover, locating it in the splined connector on the gearbox replace the protective rubber sleeve. The pinion and circlip are still in situ; the shaft will engage in the bush in the outer cover and lie at a slight angle to clear the clutch chainwheel.

36 Offer up the outer cover, engaging the foot-shift gear and cross-shaft pinion with the pedal in desired position, and ensuring the joint washer is intact, assemble the eleven posidrive screws, the long screw securing the electric starter.

37 In order that the point is not overlooked it is recommended that lubricant is added to the chaincase at this stage.

38 Refit L.H. footrest with red earth wire terminal from zener diode on rear bolt.

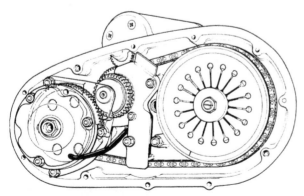

Fig. C49 *General view of primary drive assembly and chain tensioner: outer cover removed.*

SECTION C35

CLUTCH OPERATING MECHANISM

The clutch is connected from the left handlebar control to the clutch operating lever within the gearbox cover. As the lever is withdrawn, the clutch operating lever is lifted, exerting pressure on a ball bearing against the end of the clutch push rod. The push rod forces outwards the centre of the diaphragm spring, relieving the pressure and allowing the clutch plates to separate. For the clutch to operate correctly, the degree of free movement on the cable and clutch push rod must be controlled. Excessive slack may prevent the clutch freeing completely and excessively tight adjustment will result in the clutch plates being held apart. Adjustment is provided on the cable and push rod.

Clutch Adjustment

1 Slacken cable adjustment at the handlebar control as far as possible.

2 Remove the clutch adjuster inspection cap from the chaincase.

3 Remove the inspection cap from the gearbox end cover.

4 With the index finger, move the clutch operating lever to and fro inside the gearbox cover to establish whether or not there is slight movement. If there is, clutch push rod adjustment is correct. If there is not, rectify as follows.

5 Release nut (B) in *Fig.* C51 then turn the screw (C) gently anti-clockwise until movement is felt on the right side operating lever.

6 Turn screw (C) in a clockwise direction until it is felt that the screw just touches the push rod.

7 Unscrew adjustment screw (C) one full turn and, holding in this position retighten locknut (B). This ensures the correct free movement on the clutch push rod.

Engine/Primary Transmission C

8 Adjust the clutch cable at the control to provide $\frac{3}{16}$ in. to $\frac{1}{4}$ in. (4·76 to 6·35 m m) free movement between the cable outer casing and adjuster.

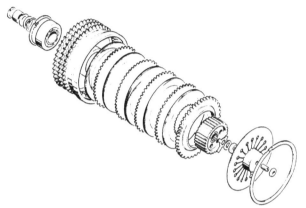

Fig. C50   Mark III clutch arrangement showing order of assembly

CLUTCH PLATES

The clutch dismantling procedure is covered as part of Section C13 "Dismantling Primary Transmission and Clutch." However, it is sometimes considered necessary to remove the plates separately for inspection.

To gain access to the clutch plates, follow Section C13 & C14 items 1 to 9. Next remove the clutch pressure plate followed alternately by the internal splined friction plates and external splined plain steel plates.

After removal, wash all the clutch plates and the pressure plate in gasoline (petrol) until perfectly clean, then allow to dry.

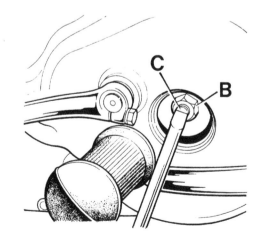

Fig. C51   Clutch adjustment

Reassembly is a reversal of the foregoing but full instructions are given in Section C34.

Plate Inspection

Examine the friction plates for obvious wear to the splines and for "charring" of the surface such as would occur during prolonged clutch slip. Examine the plain steel driven plates for deep scoring or grooving. Check the external splines for obvious wear, and check each plate in turn on a surface plate for flatness. Any badly worn or distorted plates must be renewed before reassembly.

SECTION C36

TACHOMETER DRIVE

The tachometer drive is taken from the worm drive at the right end of the camshaft. The cable has an adaptor for the cable between the lower end of the cable and tachometer driven gear. The driven gear is removable after removing two screws and lifting clear the housing and 'O' sealing ring but damage to the drive gear can only be corrected by replacing the camshaft.

SECTION C37

ELECTRIC STARTER MECHANISM

The Mark III Electric Starter is permanently engaged with its reduction gear-train, but only transmits drive to the engine shaft as permitted by a sprag clutch/free-wheel which disengages automatically immediately the engine starts.

The reduction gears are fully enclosed and lubricated within the primary chaincase and require no attention.

The drive "sprag" (or clutch) runs on the engine mainshaft engaging the drive between a sleeve on the final reduction gear and the inside diameter of the engine sprocket. The final reduction gear contains a needle roller bearing which runs on a hardened sleeve, close fitting the engine mainshaft.

Engine/Primary Transmission C

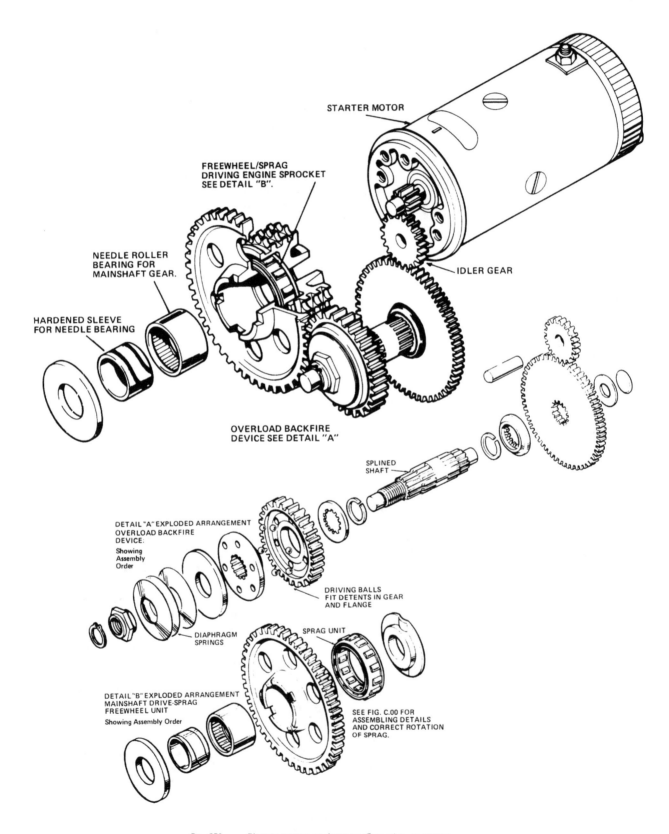

STARTER MOTOR

FREEWHEEL/SPRAG
DRIVING ENGINE SPROCKET
SEE DETAIL "B".

NEEDLE ROLLER
BEARING FOR
MAINSHAFT GEAR.

HARDENED SLEEVE
FOR NEEDLE BEARING

IDLER GEAR

OVERLOAD BACKFIRE
DEVICE SEE DETAIL "A"

SPLINED
SHAFT

DETAIL "A" EXPLODED ARRANGEMENT
OVERLOAD BACKFIRE
DEVICE.
Showing
Assembly
Order

DRIVING BALLS
FIT DETENTS IN GEAR
AND FLANGE

DIAPHRAGM
SPRINGS

SPRAG UNIT

DETAIL "B" EXPLODED ARRANGEMENT
MAINSHAFT DRIVE-SPRAG
FREEWHEEL UNIT
Showing Assembly Order

SEE FIG. C.00 FOR
ASSEMBLING DETAILS
AND CORRECT ROTATION
OF SPRAG.

Fig. C52   Electric starter mechanism: General arrangement

Engine/Primary Transmission C

It is important to check when assembling the drive sprag-cage inside the sprocket recess that this is the right way round. Obverse assembly will not drive!

See illustration C.52 for arrangement of mechanism and diagram C.52(a) for layout of the drive.

See Section J25 for Electric Starter Motor.

SECTION C38

REMOVING AND REFITTING ENGINE COMPLETE

For ease of handling the engine unit may be removed from the mounting plates as a unit so that it can be dealt with on the bench. Proceed as follows:

1   Remove the left footrest.

2   Drain and remove the outer primary chaincase, cross-shaft, alternator rotor nut and alternator stator. The stator can be left attached to the inner chaincase by the lead but disconnect the two connectors beneath the airbox and lever off the rotor.

3   Remove alternator mounting plate, outer thrust washer (behind rotor) large starter gear. With-

draw sprag cage, needle roller bearing sleeve and thrust washer from sprocket recess.

4   Extract the starter intermediate shaft from spline in back gear and remove previous chain tensioner (wire-in skates to avoid mixing fits).

5   Slacken off clutch adjustment, compress the clutch diaphragm spring (this requires tool 060999) and remove circlip.

6   Fit clutch hub tool 061015 and remove clutch centre nut and fit engine sprocket extractor tool 064297. Remove engine sprocket and lift entire engine sprocket – primary chain – clutch assembly away.

7   Remove clutch abutment circlip and internal fixing nut allowing inner chaincase to lift off its four studs.

8   Remove rubber breather hose at rear of timing chest.

9   Detach engine ground wire attached to lower left crankcase stud.

10   Remove fuel tank, ignition coils, carburettor top caps and withdraw slide assemblies. Remove exhaust pipes and upper Isolastic head steady and suspensory spring device.

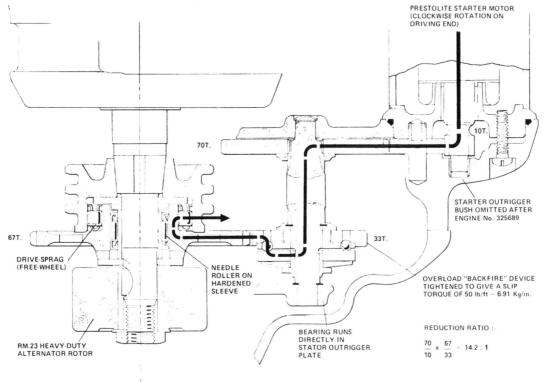

Fig. C52(a)   Diagram of starter gear reduction (and drive track)

Engine/Primary Transmission C

11 Drain oil from oil tank and remove oil feed lines from boss beneath timing cover. Remove rocker oil feed pipe, and oil-pipe from balance pipe tee-piece.

12 Disconnect the contact breaker lead wires, tachometer drive cable, and electric starter terminal, and remove starter.

13 Slip a sturdy support (wood block or metal rod) between engine and lower frame tubes.

14 Remove bolts holding rear of engine to engine cradle so engine hinges on front Isolastic mount.

15 Loosen small bolts holding front engine mount STEADY ENGINE and remove large Isolastic mount bolt, then the small bolts and lift out front Isolastic unit.

16 Engine is now free and can be lifted clear of frame to right side on to work bench.

Refitting is a direct reversal of the foregoing.

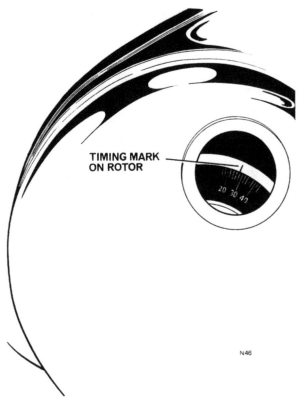

TIMING MARK ON ROTOR

N46

Fig. C 53   Timing plate visible after removal of inspection cap from chaincase

SECTION C39

IGNITION TIMING

Ignition timing can be checked and if necessary reset either with the engine stationary or, using a stroboscope, with the engine running. The stationary method is quite satisfactory where a stroboscope is not available. However, for greater accuracy, the stroboscope method is preferable, since it also checks auto advance function. A timing indicator plate is attached to the outer primary chaincase to align with the corresponding mark on the rotor, the marks being visible after removal of the chaincase inspection cap (see Fig. C53). The latest Lucas rotor has two timing markings opposite each other. Note that the presence of the surplus marking will not affect timing, either static or with a stroboscope.

To explain – the engine must be running for a stroboscope to be used. Setting the timing by the wrone marking would mean the spark was timed at bottom dead centre and the engine would not run. If the enging is timed on the correct stroke, the stroboscope will not pick up the wrong marking. Similarly with static timing, only the correct marking will align with the calibrated scale in the primary case with the piston near top dead centre on the firing stroke for the cylinder being timed.

Ignition Timing Basic Procedure Prior to Checking

Straightforward assembly of the auto-advance mechanism and contact breaker assembly is covered in Section C31 as part of the Timing Cover reassembly procedure. It is however, necessary to locate the auto-advance cam approximately prior to timing. It is assumed that the auto-advance mechanism is loose assembled to the taper in the camshaft and that the contact breaker backplate screws are central in the adjustment slots. Remove the inlet rocker cover and the right hand exhaust rocker cover and both sparking plugs then turn the engine forwards on the kickstart until T.D.C. is located on the right cylinder with both valves closed at the firing position. Identify by wire colouring the contact breaker points for the right cylinder then turn the auto-advance cam until it just starts to open this set of points. Secure the cam with washer and centre bolt. The engine is now ready for accurate timing.

Engine/Primary Transmission C

Ignition Timing Procedure – Engine Static

1   Remove both spark plugs.

2   Remove the inspection cap on the chaincase.

3   Remove the contact breaker cover.

4   Clean and adjust the contact breaker points as described in Section C40.

Note that if, at any later time, contact breaker adjustment is disturbed or allowed to vary, ignition timing will be altered. This necessitates retiming of the engine.

5   Remove the auto advance cam centre bolt.

6   Replace the washer from this bolt with the special washer 06·0949 having a hole large enough to clear the central portion of the unit and thus abut to the cam.

7   Replace the auto advance cam bolt with special washer, rotate the auto advance to the full advance position (it will rotate only one way), hold and tighten the bolt. The washer bearing against the cam will hold this in the full advance position.

8   Establish that the cylinder on which the timing is being checked has both valves closed at Top Dead Centre (T.D.C.) and rotate the engine forwards by engaging top gear and turning the rear wheel, until this is the case.

The contact breaker points leads are black and yellow or black and white and this feature allows the operator to check which set of points are feeding which coil and cylinder. The factory standard arrangement is for the left coil and cylinder to be fed by the yellow/black rear set of points.

9   Rotate the engine backwards gently until the machined mark on the rotor registers with 28° on the indicator plate. At this precise moment the contact breaker points should start to open in which case timing is correct.

The exact point of separation can be determined by inserting a strip of very thin paper between the points. The points will grip the paper when closed. By moving the engine *slowly*, a light pull on the paper will dislodge this at the exact point of separation. Take care not to leave a shred of paper between the points when using this method.   A preferable method is to use a low wattage bulb and holder with a short length of wire attached to the bulb body with a second length of wire attached to the bulb connection. Crocodile clips should be attached to the loose end of both wires. Connect one wire to the contact breaker spring of the set of points being checked and the second wire to a suitable earth point on the engine. Switch on the ignition and as the engine is turned, the bulb will light at the exact point of separation.

10   If the timing is incorrect, i.e. the points do not open at 28° before T.D.C., release the two screws in elongated holes which secure the main backplate and rotate it in the housing. To advance the timing, move the baseplate clockwise and to retard, move the baseplate anti-clockwise. When the timing is correct, secure the backplate screws.

11   Using the same technique, check that the contact breaker points open at 28° B.T.D.C. on the firing stroke for the second cylinder. If incorrect, make adjustment by movement of the secondary back-plate. To do so, slacken screws (A) in *Fig.* C54 and use the eccentric headed adjusting screws (B) to move the mounting plate. When timing is correct, re-secure the screws (A).

Ignition Timing Procedure – Engine Running

(Stroboscope Method)

This method is greatly preferred for extreme accuracy in setting. Prior to checking timing, clean and set both sets of contact breaker points to the figure given in "General Data."

Note that late models have two marks on the rotor but that if the ignition timing is sufficiently correct for the engine to run at all, the stroboscope will only detect the correct marking. If the engine has been rebuilt and ignition timing is being set from scratch, firstly follow the basic procedure in the preceding text. Commence stroboscopic timing as follows:

Engine/Primary Transmission **C**

1 Remove the inspection cap on the chaincase to reveal the degree indicator plate and timing mark on the rotor.

2 Connect the stroboscope to the H.T. lead on the right cylinder and use a battery separate to that on the motorcycle to power the lamp, thus eliminating possible incorrect readings. For the full method of connection follow the stroboscope lamp manufacturer's instructions.

3 Identify by lead colours the set of contact breaker points on which timing is being set by the colour of the wiring at the points and the ignition coil.

4 Start the engine and run at a steady 3000 r.p.m. indicated on the tachometer.

5 Shine the stroboscope lamp on the indicator plate. If timing is correct, the rotor marking will register with the 28° marking on the indicator plate. If the marks do not align, the timing must be adjusted.

6 To adjust the timing at the first set of points, release the two screws in elongated holes which secure the backplate and rotate it in the housing. To advance the timing, move the baseplate clockwise and to retard, move the baseplate anticlockwise. Move the backplate on its slots until the rotor mark and 28° marks align when checked with the stroboscope then secure the backplate screws.

7 Reconnect the stroboscope for the left cylinder and again check for rotor mark alignment at 28°.

8 If timing is incorrect for the left cylinder, correct by slackening off the clamping screw for the secondary backplate for this set of points then use the eccentric headed adjusting screw to move the secondary backplate (see *Fig.* C54—secondary backplate screws are marked "A" and eccentric screws are marked "B"). Recheck timing with the stroboscope and when correct, secure the screws "A".

SECTION C40

AUTO ADVANCE UNIT

The auto advance unit fitted behind the contact breaker plate in the timing cover automatically and progressively advances the ignition timing as the engine speed increases, and returns it to the fully retarded or static position when the engine stops.

To expose the mechanism, it is necessary to remove the contact breaker plate complete, but before doing so mark the exact position of the plate so that when it is refitted the timing is not disturbed.

Remove the contact breaker plate fixing screws and take off the plate complete with the contact sets. Ensure that the springs of the auto advance unit are intact with the taper loops attached to the pins. Check the automatic action by turning the cam by hand to the fully advanced position in which the bob weights will be fully extended. When the cam is released, the springs should return the bob weights to the static position.

Lubricate the mechanism sparingly. Do not over lubricate as an excess of oil may reach the contact breaker points. If the contact breaker plate has been removed from its original position without being marked, the ignition timing should be checked and reset as in Section C39 when the plate has been refitted.

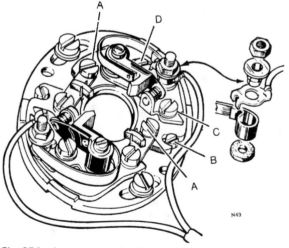

Fig. C54   Lucas contact breaker

Engine/Primary Transmission C

SECTION C41

CONTACT BREAKER ASSEMBLY

Mark III models have the Lucas 10 CA contact breaker assembly, providing a separate and independently adjustable contact set for each cylinder, see *Fig.* C54. Each contact set is mounted on its own crescent-shaped assembly plate that is fixed to the circular base plate by two screws (A). When these screws are loosened, the assembly plate can be moved in relation to the ignition cam (and the base plate) by the eccentric screw (B). This permits a very accurate setting of ignition timing for each cylinder, independently.

Screws C and D are contact plate fixing screws. They fit into slots in the plate allowing the plate to move and adjust the contact points.

The circular base plate is secured by two pillar screws in elongated holes allowing the base plate to move. To move the baseplate clockwise. To retard, move the baseplate anticlockwise.

Adjusting Contact Breaker Points Gap

rotated easily by means of the kickstart pedal. A small mark located near the lubrication slot on the cam marks the highest lift position on the ignition cam. Rotate the engine until this mark aligns exactly with the nylon heel of the contact breaker; at this position the points will be fully open. Check the gap with a 0·015 in. (0·38 mm) feeler gauge. If adjustment is necessary, slacken the contact breaker fixing screws C and D. Move the contact set by turning the eccentric screw B until the correct gap is obtained. Tighten the securing screws. Recheck the gap to ensure that the adjustment was not disturbed by the fixing screws. Adjust the other contact set in a similar manner.

Maintenance of the Contact Breaker

Every 5,000 miles (8,000 kilometres) the contact breaker points should be examined to determine their condition. Remove the nut securing the contact breaker spring to the anchor post and lift off the spring heel, together with the terminals, insulating bush and the insulating washer. Remove the fixed contact plate locking screw and take off the fixed contact plate.
Points which are slightly burnt or pitted can be smoothed with a fine carborundum stone and afterwards cleaned with a brush moistened in petrol or white spirit; if they are badly affected they should be renewed.
Before reassembly, smear the contact breaker pivot post and the cam very sparingly with Retinax "A" grease and add three drops of engine oil to each lubricating felt. When reassembling ensure that the insulating washer, contact breaker spring, terminal and insulating bush are fitted in the order shown in *Fig.* C54 and that the terminal tags are inside the curve of the spring. Finally retime the ignition as described in Section C39.

SECTION C42

CHAINS

1   The Mark III model has a fully automatic primary chain tensioner which maintains the chain in correct adjustment throughout its permissable life. See description C14 paragraph 7. *Fig.* C47

2   The primary chain operates in an oil bath formed by the primary chaincase and requires no lubrication from an outside source providing the chaincase level is maintained. The rear chain is lubricated by aerosol. A can of chainspray is produced in the tool-kit. However, the rear chain is not fully enclosed and from time to time requires cleaning before lubricating.

Chain Serviceability

Both in the case of single row (rear) chain and triple row (primary) chain, chain length extention of 2% is permissible before the chain is considered to have reached the end of its usefulness. This figure presumes that extension is checked only when the chain has been cleaned thoroughly and that any chain showing evidence of broken rollers has been discarded.

Engine/Primary Transmission C

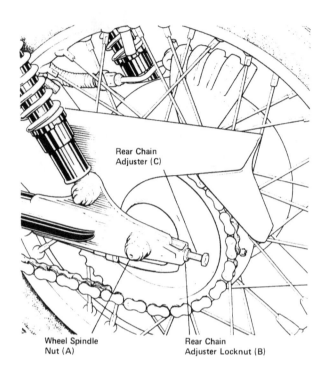

Rear Chain
Adjuster (C)

Wheel Spindle
Nut (A)

Rear Chain
Adjuster Locknut (B)

Fig. C55   Rear chain adjustment

3   Pull downwards on the bottom run of the chain to bring the spindle hard up against the adjusters (C).

4   Turn each adjuster an equal amount until, with the rider seated, there is a total up and down movement, measured in the centre of the bottom chain run of $\frac{3}{4}$ in. to 1 in. (19·05 to 25·4 mm).

5   Tighten securely the adjuster locknuts (B).

6   Tighten the wheel spindle nuts and recheck the adjustment in at least three places. Should there prove to be a tight spot, readjust to give the correct up and down movement at this point.

Rear Chain Adjustment

This adjustment is made by movement of the rear wheel. *Fig.* C55 shows the adjustment points. Proceed as follows:

1   Slacken the rear wheel spindle nuts (A).

2   Release the chain adjuster locknuts (B).

7   Finally, resettle rear brake pads as in Section H10, applying full pressure to the brake pedal a number of times. Whenever adjustments are disturbed, always check for satisfactory operation of your brake before riding machine.

Gearbox

Gearbox

D

SECTION D1

GEARBOX DESCRIPTION : MARK III CHANGES

The transmission (gearbox) is a self contained 4 speed unit, completely separate from the engine crankcase and thus simple and inexpensive for servicing. A robust aluminium alloy casing with separate inner and outer covers contains a gear cluster of extra tough nickel chrome steel. The kickstart drives through an internal ratchet on the layshaft first gear which in turn drives the mainshaft and clutch. Selection is foot controlled through a positive stop mechanism to a rotating cam plate. Hardened steel selector forks operated by the camplate position the gear pinions. The basic design of the Commando gearbox remains substantially unchanged but the Mark III foot shift is removed to the left hand side of the machine to conform with recent mandatory requirements in major markets. The modification has been achieved with a minimum of new components in the interest of spares interchangeability. A simple cross-shaft transfers the operation from the back of the original inner cover, across the machine (at a slight angle), through an oil-seal in the primary cover emerging forward of the clutch. The knuckle pin roller has been modified to a spherical form to cope with the slight angle of the new shaft and ensure a smooth, easy operation.

A small gear on the foot pedal spindle engages a pinion on the cross shaft conveniently moving the operating pivot rearwards towards the footrest (now moved back $\frac{3}{4}''$ for improved riding position) and simultaneously reversing the direction of shift which now conforms with the standard "Down to change down – and up to change up" viz: 1st "down", 2nd, 3rd and 4th "up" (from neutral).   (see Fig. D1)

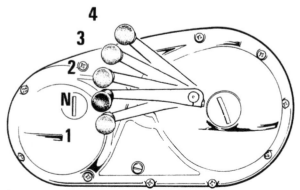

Fig. D1 Gearshift positions

Other refinements include plated shafts on kickstart and footshift to prevent corrosion and both have LIP oilseals to obviate seepage.

Sleeve gear bearings are circlip located, and a green light neutral indicator in the instrument panel is actuated by a switch and button on the camplate.

With the fixed-centre cross-shaft the gearbox is no longer adjustable and a fully automatic, oleomatic, primary chain tensioner – self adjusting – is housed within the chaincase.

SECTION D2

GEARBOX DISMANTLING

It is not necessary to remove the exhaust system whilst giving attention to the gearbox, providing the gearbox is not to be removed from the engine plates.

SECTION D3

REMOVING GEARBOX OUTER COVER

Prior to gearbox dismantling it is recommended that the gearbox should be drained into a suitable sized drain tray using the drain plug at the bottom rear of the gearbox casing. Proceed then as follows:

1 Remove the kickstart by releasing the single securing bolt. The bolt locates into a groove in the kickstart spindle and thus it is necessary to remove this bolt completely.

2 If the battery is still connected, disconnect by removing the fuse before proceeding to the next operation. *Disconnect all connectors from diode and pressure switch.*

3 Remove the two nuts and one bolt securing the right hand footrest and note that the bolt also secures the red earth lead tag from behind the footrest mounting plate.
A nut without washer is used on the footrest securing bolt. It is vitally important during re-assembly not to overlook the refitting of this earth lead or otherwise a short circuit may result in the fuse being blown, or damage to the Zener diode.

Gearbox

4 Lift the footrest and brake pedal away and tie up the assembly clear of the outer cover, allowing good access. This will avoid disturbing the hydraulics. The flexible hose gives reasonable latitude but avoid twisting the hydraulic hose and always re-assemble without stress in the rubber.

5 Remove the five cheese headed set screws from the gearbox outer cover.

6 Remove the two screws securing the outer cover inspection cap which may then be lifted away complete with gasket.

7 Disconnect the clutch cable from the fork within the gearbox outer cover.

8 Place the oil drain tray under the gearbox, and, using the kick shaft as a handle, pull the outer cover off. It may be necessary to tap the cover gently to free it.

9 Withdraw the shift ratchet plate and spindle.

SECTION D4

REMOVING GEARBOX INNER COVER

Prior to removing the gearbox inner cover it is necessary to mark clearly the position of the clutch operating body by two punch marks which are shown in *Fig. D1*(a). This is due to the fact that the clutch operating body has no positive rotational location. Proceed as follows:

1 Remove the small lever, screw and nut securing the clutch operating arm and collect the arm, roller and bush.

2 Remove the clutch operating body locking ring as in *Fig. D1*(a) and lift away the clutch operating body and the ball.

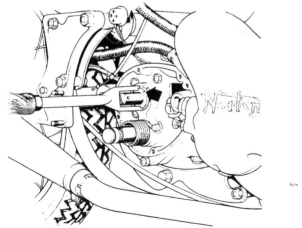

Fig. D1(a) Removal of clutch body lockring. Note alignment marks on lock ring and cover

3 Prevent the gearbox from turning by engaging top gear as follows:
Top gear can be engaged by levering the end of the quadrant carefully to the top of the window in the gearbox inner cover whilst rocking the rear wheel. At this stage the mainshaft nut can be removed. (Enlist the assistance of someone to hold the rear wheel as the brake lever is dismantled.)

4 In order to remove the gearbox inner cover it will be found simpler to revert to the neutral position, again by moving the end of the quadrant down the window.

5 Remove the seven securing nuts to the gearbox inner cover. These nuts are all of equal size, five within the case and two outside.

6 Remove the gearbox inner cover, if necessary tapping the end of the mainshaft to ease separation.
The inner cover should then be lifted away, complete with kickstart spindle, with the pawl assembled and also the return spring.

SECTION D5

DISMANTLING GEAR CLUSTER AND CAM PLATE

To dismantle the gearbox further it is necessary to remove the clutch from the gearbox mainshaft and if the sleeve gear is to be removed from the gearbox, the countershaft sprocket must also be removed. Clutch removal is covered in items 1 to 6 of Section C13 and C14 and countershaft sprocket removal in Section D8.

1 Remove any clutch locating shims, the clutch locating spacer, and circlip from the mainshaft end.

2 Remove the low gear pinions from the shafts.

3 Unscrew the selector fork spindle and remove.

4 Remove selector forks and withdraw mainshaft with gears.

5 Withdraw the layshaft with gears. If the shaft is a tight fit in the bearing heat the case and withdraw the shaft complete with bearing. The bearing can then be removed to complete disassembly.

6 Remove countershaft sprocket (Section D8).

7 Remove sleeve gear by tapping gently through the bearing into the gearbox.

Gearbox

8 Remove the acorn shaped detent plunger spring bolt. This will release the camplate detent plunger and spring.

9 Remove the bolt and circlip securing the camplate and quadrant to the gearbox shell.

10 Remove camplate and quadrant and collect "O"-rings.

11 Withdraw the sprocket spacer from inside the countershaft oil seal.

12 The bearings can be withdrawn for inspection or replacement by gently heating the case and tapping the open end on a soft wooden surface.

13 Prise out the countershaft oil seal.

SECTION D6

INSPECTION OF GEARBOX PARTS

After cleaning all components very thoroughly such as in gasoline (petrol) or kerosene (paraffin) check all items thoroughly as below :

1 Inspect the two mainshaft and one layshaft ball journal bearings for roughness indicating ball or ball track damage on either the inner or outer races. Feel for side play between the inner and outer races. If the bearings are in good condition, such play should be negligible.

2 Inspect both the layshaft and mainshaft for wear on the splines, damage to the threads, out of truth and severe wear and grooving on the bearing diameters.

3 Inspect all pinions for chipping or obvious wear to the teeth. Ensure that the dogs are not badly rounded and that the inner splines are a satisfactory fit to the shafts. Bushed pinions should be offered to the shafts and checked for excessive wear by attempting to rock them on the shafts.

4 Inspect the gearbox shell and gearbox inner cover bushes for obvious wear. Note that wear on the bushes in the shell supporting the camplate and quadrant can result in bad gear indexing and a tendency to jump out of gear engagement.

5 Inspect the selector forks and mating grooves in the sliding pinions for seizure or wear.

6 Especially in cases of bad selection, inspect the camplate tracks for wear or distortion and ensure that the camplate spindle is a good fit in the bush in the gearbox shell.

SECTION D7

REMOVAL OF GEARBOX COMPLETE

Though not normally necessary during overhaul, we recognise that circumstances may arise which make it desirable to remove the complete gearbox without disturbing the engine although the primary transmission must be dismantled fully. In these circumstances remove the rear three crankcase to engine plate bolts, the rear wheel and support the motorcycle by the lower frame rails on a strong box and remove the centre stand. Remove completely the gearbox top and bottom mounting bolt and stud and turn the gearbox anti-clockwise in the engine plates viewed from right side. Force the rear engine mounting rearwards until the cutaway part at the bottom right hand side is clear of the crankcase. The gearbox can then be turned further and withdrawn horizontally from the right hand side. Only in isolated cases will it be necessary to take out the front mounting main bolt to provide still further working space.

SECTION D8

COUNTERSHAFT (GEARBOX FINAL DRIVE) SPROCKET

The countershaft sprocket is mounted on the mainshaft sleeve (high) gear and secured by a tab washer and L.H. threaded nut. The Commando overall gearing should be varied by changing the sprocket size. For the road going editions of the Commando, the following sprockets are available :

Gearbox

D

040480	Sprocket	19 teeth
060931	Sprocket	20 teeth
060721	Sprocket	21 teeth
060759	Sprocket	22 teeth
063420	Sprocket	23 teeth
063421	Sprocket	24 teeth

Changing the countershaft sprocket

1 Remove the outer primary chaincase, cross shaft, chain tensioner, starter gear mechanism, clutch and primary transmission and inner primary chaincase as in Section C14 to gain access to the sprocket.

2 Remove set screw and lockplate from sprocket.

3 The sprocket must be prevented from turning whilst the left hand nut is released. If the gearbox is in the frame, leave the rear chain connected and wedge the rear brake fully. If the gearbox is out of the frame, pass a length of chain round the sprocket, holding the ends securely in a vice.

4 Noting that the sprocket nut is *left hand* threaded, remove the nut and lift the sprocket clear.

5 Before refitting the sprocket, ensure that the sprocket spacer is in place on the sleeve gear bearing sleeve.

6 Place the sprocket in position and if necessary tap fully home with a tube drift.

7 If the original lockplate has been scrapped in removal, have a new one available.

8 Fit and tighten the left-hand nut fully, whilst preventing the sprocket from turning.

9 Secure the lockplate with the locating screw.

10 Refit the inner chaincase, cross shaft, primary transmission, starter gear mechanism, primary chain tensioner, gearshift pedal (engaging gears) and outer chaincase as in Section C34 and fit and connect the rear chain.

SECTION D9

REFITTING GEAR CLUSTER AND SELECTORS

After inspection of components as in Section D6 commence reassembly as follows:

1 Heat the gearbox shell and press the sleeve gear and layshaft bearings fully into position.

2 Fit the sleeve gear bearing seal squarely into the housing, lipped side first.

3 Fit detent plunger, spring, and acorn nut loosely.

4 Fit the quadrant with "O"-ring and secure with circlip and washer.

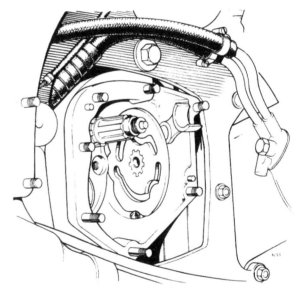

Fig. D2 *Location of camplate to index plunger. Knuckle end of quadrant is aligned to top front cover stud*

5 Lift the knuckle end of the quadrant until the top inside radius is directly in line with the top front cover stud (see *Fig. D2*), fit the camplate and sealing ring, engaging the teeth of the quadrant and camplate so that the notched edge of the camplate is towards the gearbox sprocket and the blank smooth edge towards the gearbox inner cover, the last notch at the bottom engaging with the camplate index plunger (see *Fig. D2*).

6 Secure the camplate with "O"-ring, washer and bolt. N.B. A button on the camplate operates the neutral indicator switch, now housed in the gearbox shell, and connected to the green light on the instrument panel.

Gearbox

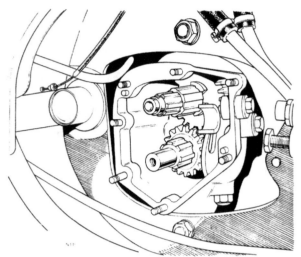

Fig. D3   *Mainshaft and layshaft fitted to gearbox shell*

7   Tighten detent plunger acorn nut.

8   Fit the countershaft (sleeve gear) through bearing and seal. Fit sprocket spacer in place inside seal.

9   Fit countershaft sprocket (Section D8).

10   Fit mainshaft through sleeve gear.

11   Fit the 3rd gear free pinion and bush to the layshaft (dog side first to face out of assembled gearbox).

12   Fit the fixed high gear pinion to the layshaft, flat side first (toward 3rd gear pinion). The shoulder is to fit against the bearing.

13   Push the layshaft into the bearing in the gearbox shell.

14   Assemble the mainshaft 3rd gear with selector fork to the mainshaft (selector fork groove side outwards) and engage the pin with the inboard cam track (see *Fig.* D4).

15   Assemble the main shaft 2nd gear with bush to the mainshaft, dogs inwards.

16   Assemble the layshaft 2nd gear with selector fork (selector fork groove side inwards) and engage the pin with the outboard cam track.

17   Fit the selector fork spindle through the selector forks and screw home into the gearbox shell.

18   Fit the layshaft 1st gear.

19   Fit the mainshaft 1st gear with shoulder outwards.

20   Since the quadrant roller cannot be fitted after the inner cover is fitted, it is imperative that the roller is fitted into the quadrant knuckle at this time.

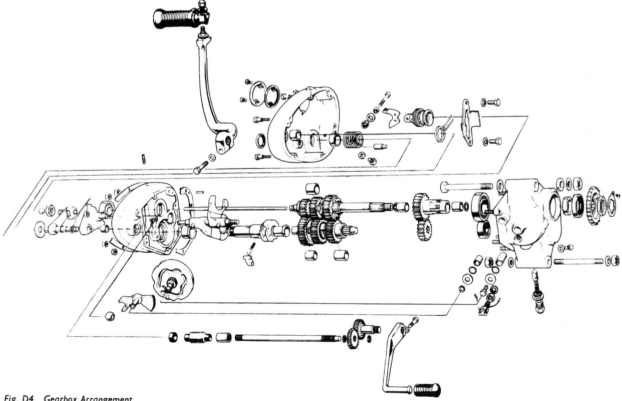

Fig. D4   *Gearbox Arrangement*

Gearbox

D

SECTION D10

REFITTING GEARBOX INNER COVER

Ensure that the gearbox inner cover is clean on both inner and outer joint faces prior to assembly. Proceed as follows:

1 Fit the inner cover gasket.

2 If the kickstart spindle has been removed from the gearbox inner cover, it must be refitted at this stage. Assemble the kickstarter spindle to the inner cover, ensuring that the pawl is behind the stop on the inner cover as shown in *Fig. D5*.

3 Assemble the kickstart return spring, aligning the outboard end of the spring with the mating hole in the spindle and sliding the spring down until the spring engages in the hole. Wind the spring as illustrated in *Fig. D6* to tension and engage on the spring anchor pin.

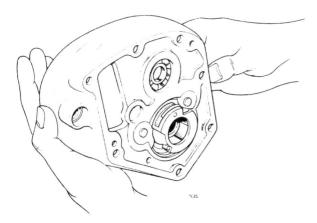

Fig. D5   *Showing kickstart pawl stop on inner cover*

4 Fit the inner cover gasket and hold in place with grease.

5 Ensure that the two shafts are fully home prior to attempting to assemble the inner cover to the gearbox shell.

6 Assemble the inner cover, ensuring that it enters over the location dowels, and fit snugly home during assembly, at the same time guiding the cover over the unsupported outboard end of the selector fork spindle.

7 Fit the seven nuts securing the inner cover, noting that two of these fit outside the casings. The seven nuts should be tightened to a torque setting of 10 to 15 lbs./ft. (1·383 to 2·074 Kg/m).

8 Engage top gear, apply the footbrake, and tighten the gearbox mainshaft nut to a torque reading of 70 lbs./ft. (9·678 Kg/m).

9 Assemble the clutch operating lever body complete with lock ring and ball to the gearbox inner cover.

10 Tighten the operating lever body ring until the body is fully engaged and finally tighten the lock ring to bring the body slot directly into line with the marks previously applied to the boss in the cover. *Fig.* D6 illustrates the alignment procedure during tightening of the lock ring. If a new cover is being fitted and no alignment marks are present, hold the body in the position where the clutch cable can exert a straight pull, as the lockring is tightened.

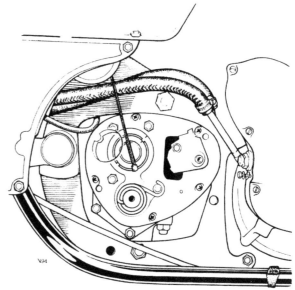

Fig. D6   *Kickstart spring located. Note alignment of clutch body to permit straight pull on clutch cable and operating lever*

Gearbox

11 Assemble the withdrawal lever, roller, bush and pivot screw and secure the lock nut. Assembly should be in accordance with *Fig.* D7.

12 Assemble the ratchet plate and spindle, locating the peg into the knuckle pin roller. Ensure that the 'O' ring is fitted to the ratchet plate spindle.

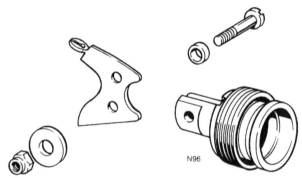

Fig. D7   Order of assembly of clutch withdrawal lever

SECTION D11

DISMANTLING AND RE-ASSEMBLING GEARBOX OUTER COVER

To dismantle the outer cover, remove the pawl carrier assembly and disengage the spring peg from the legs of the pedal return spring. The pedal stop plate set screws can now be removed and the stop plate lifted away, complete with spring.

During re-assembly ensure that the spring retaining washer is fitted over the main spindle of the pawl carrier and that the spring has been assembled over the ratchet plate as illustrated in *Fig.* D8. Tighten the stop plate set screws and assemble the splined end of the pawl carrier past the 'O' ring in the cover. Locate the spring peg between the legs of the spring and push the pawl carrier fully home, engaging between the legs of the spring. Check the carrier action and that the spring is correctly located. The set screws should be tightened only when the action of the pawl carrier has been checked for full freedom of movement. Now fit the pawl spring with its double cranked leg downwards, ensuring a minimum but perceptible clearance, between the two legs of the spring and the pawl.

SECTION D12

REFITTING THE GEARBOX OUTER COVER

Having dealt with the outer cover as described in Section D11, ensure that the joint facing is perfectly clean and proceed with assembly as detailed below:

1 Fit the inner cover to outer cover gasket, retaining in place during assembly with a smear of grease.

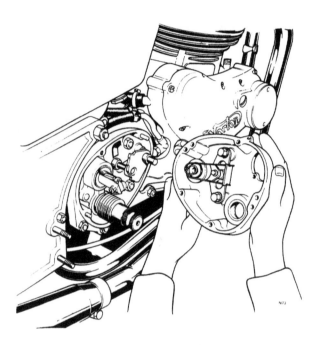

Fig. D8   Pawl carrier, spring and ratchet plate assembled

Ensure that the gasket engages satisfactorily over the cover dowels.

2 To ensure cover alignment during assembly, retain the ratchet spring in the central position with the index finger of the right hand and guide the case over the kickstart shaft with the thumb of the left hand engaged through the filler cap hole.

3 Drive the outer cover fully home and assemble the five screws of equal length to retain the outer cover in position. If the cover is very difficult to push into position, check whether the pawl has rotated due to the pawl scissor spring not having been held securely in position, during final assembly. The cover should be removed, the ratchet pawl reset and re-assembly undertaken.

4 Fit the kickstart crank, then, operating the gear-shift pedal on the left hand side of the machine, check the action of the gearbox, rotating the rear wheel as the gear pedal is moved to the various gear positions. Ensure the rubber sleeve is covering the cross-shaft connecting-piece. If all is well, replenish the gearbox with oil.

5 Connect the clutch cable through the inspection hole in the gearbox outer cover, engaging and locating the nipple in the operating lever.

6 Finally assemble the gasket, inspection cover and screws to the gearbox outer cover, and check the security of the drain and level plugs.

Carburetor

Carburetor

E

SECTION E1

DESCRIPTION

The Amal concentric float carburetor proportions and atomises the correct amount of fuel, mixing it with the air drawn in through the air intake. The jet sizes, choke bore, throttle needle, and throttle slide cut away ensure that the correct fuel/air mixture is maintained at all throttle openings. Initial opening of the throttle brings into operation the mixture supply from the pilot jet system which controls the idling speed. As the throttle is progressively opened the mixture supply is augmented from the main jet which discharges through the

needle jet into the primary air chamber and goes from there as a rich fuel/air mixture through the primary air choke into the main choke. The earlier stages of the throttle opening are controlled by the throttle cut away and the taper needle which passes through the needle jet, the taper allowing more fuel to pass through the needle jet as the throttle is opened.

Type 932 Amal concentrics of 32 mm bore size are fitted to the 850 cc Mark III Commando. An exploded layout (illustrating both hands) with part descriptions is shown in *Fig.* E1. A common airbox serves both carburetors, this being covered in detail in Section E9.

The Mark III now incorporates a low friction throttle cable lined with P.T.F.E. and easy entry into twist grip.

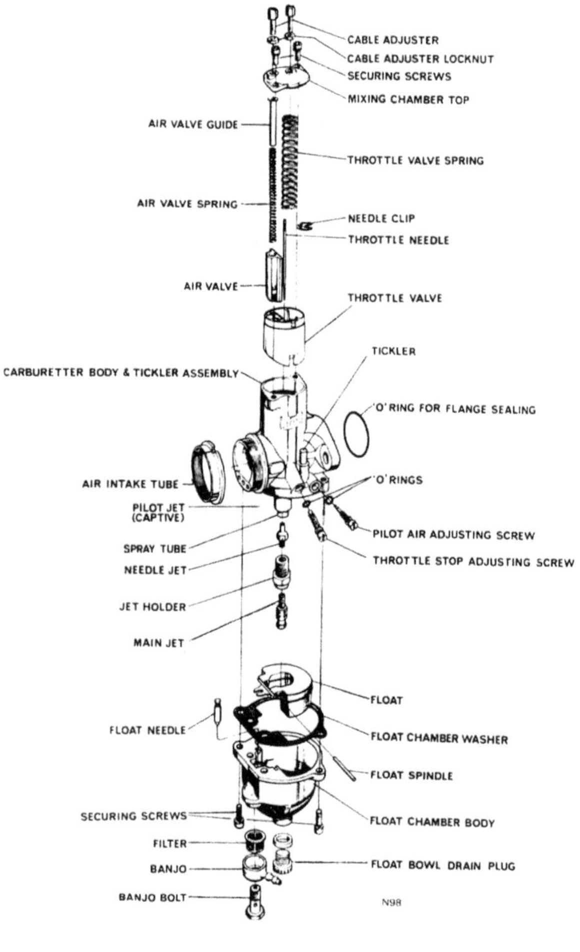

Fig. E1   Amal concentric float carburetor

SECTION E2

CARBURETOR REMOVAL

For ease of handling it is recommended that the carburetors are removed attached to the spacers as a pair as follows :

1 Disconnect the fuel lines from both fuel taps, also disconnect oil separator pipe from balance pipe tee-piece.

2 Remove four socket screws and washers securing the spacers to the head – a shortened socket key is needed for ease of access.

3 With the balance pipe and cables still connected, lift the carburetors and manifolds away from the cylinder head, disengaging the flexible air hoses at the same time. To service the carburetors individually :

4 Disconnect the balance pipe at one end.

5 Remove the two cross head screws and washers securing the carburetor top.

6 Lift off the carburetor top throttle and air slides with cables attached.
   The top and slides can be left hanging from the cables but the exposed parts should be protected from damage by wrapping in clean cloth.

7 If required, remove the second carburetor in similar fashion. removing the fuel line by taking off the banjo bolts.

Carburetor

E

SECTION E3

CARBURETOR DISMANTLING

The carburetor as detached from the motorcycle is partially dismantled, in that the mixing chamber top and both throttle and air slides have been removed. If the top and slides are to be removed from the cables, proceed as follows:

1 Lift the throttle return spring, note the groove in the needle to which the clip is engaged then remove the clip. Collect the needle.

2 Disengage the throttle cable nipple and collect the throttle valve.

3 Lift the air valve cable and spring, disengage the cable nipple and collect the air valve.

4 The top is now free to be lifted clear. Dismantling of parts from the mixing chamber should proceed as follows:

5 Remove the two screws securing the float chamber to the carburetor body and collect the float chamber complete with float and float needle, also the joint washers.
   The float and float needle are manufactured from white nylon. Lift the float, float needle and float spindle clear for later examination and drain the float chamber.

6 Remove the main jet, needle jet.

Throttle Valve: Remove any burrs and burnish carefully any scores. Deep scoring renders the valve unfit for re-use.

Throttle Needle: Ensure the needle is not bent or worn badly on the taper. Check that the clip grooves are clear and "sharp."

Carburetor Body: Blow out all internal galleries with compressed air. Check that all threads are sound. Examine for excess wear on the throttle valve bore.

Pilot Air Screw: Check for wear on the taper.

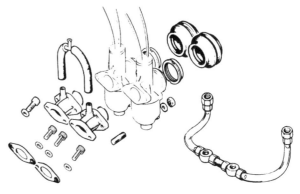

E2   Carburetor intake items

SECTION E4

EXAMINATION OF CARBURETOR PARTS

The following parts should be examined and replacements made where necessary:

Float: Check for leakage – fuel can be seen in the float if this condition exists. Check also that the float needle fits securely.

Float Needle: Check for wear on the seating taper.

Main, Needle and Pilot Jets: Examine for damage and blockage – never use wire to clear a blockage but instead use compressed air.

SECTION E5

CARBURETTOR REASSEMBLY

Assuming all parts are clean and in sound condition commence reassembly as follows:

7 Using new friction 'O' rings on both screws if the originals have deteriorated, refit the pilot air screw and throttle stop screw.

8 Fit the needle jet to the jet holder and jet holder to the carburetor body.

9 Fit the main jet.

Carburetor

10 Position the float, with float needle and spindle, in the float bowl.

11 If the original is damaged, fit a new float bowl joint washer ensuring it is the correct way round with the holes aligned to the jet passages in the bowl.

12 Fit the complete float bowl and secure with the two screws and washers.

Where the originals have deteriorated, replace the 'O' ring in the mounting flange of both carburettors and couple the carburetors to the manifolds, securing with two nuts and plain washers for each instrument. Connect the balance pipe to both manifolds. If the air and throttle valves and mixing chamber tops have been detached from the control cables, they should be re-connected as follows:

13 Place the air valve guide tube and spring over the air cable (the brass guide assembles with the flanged end towards the cap).

14 Compress the spring to expose the maximum of inner cable then pass the nipple through the air valve to engage at the bottom.

15 Place the throttle valve spring over the throttle cable and compress it.

16 Feed the throttle cable nipple through the throttle valve centre hole then engage the nipple in the adjacent hole.

17 Fit the needle clip to the correct groove.

18 Compress the throttle spring to clear the throttle valve then place the needle and clip into the throttle valve from the top with the needle in the centre hole of the slide. Release the throttle spring and ensure that the spring fits over the needle clip.

19 Locate the air valve into the channel of the throttle valve. The carburetors with manifolds are ready to refit to the cylinder head. Proceed as follows:

20 Offer the throttle and air valves, assembled to the cables and tops to both instruments. Ensure that the throttle needle passes easily through centre hole of the body and that the key on the throttle valve mates with the keyway in the carburetor body. Ensure that the return spring fits over the abutment in the top.

21 Secure each carburetor top with two cross headed screws and washers.

22 Mount the carburetors on the cylinder head using the heat insulators between the manifolds and cylinder head. Secure with socket screws and washers.

23 Reconnect the fuel pipes to both petrol taps.

24 Fit both carburetors to the airbox flexible connectors and take great care that these locate both in the airbox front plate and over the carburetor intakes.

25 Reassembly is now complete and slack should be taken up in the control cables and the carburation adjusted as in Section E7.

SECTION E6

FUEL TAPS

Twin taps are fitted. The one on the left side provides the reserve supply and is recognised by the lack of a stand pipe inside the tank. Fibre washers seal the taps to the tank and must be checked that they are undamaged before being re-used.

Both taps operate forwards for OFF. The left tap moves UP for reserve. The right tap operates DOWN for main supply.

Always turn tap off when machine parked or stored.

SECTION E7

CARBURETOR ADJUSTMENT

Adjustment should be carried out in the sequence described below with the engine at operating temperature. The exhaust system to be used must be fitted and preferably the test should be carried out on a slight up grade so that the engine is pulling. The air lever must be fully to the tight wire position before adjustment takes place.

1. Main Jet – Throttle threequarters to full open.
If at full throttle, the engine runs "heavily" the main jet is set too large. If by slightly closing the throttle valve, the engine power seems to improve, the main jet is too small. With a main jet of the correct size the engine should run evenly, and be delivering maximum power at full throttle.

Carburetor

E

The appearance of the sparking plug is one of the best indications of mixture strength. To check, set the carburetors to shut off completely on closing or false readings will be obtained, then run the machine at full throttle over the test course, declutching and stopping the engine quickly. Then examine the spark plugs. If the plugs have a cool appearance with the central insulator free from loose black carbon and a light chocolate colour on the insulator, the mixture is correct. A rich mixture will be indicated by a black, wet oily appearance with deposits on the central insulator. Weak mixture will be indicated by a dry whitish deposit and the points may appear to have been overheated.

2. The Pilot Jet – Throttle up to one-eighth open.
Set the engine to run at a fast idling speed with the throttle shut by using the throttle adjusting screw. Turn this screw outwards until the engine runs slower and begins to falter, then screw the pilot air adjusting screw in or out to make the engine run more evenly and faster. If the idling speed is still too fast reduce it by means of the throttle adjusting screw and again adjust the pilot air adjusting screw until the idling is satisfactory.

Note: When new or re-assembled carburetors are used, start with pilot screw $1\frac{1}{2}$ turns out from the fully-in position.

3. Throttle Cutaway – Throttle one-eight to one-quarter open.
If, as the machine pulls away from the idling position, there is spitting back from the carburetors, slightly richen the mixture by screwing in the pilot air adjusting screw slightly. If this is not effective, return the screw to its former position and fit a throttle slide with a smaller cutaway. If, with the throttle in this position, the engine jerks under load and there is no spitting, either the jet needle is much too high or a throttle slide with a larger cutaway is required to cure richness.

4. Throttle Needle – Throttle one-quarter to three-quarters open.
The needle controls a wide range of throttle opening and therefore the acceleration. Placing the needle in the lower position, that is, with the clip in the top groove gives a weaker mixture. Placing the needle in the higher position, that is, with the clip in the bottom groove, richens the mixture. If the mixture is too rich with the needle in the lower position, the needle jet should be replaced and if the needle itself has had a great deal of use, replace it also.

5. Pilot Jet
Check again pilot adjustment as the last operation.

SECTION E8

ADJUSTMENT FOR ALTITUDE

It is necessary to adjust carburation on a motorcycle operated continuously in altitudes greater than 3,000 feet approximately. Motorcycles as supplied from the factory are already equipped for correct carburation up to 3,000 feet.

The main jet requires a reduction in size of 5 per cent at altitudes between 3,000 and 6,000 feet. Beyond 6,000 feet further reductions of 4 per cent should be made.

Altitude adjustments should only be made if the motorcycle is used permanently at high altitudes. It is not necessary to adjust merely for a journey through mountainous areas.

SECTION E9

TWIN CARBURETOR ADJUSTMENT

It is necessary periodically to synchronise the carburetors so that they open and close simultaneously. Start with the handlebars in the centre position so that there is no "pull" on the throttle cable which will interfere with adjustment. Proceed as follows:

1   Take up any slack in the throttle cables using the adjuster on the top of each mixing chamber, then tighten the adjuster locknuts.

2   Start the engine – this must be thoroughly warmed up before adjustment commences.

3   Follow the main adjustment sequence in Section E7 before setting slow running. It is all-important to have both throttle valves opening simultaneously. To ensure that this is the case, the twist-grip should be set to allow the engine to run fractionally over idling speed. Gently screw in the throttle stops in that position. Return the twist-grip to the closed position so that the engine runs on the throttle stops. Now proceed as follows:

4   Lift off one spark plug lead and commence setting the carburetor on the other cylinder as a single unit.

Carburetor

5   Adjust the pilot air screw and stop screw on the cylinder which is firing.

6   Reverse the process by replacing one plug lead and removing the other.

7   Adjust the pilot air screw and stop screw on the second cylinder.

8   Replace the plug lead – at this stage tickover may be too fast. If so, lower both throttle stop screws by an equal amount until idling is correct. Ensure there is about $\frac{1}{8}$" (3 mm) slack in throttle cable. This slack must be equalized so that throttles open together.

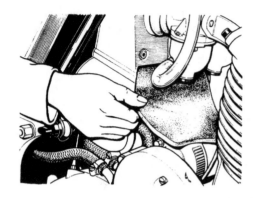

Fig. E3   Removing air cleaner element

SECTION E10

AIR FILTER

The airbox fulfils the dual roles of air cleaner and air silencer. It incorporates a micro-cellular plastic foam element which must be oil wetted.

Removing and Refitting the Element:

1   Access to the filter is through the front cover plate

    which can be detached by removing three bolts.
2   Take out the three set screws bolts securing the air filter front plate.

3   The foam element has a wire reinforcement and can be easily withdrawn through the aperture. Care should be observed not to tear the foam on the float-bowl drain plugs.

5   The element should be cleaned as described below or replaced.

6   Reassembly is a reversal of the dismantling procedure.

Cleaning the Air Filter Element:

1   In normal conditions (every 3,000 miles – 4,800 Km) the foam should be washed in clean petrol, expelling all dirt; then be squeezed out to dry before immersing in fresh engine oil.

2   Squeeze out surplus oil and refit into airbox.

3   Cleaning should be undertaken more frequently in dusty conditions.

OIL SEPARATOR

The new oil separator (illustrated in the Engine Lubrication System Diagram *Fig. C29* is designed to separate oil and air expressed by the engine breather system. Mixed oil/air passes first to the oil tank where initial separation takes place. The fine mist that comes from the oil tank breather tower is then passed through the separator. The remaining vapour is drawn to the airbox and any residual oil droplets are sucked into the inlet manifold via the balance-pipe tee-piece, to be burnt in the combustion, obviating breather drip and deposits on road or machine.

The device requires no attention except to ensure that the connections especially into the airbox, have not become disengaged.

Continued use of the machine on short trips in cold, humid weather may result in "sludging", requiring a clean-out to prevent blockage of the pipes.

Frame

and

Ancillaries

Frame and Ancillaries

F

SECTION F1

REMOVAL OF POWER UNIT

In some types of repair, for example, during an accident repair, where the frame must be changed, it is desirable to remove the engine/gearbox/primary drive and engine plates as a group. To remove this assembly, proceed as below:

1 Turn the seat-lock forward with the key provided and lift the seat. Release the check cable one end, and remove the four posidrive screws attaching the hinge. Lift off the seat clear of oil and grease·

2 Turn the ring of the twist fastener to release the top forward end of the left hand battery cover and lift the cover forward off the rear mounting peg.

3 Disconnect the battery by removing the fuse from the fuseholder adjacent to the battery.

4 Remove the right side panel which is secured by two screws at the top and a peg and rubber at the bottom.

5 Remove the fuel tank (Section F9).

6 Remove both exhaust pipes with mufflers by detaching balance-pipe and unscrewing the finned lockrings using service tool 063968. Collect the split-rings and spherical seating washers from inside the ports, to avoid loss. Remove the nuts and washers holding the muffler bracket to the two mounting rubber studs and lift each system away in turn.

7 Disconnect the rear chain at the split link and remove the chain completely.

8 Remove snap connector from right hand diode and red earth wire at nut. Detach both pressure-switch wires. All from inside of light-alloy rear footrest-support plate.

9 Slacken the right hand suspension unit and withdraw as far as the locating circlips.

10 Unscrew and remove axle from right hand side. Ease the wheel over to the left and withdraw the chain tensioner clevis. Move the caliper and mounting plate upwards and insert the tensioner

(pushing together with finger and thumb) between the friction pads before they clear the disc, to prevent them falling out.

11 The Caliper and mounting plate (still attached to the hydraulic hose) should now be withdrawn through the frame, inverted and hung by the mounting plate boss (outside) from the hook on the rear frame loop.

12 Leaning the machine to the left on the centre-stand foot, extract the wheel off the shock-absorber paddles and withdraw from the "right-hand rear".

13 It is now possible to remove the right hand (light alloy) rear support plate complete with the entire hydraulic brake, pedal, and footrest – threading the caliper through the frame, forward of the sus-pension strut. This is not essential but prevents damage and avoids mishaps to the vital brake system, during this major rework.

14 The swinging arm must now be removed. The Mark III pivot is lubricated by felt-wicks impreg-nated with SA140 oil inserted each end of the cottered spindle. These contact felt discs which feed the oil out to the bushes. Oil drips are unlikely during dismantling.

15 Proceed as follows: The new swinging arm bearing is sealed by welch-washer type end-caps which require renewing when removed. To avoid drilling we recommend piercing the right hand cap with a sharp punch and prising out the disc. This obviates swarf from entering the bearings. Remove the felts from behind the disc. The left hand cap can be knocked out with a long bolt or similar, if necessary, when the arm is removed from the frame.

16 The Mark III "King-Pin" – swinging arm spindle is now located by two cotter-pins engaging in flats, ensuring a more positive and rigid mounting. To gain access to these it is desirable to remove the rear mudguard lower front fixings, swinging it downwards and rearwards on its top-rear bridge, – clear of the working zone.

Frame and Ancillaries

F

17 Detach oil-filter and oil-pipes (this is on the return side of the system and will not drain the tank).

18 Disconnect terminals and detach electric-horn (above filter).

19 Remove both cotter-pins — driving up from below. Do not damage threads on cotters. Collect rubber plugs — one each boss.

20 Remove the suspension unit bottom bolts.

21 Take out the swinging arm pivot spindle. It will be noted that the pivot spindle is threaded internally to aid removal. Screw a bolt with locking nut into thread (the $\frac{1}{2}''$ UNF main front mounting bolt will be ideal) tighten the nut and twist and pull the spindle out. The left hand welch-washer felt disc will remain undisturbed. See *Fig.* F6.

22 Detach tachometer cable from hub unit on axle. Lift away the swinging arm complete with chain-guard and left hand wheel components.

23 Disconnect the tachometer cable (at the top front of the crankcase).

24 Dismantle the engine steady (see C1) by removing the nuts and washers from the rubber mountings first, to prevent them turning in the frame. Release the two studs and lift away with the side plates. Remove the main engine steady plate

by taking out the three socket screws and washers, releasing the suspensory spring device as in C 'O'. Note that the centre screw secures the ground (earth) lead tag.

25 Remove the rocker feed pipe after taking out the three banjo bolts. Collect the copper washers for re-use.

26 Release the coil cluster from the frame as an assembly: (four bolts are used). Disconnect the H.T. leads at the sparking plugs then tie the cluster clear of the engine unit with all other leads still attached.

27 Remove oil separator pipe from tee-piece on balance-pipe. Detach the carburetors from the cylinder head complete with manifolds and balance pipe. Either removal or refitting of the securing screws is facilitated by the use of a shortened socket screw key. Lay the carburetors and manifold assembly still attached to the throttle and air cables over the headlamp clear of the engine unit.

Fig. F1   Removing oil junction block securing bolt

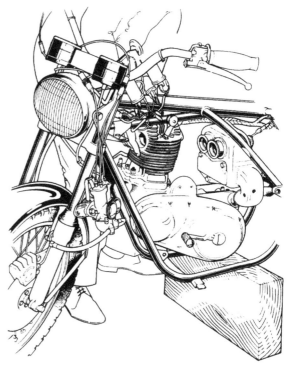

Fig. F2   Lifting out power unit to right side

Frame and Ancillaries F

28 Disconnect the contact breaker leads from the main harness in the area of the frame top rails. Disconnect starter wire and remove starter (and sealing ring) by withdrawing three posidrive screws in primary cover mounting. This enables engine to be removed under the new airbox.

29 Disconnect the oil tank end of the engine breather pipe.

30 Place a receptacle of sufficient size to contain the contents of the oil tank below the rear of the crankcases, remove the bolt securing the oil junction block to the crankcases, pull the block and pipes away from the crankcases and allow the oil to drain. Alternatively after parting the junction block from the crankcases, raise the junction block and tie with wire to the airbox to prevent oil draining from the tank, or protect the feed pipe with cardboard and compress the pipe with grips to prevent oil draining (see *Fig.* F1).

31 Slacken clutch cable adjustment and lift the cable nipple from the handlebar control.

32 Remove the front engine mounting by taking out the centre bolt. Remove the two mounting-to-crankcase bolts and lift away the mounting. The Mark III rubbers are all bonded to the hollow spindle and the two end-caps retain the units in one piece.

33 Remove the centre stand. This is secured by bolts fitted from inboard. Lift the spring clear as the stand is removed.

34 Disconnect the two alternator leads at the snap connectors.

The power unit assembly is now secured to the frame only by the rear mounting. Before removing the rear mounting stud, coil the clutch cable by the gearbox. Unclip the C.B. leads from the frame and coil them by the timing case. Protect the lower frame rails against damage using cardboard or thick cloth.

35 Support the weight of the power unit and use a soft drift to drive out the rear mounting stud.

36 As shown in *Fig.* F2, lift the power unit bodily from the frame to the right hand side. Raise the front of the power unit and lower the rear to clear the airbox. The clearance is minimal but with the electric-starter removed the operation is possible.

SECTION F2

ISOLASTIC ENGINE MOUNTINGS

The Norton Isolastic principle built into the Commando couples together the engine, transmission, swinging fork and rear wheel. This assembly, parted from the main frame is seen clearly in *Fig.* F3.

Isolation of the engine transmission swinging fork and rear wheel is achieved by the use of resilient mountings shown as A, B and C. Unlike earlier attempts at rubber mounting, the Commando is unique in that the swinging fork is mounted on the engine cradle and thus isolated from the main frame. This prevents twisting between the engine and rear wheel sprockets under load which would otherwise cause premature chain wear or displacement of the chain.

The power unit in its mounting plates oscillates on the rear mounting (B). This arrangement provides maximum support, particularly to the swinging arm and rear wheel, whilst isolating the power unit from the frame.

The front mounting (C) controls the degree of movement of the power unit on the rear mounting and the two main and two "buffer" rubbers allow more flexibility than does the rear mounting. All rubbers are now bonded and positively located to prevent shuffling.

Frame and Ancillaries

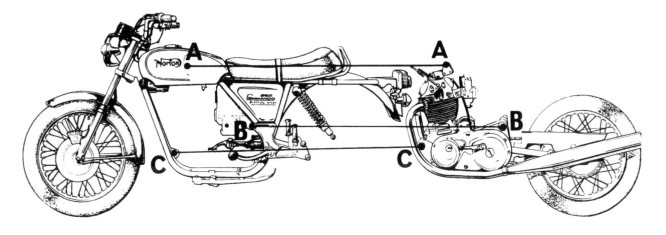

Fig. F3   Commando parted to show isolastic mounting points

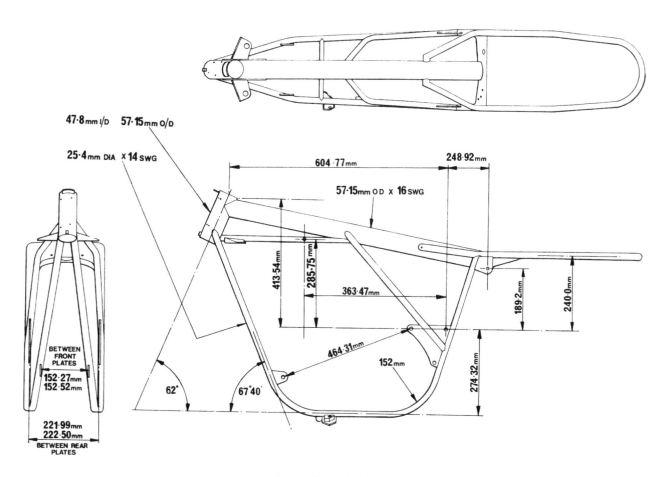

Fig F4   Frame checking charts

Frame and Ancillaries

Both the front and rear mountings incorporate plastic thrust washers to permit side play to be kept within very restricted limits without transmitting engine and transmission vibrations to the rider. The degree of side play is controlled by adjustable, lockable collars – a new feature on the Mark III – enabling the clearance to be kept within design limits even after considerable mileages. (See Technical Data for Adjustment dimensions and method) and Frame Section F12 for full details of Isolastic Adjustable mountings.

The engine head steady (A) completes the triangular formation of the resilient mountings and controls lateral movement of the engine unit in the frame. The insulating rubbers are fitted between the side plates and frame tube. An additional suspensory spring device is incorporated on the Mark III to improve isolation at low engine r.p.m. See Section C1 for particulars.

SECTION F3

FRAME CHECKING DIMENSIONS

During the course of an accident repair, the frame must be examined most carefully for damage to tubes, welds and fixing lugs. It is then essential to check for distortion and misalignment. *Fig.* F4 shows the Commando frame measurements which should be used to establish whether or not damage has occurred. However, before stripping out the frame from the motorcycle, one quick visual check can be made on vertical alignment at the steering head tube after removal of the front fork assembly. This is accomplished by a long tube (approximately 4 ft. (121 cm)) inserted as a tight push fit through the steering head races. Viewed from the front, the tube should be seen to be perfectly aligned to the motorcycle centre line. Severe damage will immediately be shown up by this method and will obviate unnecessary dismantling at the estimating stage.

It is recommended that the frame is checked more accurately when removed from the motorcycle, to the dimensions given in the checking chart.

SECTION F4

REFITTING POWER UNIT

Prior to refitting the power unit, if any major mechanical attention has been given, wash the oil tank and oil pipes out very thoroughly to remove dirt and foreign matter. As with dismantling, protect the lower frame rails against damage. Proceed as follows:

1   Pass the power unit into the frame from the right side, raising the front slightly and lowering the rear to clear the airbox.

2   With the power unit loosely in position, move the rear end as far as possible to the right side of the frame to facilitate assembly of the rear mounting.

3   The new Mark III adjustable, fully bonded engine mountings, see F12–,16 are unlikely to need attention except for final adjustment and can be re-assembled after inspection of plastic washers.

Where they are to be assembled without further attention proceed as follows:

4   Grease, using silicone grease such as Releasil No. 7, on all faces of washers, face rings and end caps. Position the spacer between the left hand alloy footrest mounting plate and battery tray bracket and slide in the mounting stud from the left side, moving the power unit as necessary to align the stud holes.

5   Tap the main stud right through aligning with the right frame bracket, insert the footrest plate and spacer, then fit the washer and nut. Tighten to 30 lbs./ft. (4·15 Kg/m).

Frame and Ancillaries

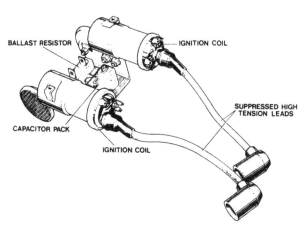

Fig. F5   Coil cluster from rear beneath

6   Fit the front engine mounting plates to the crank-cases, sliding the long end of the mounting over the lower crankcase bosses. With the stud or bolt fitted, pivot the mounting up into position to insert the second stud or bolt. Almost certainly the power unit will need to be lifted to insert the crankcase studs (or bolts).

7   Grease the end caps with a silicone grease and reassemble the front mounting as in Section C32. Adjust front and rear mountings as described in Technical Data. This will give 0·005 in to 0·006 in clearance as recommended by "Engineering".

8   Tighten the centre bolt to a torque of 30 lbs./ft. (4·15 Kg/m).

9   Refit the oil pipe junction block, using a new gasket if necessary and securing with the single bolt which must not be overtightened. (8 lbs/ft. 1·10 Kg/m)

10   Prior to refitting the carburetors and spacers, grease the manifold screws lightly and run them into the cylinder holes to ensure that they can be tightened by finger pressure only when the car-burettors and manifolds are assembled. During this operation and before attempting to fit the engine to the frame block the inlet ports with clean non-fluffy cloth to prevent a screw dropping down one of the ports. Remember to remove the cloth before fitting the carburetors.

11   Holding the Tuffnol insulating block in place fit the air hose to the airbox using a screwdriver blade to enter the lip, then assemble the right carburetor and manifold to the head tightening the socket screws completely.

12   Fit the air hose to the airbox, then offer the insulating block, carburetor and manifold to the cylinder head, tightening the socket screws as far as possible with the fingers. When locking up the screws an abbreviated socket key is essential.

13   Attaching the suspensory spring unit with its loop positioned as previously (See C1(a).
Fit the main head steady plate to the cylinder head, securing with three socket headed screws. Note that the centre screw secures the ground (earth) tab on the red leads.

14   Position the two spacer tubes in the head steady plate and offer the side plates over the rubber mounting studs. Pass the two studs through the side plates and spacer tubes and secure with the washers and nuts. Lastly, fit and tighten the nuts at the rubber mountings.

15   Pass the rocker feed pipe behind the fuel line 'T' piece and between the manifolds. The double end of the pipe fits to the right side of the rocker box. Ensure copper washers are fitted to both sides of each banjo and secure with the banjo bolts.

16   Refit the coil cluster, (the cluster is illustrated in *Fig.* F5) and reconnect the contact breaker leads colour to colour.

17   Reconnect the crankcase breather pipe at the oil tank and the separator pipe to the tee-piece on balance-pipe. Refit the earth wire to the top left nut on the crankcase stud.

18   Reconnect the tachometer cable to the abutment at the top front of the crankcase, ensuring that the cable adaptor is fitted square upwards and that it has engaged with the drive before the cable union nut is tightened.

19 Reconnect the clutch cable at the handlebar control and adjust the cable to give $\frac{3}{16}$ in. to $\frac{1}{4}$ in. (4 to 6 mm) free play.

felt plugs, previously soaked in SAE140 oil must be fitted in the $\frac{1}{2}$" dia tapped bores in the King-Pin and the "penny-washer" felts assembled under the end-cap welch-washer providing sealed-in lubrication for the bearing.

20 Reassemble the starter motor (making sure the rubber sealing ring is over the spigot). Tighten the three posidrive screws, one through the primary cover joint, and two through the mounting flange. Re-connect the starter wire to the terminal on the body and replace the rubber boot.

N.B. The presence of an outrigger journal on the armature shaft may cause confusion. It has been found that the starter motor functions more satisfactorily and freely without the additional bearing, and the bush has not been fitted in the mounting flange since Engine No. 325689.

23 With the left-hand welch-washer and felt "penny-washer" already fitted, and the moulded sealing rings trapped under the bush-flanges, push the swinging arm forward to align the bushes with the bore.

24 Using a $\frac{1}{2}$" UNF bolt (the main isolastic bolt is suitable) with a locknut screwed into the right-hand end of the swing-arm pivot spindle (King-Pin), insert the left-hand cotter from above — flat facing flat, — and push the spindle home. Making sure the oil soaked felt plug is fitted in the $\frac{1}{2}$" tapped recess, forward. The spindle can be felt carefully past the cotter which will stop the initial progress through the bore, and, with care, obviate the annoyance of knocking out the left-hand welch-washer, and a time-wasting rework. If there *is* any doubt after an "over-shoot", always check and re-affirm a satisfactory end-seal before reassembling the arm as the exclusion of road grit and water is essential to ensure the full life of this heavily loaded bearing.

21 Refit the centre stand with the pivot bolts passing through the engine plates, spacers and stand, inboard to outboard. Fit the nuts and tighten fully on to the spacers. Hook the long end of the centre stand spring into the L.H. rear engine plate then use a length of twine over the stand end of the spring to expand it whilst locating the hook in the stand cross tube.

25 With the spindle home and the left-hand cotter located draw in the second cotter. The right-hand pin has a wider side tolerance to ease assembly — the left-hand cotter is the lateral locator.

22 Prior to refitting the swinging arm (which in this exercise still has the sprocket, speedo gearbox, and chain-guard attached) ensure that the pivot area is perfectly clean, that the sintered bushes are oiled lightly and that the special moulded sealing washers are interposed under the bush flanges on the inside joints. Eventually, lubricating

26 Remove the bolt and nut used during fitting of the pivot spindle.

Frame and Ancillaries

F

27 Fit the right-hand felt-plug impregnated with
    *SAE140 oil into the tapped recess in the King-Pin,
    install the flat felt washer (also oiled) and knock
    in the welch-washer to effect a permanent seal
    and exclude all road-grit and tire-splash.
    (The bushes are sealed and lubricated for life)
    Insert rubber plugs in the top of each cotter boss.

    *N.B. The assembly department at the factory use
    140EP oil and 2% Molybdenum Disulphide
    additive.

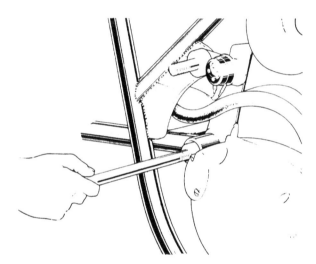

Fig. F6   Removing (or aligning) swinging arm spindle

28 Refit the rear chain to the Sprocket unit, now
    installed with the swing arm. The chain must pass
    over the bolts within the chainguard and over the
    countershaft (gearbox) sprocket. This is facilitated
    by engaging top gear, tying the clutch lever back
    to the handle-bar then cranking the kickstart to
    revolve the sprocket and pull the chain over.

29 Engage neutral and pull the chain through suffici-
    ently to connect the bottom run. Release the
    clutch lever.

30 Refit the right-hand support plate complete with
    the hydraulic master cylinder, brake pedal and
    footrest (previously dismantled as a complete
    sub-assembly) threading the caliper through the

frame, inverting and supporting it on the hook
provided. Ensure that spacers are correctly fitted
behind the plate. This requires some dexterity but
is easier with the wheel removed. Re-connect
"lucar" to the diode, red wire to the earth-nut, and
the two contacts to the master cylinder-pressure
switch.

31 Refit electric-horn and reconnect terminals.

32 Refit oil filter and reconnect return pipes.

33 Reassemble rear mudguard to forward fixings.
    The tail lamp harness has remained undisturbed
    along the frame loop.

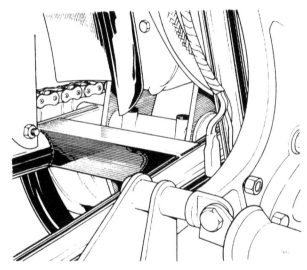

Fig. F7   Swinging arm pivot (king pin) and cotters.

34 Refit the rear wheel (see Section H0). Take care
    to untwist the hydraulic hose and when the caliper
    is reassembled to the disc apply the rear brake
    forcibly a number of times to settle the friction
    pads back in correct relationship to the disc.
    THIS IS MOST IMPORTANT AND MUST BE
    DONE AFTER ANY WORK INVOLVING THE
    BACK WHEEL (INCLUDING REAR CHAIN
    ADJUSTMENT).

Frame and Ancillaries **F**

35 Refit the exhaust system, (see Section F19) ensuring that the spherical seating rings are in position in the ports and the split rings behind the finned lockrings adjacent to the pipe-flanges. Tighten the finned lockrings with service tool 063968 or a similar suitable 'C' spanner.

36 Refit the fuel tank (see Section F9) and reconnect the fuel pipes.

37 Refit the fuse.

38 Refit the battery cover and right side cover.

39 Check all oil levels and top up or refill as necessary.

40 Replace the seat and check wire, and secure with the knurled side knob, after engaging lock-claw with key turning anti-clockwise to lock.

SECTION F5

REMOVING AND REFITTING SUSPENSION UNITS

In order to replace or dismantle the suspension units it is necessary to remove them from the motorcycle as follows:

1 Remove the nut securing the bottom of the suspension unit and pull the unit clear of the swinging arm.

2 Unlock and lift the seat. Removing altogether by dismantling the four posidrive screws at the hinge, if preferred.

3 Slacken off the knurled knob as far as possible to gain spanner access to the integral hexagon of the suspension unit top bolt.

4 Holding the bolt by the hexagon to prevent turning, remove the nut and plain washer from behind.

5 Support the weight of the suspension unit and remove the bolt.

The suspension unit is now free to lift clear of the top frame lugs.

Refitting is a reversal of the foregoing but on re-assembly ensure adequate clearance between the suspension unit top collar and any carrier equipment which may be fitted.

SECTION F6

REAR SUSPENSION UNITS (GIRLING)

The rear suspension units are of the spring controlled, oil damped, telescopic type. Adjustment of static spring loading is accomplished by rotating the three position castellated cam ring at the bottom of the spring. To adjust, support the motorcycle on the centre stand and use a 'C' spanner to turn the cam ring. Turning the cam ring to the left increases the loading to cope with additional loads and vice versa. Both units must be on the same loading – if in doubt, start both units from the light load position. The damper units are factory sealed thus cannot be serviced. The springs can however be removed. Bonded rubber bushes are used top and bottom for mounting the suspension units. These can be pressed out for replacement and new ones pressed in, smeared with a lubricant such as soap to ease entry.

IMPORTANT NOTE

It is important always to check the assembly and function of the rubber mounting bushes on suspension units.

As designed the inner sleeve is proud of the outer, and will always oscillate freely within its rubber when clamped up.

In the unlikely event of misuse or damage resulting in a shortening of the inner sleeve, (or incorrect replacement of the sleeve by a shorter version), the bush could be clamped up solid, preventing torsional freedom and eventual fatigue failure of the attachment – weld to the strut.

Frame and Ancillaries

F

Fig. F9

Fig. F10

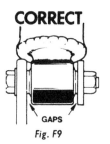

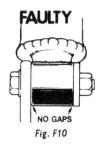

Fig. F9 *Suspension unit assembled with correct length sleeve*

Fig. F10 *Suspension unit assembled with sleeve of incorrect length*

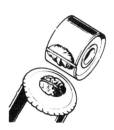

Fig. F11 *Failed suspension unit with ferrule detached*

When locked up, normal articulation of the swinging arm causes movement of the suspension unit body, not the affected ferrule, and a fatigue failure occurs. See *Fig.* F11.

Check that the top and bottom suspension unit mount-
Check that the top and bottom suspension unit mounting bolts are tightened to 28 lbs./ft. Grasp the suspension unit in the hand and turn axially in one direction then the other on the mountings as shown in *Figs.* F12 and F.13

Fig. F12

Fig. F13

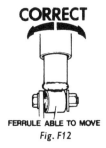

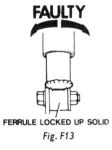

Fig. F12 *Grasping suspension unit and turning axially – showing ferrule freedom of movement*

Fig. F13 *Grasping suspension unit and turning axially – shows ferrule unable to move*

The ferrules of each suspension unit should move visibly on the bonded rubber bushes within the side plates as indicated. If there is freedom of movement, no further action is necessary since no fault is present.

If there is no movement, the inner sleeve of the bonded-rubber-to-metal-bush sleeve is of insufficient length. The comparative measurements of correct and incorrect sleeves are shown in *Figs.* F14 and F15.

Fig. F14

Fig. F15

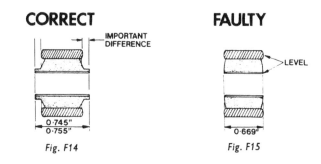

Fig. F14 *Correct length sleeve showing comparison point*

Fig. F15 *Incorrect length sleeve flush with suspension unit ferrule*

Where a suspension unit is identified as having a sleeve of insufficient length, *the whole suspension unit* must be replaced, together with the other side suspension unit which may have suffered undue stresses as a result. In these circumstances contact your dealer immediately. In bonafide cases he is authorised to replace faulty units free of charge.

When fitting new suspension units ensure that the securing bolts are tightened to 28 lbs./ft. and that there is freedom of axial movement on completion.

Fig. F16

Fig. F17

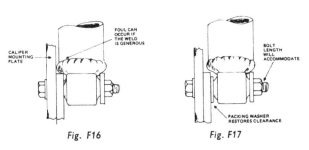

Fig. F16 *Suspension unit assembled fouling caliper plate.*

Fig. F17 *Suspension unit assembled with clearance restored.*

Frame and Ancillaries   **F**

CAUTION:

Mark III Commando rear disc brake: critical assembly. Always ensure adequate clearance between the caliper mounting plate and suspension strut where the bottom weld adjoins the plate. This is a variable and can result in a foul. A packing washer will rectify this and remove any stress from the bush. The bolt will accommodate the extra length and overhang.

wicks, washers and oil sealing rings. Renewal of these items should be dealt with as follows:

1   Remove the welch washer from the remaining boss on the swinging arm. This will press out or knock out easily from the opposite side.

2   Using a light press and a suitable shouldered press tool, press out the first bush, releasing the large bonded sealing washer trapped under the bush flange.

SECTION F7

CHANGING THE SPRING

In order to change a spring it is recommended that the suspension unit is gripped in a vice by the bottom mounting. Turn the castellated cam ring to the light load position. The help of a second operator is needed so that as the spring is grasped firmly in both hands and compressed down, the second operator lifts clear both split collars. Pressure on the spring is now released and the spring can be lifted clear. Reassembly is a reversal of these instructions.

3   Repeat for the second bush.

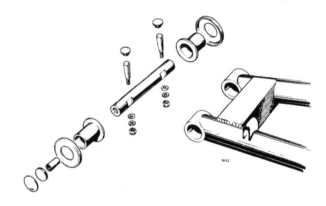

Fig. F18   Swinging arm bushes showing order of assembly

SECTION F8

REBUSHING THE SWINGING FORK

After long usage, the two flanged bushes working on the spindle may wear. After removal of the swinging fork (Section F1 (9–22) wash all parts very thoroughly in gasoline (petrol). Insert the pivot spindle and check the fit. Excessive working clearance will permit unacceptable side movement at the rear wheel and this must be rectified by renewing the spindle, bushes, felt

New bushes are pre sized and do not require reaming after fitting. Assemble as follows:

4   Place the bonded sealing washer over the bush as in *Fig.* F18 and press the bush in fully.

Frame and Ancillaries

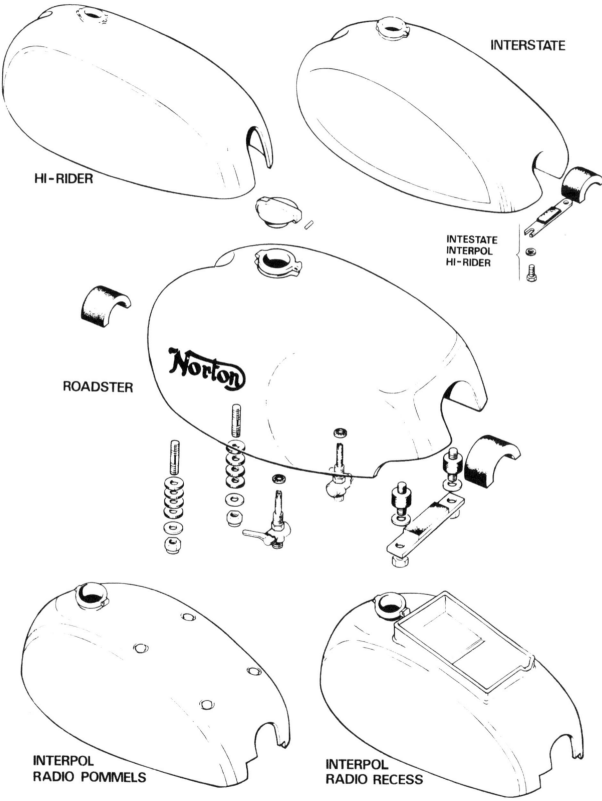

HI-RIDER

INTERSTATE

INTESTATE
INTERPOL
HI-RIDER

ROADSTER

Norton

INTERPOL
RADIO POMMELS

INTERPOL
RADIO RECESS

Fig. F19   Mark III Fuel tanks and fixings

Frame and Ancillaries   **F**

5   Repeat for the second sealing washer and bush.

6   Place the felt disc (previously impregnated with SAE140 oil) in the recess in the left-hand boss and press home the welch-washer. The right-hand set will be fitted after assembly into the machine.

The swinging arm is now ready to refit to the motorcycle, using a new spindle if the original shows signs of wear. Remember you will need new welch-washers and must ensure the "plug-wicks" and felt discs are fully impregnated with SAE140 oil before assembly. These must provide lubrication, for life, of the replacement bushes!

The rear fixing employs resiliently padded steel cross-straps straddling beneath the main frame tube secured by bonded rubber isolators. Moulded resilient paddings cap the tank top tube, fore and aft, fitting the tank channel.

The various tanks fitted to the Mark III Commando models are illustrated on Fig. F19 with model designations

FUELS

The Mark III Commando is designed to operate on fuels of *at least* 94 octane rating. (U.K. 3 star or U.S.A. premium. *See section K1: and Rider manual; P. 15/17.*

SECTION F9

REMOVING AND REPLACING FUEL TANK

Prior to removal of any fuel tank, remove the seat. This will permit easier access to the rear tank fixings. Disconnect the fuel pipes from both fuel taps at the pipe union nuts.

The method of fixing is illustrated in Fig. F19. The front mounting utilises studs, self locking nuts and loose insulating washers, providing a form of insulation from the frame front tank member. This mounting is common to all Mark III types.

SECTION F10

REMOVING AND REFITTING OIL TANK

Prior to draining the oil tank, take the motorcycle for a short run to warm the oil which should then flow more freely. Have available a receptacle of sufficient size to receive the contents of the oil tank. Remove the seat after releasing the large knurled side knob.

A common oil tank is used on all 850 Commando Mark III models and the following instructions apply to all editions.

Frame and Ancillaries

1 Remove the two hexagon headed screws and washers securing the right hand side panel.

2 Remove the drain plug and allow oil to drain into the receptacle previously obtained.

3 Pull the crankcase breather pipe and oil tank breather pipe away from the oil tank.

4 Remove the large hexagon headed oil tank filter at the rear of the oil tank.

5 Pull off the oil return pipe from the stub at the rear of the oil tank.

6 Remove the nut and washer securing the oil tank to the top rear mounting.

7 Slacken only the nut on the top front flexible mounting (the bracket is slotted and will then slide clear).

8 Using an extension socket wrench, remove completely the bolt fitting through the bottom mounting into the base of the oil tank.

9 Pull the bottom of the oil tank outwards so that the filler neck clears the frame, slide the tank forwards and outwards, lifting the bottom clear first.

10 Reassemble as a reversal of the foregoing. Take care not to omit the spacer from the bottom mounting rubber.

SECTION F11

L.H. BATTERY AND R.H. SIDE COVERS

The left hand battery cover is retained by a Dzus fastener at the lower front of the cover. To remove, pull and turn the ring of the fastener. The cover is then pulled away from the frame at the front and lifted off the rear peg. On all but certain Interpol models, the cover can be lifted clear. On Interpol models with alternating horns, the horn relays and control boxes are located within the battery cover and the cover cannot be removed completely without disconnecting the horn wiring.

Mark III models have a right hand side cover secured at the top by hexagon headed screws and washers, and supported by an extension with rubber grommet at the bottom, fitting inboard of the footrest support plate.

SECTION F12

ISOLASTIC ENGINE MOUNTINGS

The Mark III Commando Isolastic Suspension incorporates redesigned, adjustable front and rear mounting units employing fully bonded rubber bushes, simplifying assembly procedure and eliminating scuffling in service. Adjustment is straight-forward and requires no special tools. A spoke or suitable small dia. screwdriver is all that is required as a tommy bar to turn the adjustable end cap, which is located on the right hand side at the front and the left hand side of the rear mounting. The opposite side in each case has a fixed end cap located by a grub-screw lock.

ADJUSTING ENGINE MOUNTINGS

Prior to checking adjustment or dismantling note that Mark III models must be supported by a stand or strong box placed below the main frame tubes with the centre stand folded. This is necessary due to the stand being mounted direct onto the engine plates on these models. On such models the mountings would be under tension with the centre stand in use. Proceed as follows:

SECTION F13

CHECKING AND ADJUSTING FRONT MOUNTING CLEARANCE

1 Slide the right side gaiter back to give access to the adjuster and plastic washer.

2 Push or lever the engine to the right until all slack in the Isolastic mounting has been taken up. Holding the engine unit in this position, use feeler gauges to measure the clearance between the plastic washer and bright plated adjuster collar. (See *Fig.* F20).

3 If the clearance exceeds 0·010 in (·25 mm) the unit should be readjusted.

4 Following the procedure defined in Technical Data: Slack of the main mounting central bolt, and slide spring clips clear of holes in adjuster.

Frame and Ancillaries **F**

5 Insert suitable size tommy bar (spoke or similar) into a convenient hole in the adjusting collar and screw up until there is no clearance.

6 Back-off adjuster, moving 1½ holes only (to unscrew), replace spring clip and gaiter.

7 Tighten main bolt to 30 lbs./ft. (4·15 Kg/m) torque.

8 The clearance will now be approximately 0·006 in (0·152 mm) as recommended.

Fig. F20   Checking front mounting clearance

SECTION F14

CHECKING AND ADJUSTING REAR MOUNTING CLEARANCE

1 Slide the left side gaiter back to give access to the face ring and plastic washer.

2 Push the rear wheel to the left firmly and measure the clearance between the plastic washer and bright plated adjusting collar.

3 If the clearance exceeds 0·010 in (·25 mm) the unit should be readjusted.

4 Following the procedure defined in Technical Data: Slack off the main mounting central bolt, and slide spring clip clear of holes in adjuster.

5 Insert suitable size tommy bar (spoke or similar) into a convenient hole in the adjusting collar and screw up until there is no clearance.

6 Back-off adjuster, moving 1½ holes only (to unscrew), replace spring clips and gaiter.

7 Tighten main bolt to 30 lbs./ft. (4·15 Kg/m) torque.

8 The clearance will now be approximatley 0·006 in (0·152 mm) as recommended.

SECTION F15.

ISOLASTIC ENGINE MOUNTINGS DISMANTLING AND RENEWAL

Routine checking of clearances will present little difficulty with the new adjustable mountings ,and with the fully bonded rubbers and provision to take up any wear of the plastic washers, it is unlikely that replacements will ever be required.

However, where a mounting has seen long service it may be desirable to clean out the unit and/or examine the plastic washers, etc for uneven wear or damage. In this event the complete unit will have to be removed to gain access to the components.

It is no longer possible to extract the end caps (as previous practice) after removal of the centre bolt or stud.

The front mounting is reasonably accessible but the rear unit can only be dismantled after a major stripdown of the primary transmission as described in Section C13/14.

Frame and Ancillaries F

DISMANTLING FRONT MOUNTING

In order to withdraw the mounting bolt completely it may be necessary to detach the right hand exhaust pipe as described in Section 19.

1   Remove the self locking nut and plain washer from the left hand side of the central mounting bolt.

2   Align the flats on the bolt head to clear the timing cover as the bolt is withdrawn.

3   Using a soft metal drift, gently drive the bolt out to the right hand side easing and supporting the weight of the engine and avoiding damage to the threads.

4   Remove the two $\frac{3}{8}''$ dia. bolts securing the plates to the crankcase. Lift the mounting away.

5   Remove gaiters both ends.

6   Slide back the spring clip on the adjusting end and with a spoke or similar tommy bar unscrew and remove the end cap, holding the assembly in a vice if necessary.

7   The plastic washer on the right hand end and the facing ring can now be removed and cleaned or replaced as required.

8   The opposite (fixed) end cap on the left hand side is located to the centre sleeve by a grub screw. See illustration F21. It is not essential to remove this end, unless the washer needs replacing, and the inner sleeve with bonded rubbers can be withdrawn from the mounting tube sufficiently to allow examination and cleaning of the washer and faces.

If the entire unit is to be dismantled it should be possible to drive the centre sleeve out without excessive force, the operation being eased by use of a rubber lubricant applied to the bore. Additional side pressure, applied by inserting a suitable sized bar into the central sleeve will assist extraction. The front mounting's are a *tighter designed fit* than the rear rubbers.

9   The engine mounting, end-caps, facing rings and plastic washers can now be thoroughly cleaned and examined. Remove all dirt and corrosion and where excessive wear, uneven thickness or damage is evident, replacement is advised. It will be necessary to unlock the grub screw and remove the fixed end cap if new items are needed on the left hand end.

10   In the unlikely event of deterioration of the rubbers a replacement bonded unit will be required. Rubbers are no longer available separately.

REASSEMBLY: FRONT MOUNTING

1   Hold the mounting securely in a vice, left hand side uppermost.

2   (Using a silicone grease such as Releasil No. 7). Slightly grease the contact faces of the facing ring, plastic washer, and fixed (left hand) end-cap. These items will still be sandwiched between the fixed end and left hand rubber if found OK, and dismantled intact, otherwise new components will be assembled in the correct order with the end-cap flush with the sleeve and the grub screw locked-up securely.

3   Paint the edges of the large rubbers with rubber lubricant and squeeze the right hand rubber into the mounting tube. (It has been found quite feasible to assemble the new rubber units without recourse to the original tapered guide body 063971, but where this is available it should still simplify entry into the tube). Work the unit through the mounting tube until the fixed end-cap is fitting snugly on the plastic washer and face ring.

4   Replace the left hand gaiter.

5   Remove and invert the assembly in the vice, right hand side uppermost.

6   Using a silicone grease such as Releasil No. 7 lightly grease the contact faces of the facing ring, plastic washer (both sides) and adjusting (screwed) end-caps. Insert spoke or similar tommy bar in a

Frame and Ancillaries F

hole and screw down until the flange pinches the washer.

7 Replace the right hand gaiter.

8 The mounting is now ready for re-installation on the crankcase.

   N.B. Adjustment is finalised with the unit in position.

9 Grease outer faces lightly and offer the mounting to the lower crankcase lug and hold loosely in position with the bottom stud.

10 Pivot the mounting up to engage with the crankcase lug and fit the top stud.

11 Secure both top and bottom stud nuts to 25 ft./lbs. (2·07 Kg/m) torque.

12 Fit the main mounting bolt from the right side. It will be necessary to align a flat on the hexagon to pass the timing case.

   This is facilitated by levering the power unit in the frame, supporting the weight of the engine to relieve the load on the bolt.

   Push the mounting bolt fully home, fit the washer and nut. Do not tighten at this stage.

13 Ensure that the gaiters are still located properly over the mounting, using a small screwdriver to assist this operation if necessary.

14 With the main mounting nut still slack, slide the spring clip away from the holes in the adjustable end-cap. Insert suitable sized tommy bar (a spoke or similar) into a convenient hole and screw up "finger-tight", taking up all clearance.

15 Back off the adjuster, moving (unscrewing) 1½ holes only, replacing spring clip. This will give 0·006 in/0·152 mm as recommended.

16 Tighten the main bolt to 30 lbs./ft. (4·15Kg/m) torque.

SECTION F16

ATTENTION TO REAR MOUNTING

After considerable usage it may be expected that the rear mounting end groups have suffered wear and deterioration due to corrosion. If the unit is to receive attention as in Section F15 the power unit must be removed from the frame as described in Section F1. However, the need for attention to these fittings is comparatively rare, and can usually be left until the power unit has to be dismantled for a major overhaul.

With the power unit removed as described in F1 the rear mounting is accessible, and although the mounting tube is smaller in diameter and longer, the basic design is similar in every aspect to the front layout, except for opposite – end adjustment and an easier fit of the rubbers in the bore – needing no special tool for extraction or assembly.

The procedure for dismantling, cleaning, lubricating and assembly are the same as for the front.

The adjustment drill is identical – lock up lightly and "back-off" 1½ holes after reassembly in the frame. The rear mounting stud is also torqued up to 30 lbs./ft. (4·15 Kg/m). Refer to F15 for details.

Note: Mark III model Commandos have been fitted with bronze-loaded PTFE plastic washers (brown in colour) in place of the cream coloured polyurethane washers fitted to earlier models. These washers resist wear and deterioration; therefore, we recommend they always be fitted as replacements.

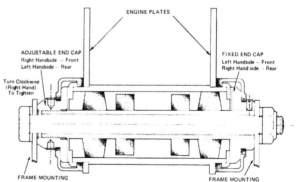

Fig. F21   Mark III adjustable isolastic mounting: Engineering diagram

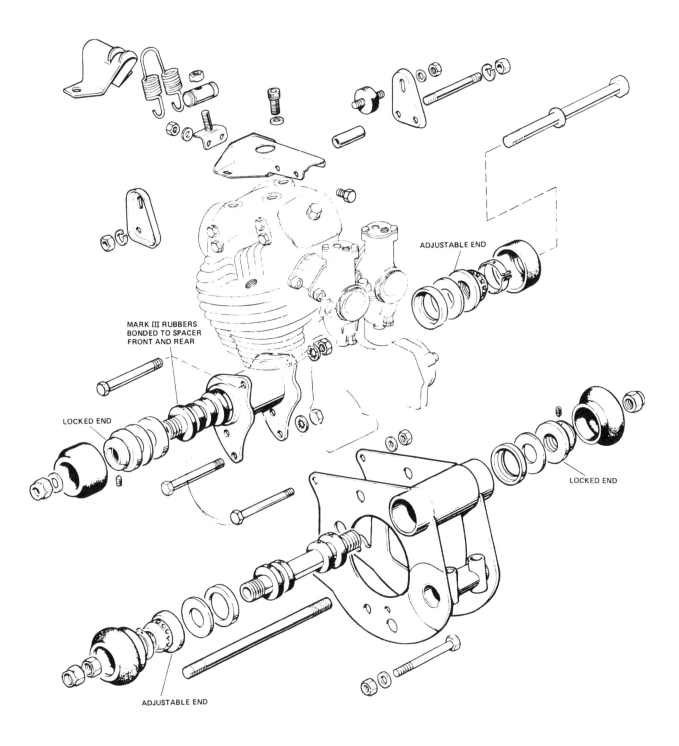

ADJUSTABLE END

MARK III RUBBERS
BONDED TO SPACER
FRONT AND REAR

LOCKED END

LOCKED END

ADJUSTABLE END

Fig F14   Isolastic mountings exploded view

Frame and Ancillaries   F

SECTION F17

REAR FENDER

Removal and refitting of the rear fender is similar for all Mark III models.

1   Unlock and lift the seat.

2   Release the tail lamp with fairing and number plate support as a group, by removal of six bolts and plain washers.

3   Disconnect the tail lamp leads (and the direction indicator leads where fitted) and lift away the tail lamp and tail lamp fairing group.

4   Remove the bottom front two self-locking nuts and plain washers securing the rear fender to the bracket from the frame gusset.

5   Reassembly is a reversal of the foregoing but do not omit to reconnect the tail lamp leads. Where direction indicators are fitted, ensure that they work correctly when reconnected.

SECTION F18

EXHAUST SYSTEM: REMOVAL

1   Slacken and slide both connector sleeves to the centre of the cross tube and remove.

2   Using service tool 063968 unscrew the finned exhaust lockrings and allow these to hang on the exhaust pipes. Collect Split rings and Sealing rings.

3   Remove the nuts securing the muffler (silencer) mounting plates to the rubber mountings, so that at the next stage the mufflers are removed with plate attached.

4   Lift each exhaust system clear.

REFITTING:

1   Place spherical seating washers in ports.
    Fit L.H. exhaust pipe complete with lockring, and split rings. Run up lockring but do not tighten at this stage.

2   Fit L.H. muffler to exhaust pipe, align the mounting pommels and assemble loosely to the L.H. muffler bracket mounting rubbers.

3   Fit R.H. exhaust pipe complete with lockring and split ring. Run up lockring but do not tighten.

4   Fit R.H. muffler to exhaust pipe, align the mounting pommels and assemble loosely to the R.H. muffler bracket mounting rubbers.

5   Slide both connector sleeves to the centre of the cross tube. Place cross tube in position and slide both connector sleeves outwards to engage with the exhaust pipe stubs.

6   Slacken off all footpeg support and muffler bracket bolts in the left and right hand aluminium support plate castings — to allow the brackets to swivel and adjust to the exhaust pipe/muffler alignment.

7   Tighten up the total exhaust system, commencing at the cylinder head lockrings and cross tube connector sleeves.

8   Finally retighten the muffler bracket/support plate bolts.

Frame and Ancillaries

F

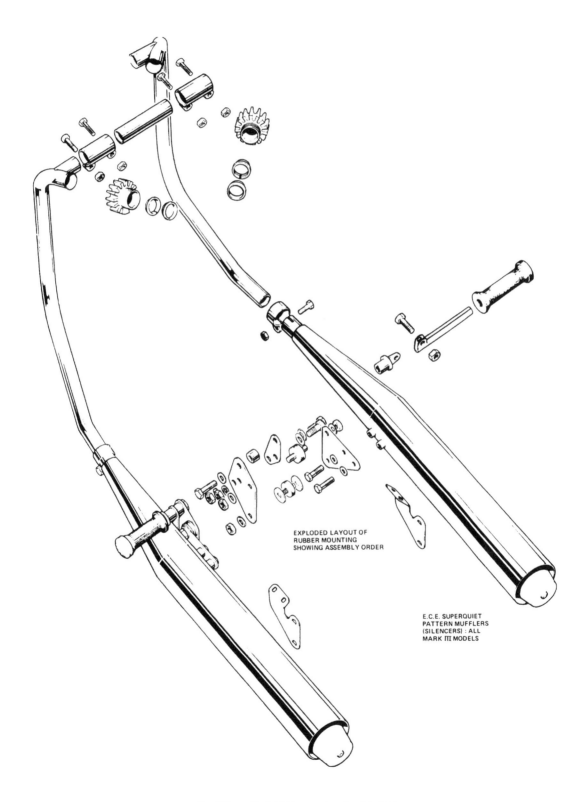

EXPLODED LAYOUT OF
RUBBER MOUNTING
SHOWING ASSEMBLY ORDER

E.C.E. SUPERQUIET
PATTERN MUFFLERS
(SILENCERS) : ALL
MARK III MODELS

Fig. F23   Mark III Commando exhaust system

NOTES

Front Forks

and

Steering

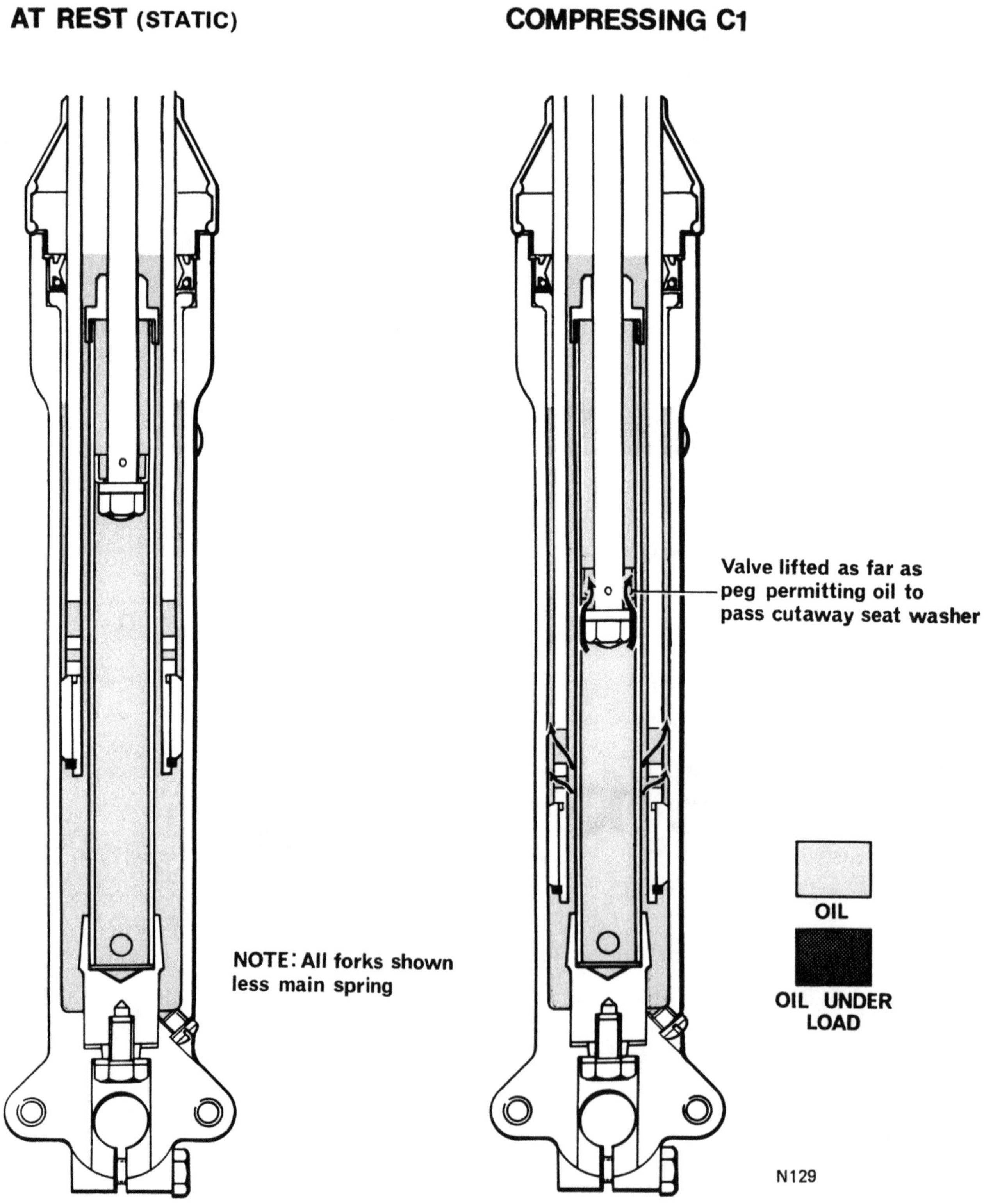

Front Forks/Steering

AT REST (STATIC)

COMPRESSING C1

Valve lifted as far as peg permitting oil to pass cutaway seat washer

NOTE: All forks shown less main spring

OIL

OIL UNDER LOAD

N129

Fig. G2   Fork at rest, compressing, extending and almost fully extended

Front Forks/Steering

FINAL COMPRESSION C2

EXTENDING

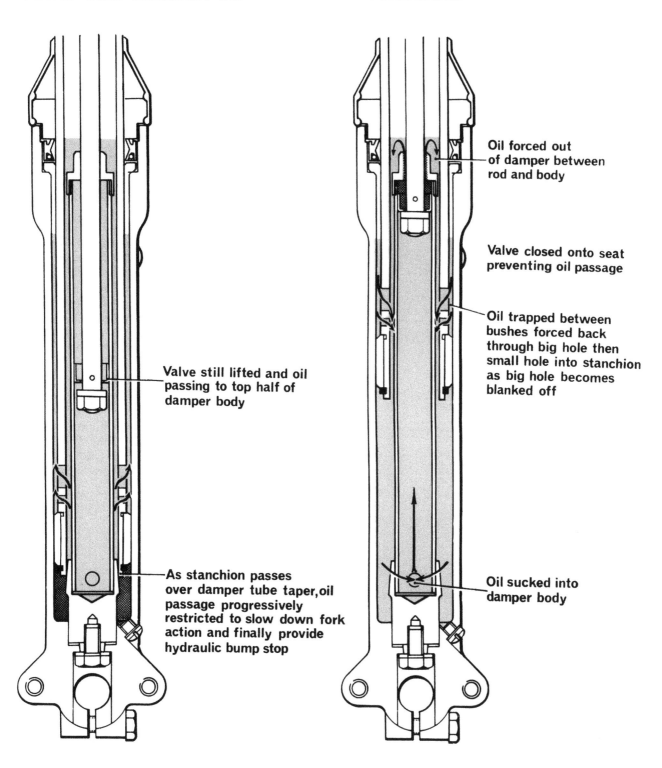

Valve still lifted and oil passing to top half of damper body

As stanchion passes over damper tube taper, oil passage progressively restricted to slow down fork action and finally provide hydraulic bump stop

Oil forced out of damper between rod and body

Valve closed onto seat preventing oil passage

Oil trapped between bushes forced back through big hole then small hole into stanchion as big hole becomes blanked off

Oil sucked into damper body

Front Forks/Steering

SECTION G1

FRONT FORK DESCRIPTION

The Commando Fork is a development of the "Road-holder" Fork which is world famous as an extremely strong and precise steering unit under all conditions. The Mark III caliper is mounted on the left side of the machine to maintain optimum steering precision and balance now that the rear disc is mounted on the right hand side, and the front mudguard stay is deleted to minimise eddy of road splash into the caliper. The forks comprise high quality seamless chrome steel main tubes with light aluminium sliding members for reduced unsprung weight. Fork movement is controlled by long single rate springs and two-way oil damping. The sliding members are supported on oil impregnated sintered bronze bushes at the top and steel at the bottom to give maximum support and to minimise wear. The fork yokes are substantial cast components which provide great rigidity. The steering head pivot comprises two pre-packed and sealed ball journal bearings.

SECTION G2

HOW FORK WORKS

Consider that as the front wheel meets a bump in the road surface the front forks are compressed against the main springs. As the wheel passes the bump the forks are permitted to return to the static position. Should the motor-cycle become "front end light" such as negotiating a hump-backed bridge, the fork extends fully but once again on level road, returns to the static position. The natural tendency for a spring controlled suspension system is to over react and oscillate before returning to static position. Such a system would result in a pitching motion on rough roads and a subsequent loss of stability. To counter this condition, oil damping is provided which in the case of the Commando fork slows down the spring return both on compression and extension. Each fork slider contains 150 cc of oil which is metered by a rod and valve damper assembly. The damping sequence is detailed in the following text and the complete fork assembly is shown in *Fig.* G4.

FORK AT REST

The oil lies in the bottom of the slider and occupies the spaces between top and bottom bushes, damper tube and main tube and occupies the lower end of the damper tube.

FORK COMPRESSES (C1 and C2)

Consider that the main tube and damper rod remains stationary thus as the fork compresses, the slider and damper tube rise. As the slider rises, oil passes into the lower end of the damper tube. There is no passage of oil between the damper rod and damper tube cap but oil passes from the slider through the main tube bleed holes between the bushes. The vacuum caused between the fork bushes during compression causes oil to be sucked from the space between the fork bushes. As the fork compresses further, the damper tube passes further into the main tube until the cone shaped bottom area enters and the oil passage into the main tube is progressively cut off until only the bleed hole into the damper tube remains. Oil is then able to pass through the bleed hole slowly, thus slowing or "damping" the fork action, finally providing a hydraulic bump stop on full compression.

FORK EXTENDING

The main tube remains stationary whilst the slider and damper tube descend. Oil remains trapped between the top and bottom bushes. The damper valve within the damper tube remains closed thus as the damper tube descends, oil passes between the damper rod and damper tube cap into the space between the damper tube and main fork tube. As the fork continues to extend, oil trapped between the fork bushes is forced back into the slider through the large hole then the small hole to slow down the fork action and prevent the fork "topping" heavily.

Front Forks/Steering

G

REMOVAL OF FRONT FORKS

Removal of the front forks is most easily achieved by dismantling in parts rather than attempting to remove the fork assembly complete.

Unfortunately it is no longer possible to remove the hydraulic system as a complete assembly, and is necessary to drain and disconnect the pipe line when dismantling the fork. The Mk III has a redesigned hydraulic pipe run with armour protective cover over the lower hose and a short hose from the master cylinder to the top yoke intended to simplify handlebar change. For convenience and to avoid spillage on paintwork it is advisable to drain the system using a small bore tube on the bleeder screw as in Brakes Section H10 — Bleeding and Flushing (*Fig.* H9). Discharge the fluid into a suitable receptacle, pumping the lever slowly until flow ceases. Remember fluid bled from the system MUST BE DISCARDED.

With the pipe line drained, proceed to disconnect the olive unions at the bridge lugs (see important note on olive unions in Section H10).

Release the hydraulic pipe bracket from the left fork slider at the fender bridge. Remove the two bolts and spring washers securing the caliper to the slider and lift the caliper away, complete with pads and still attached to the brake hose. To simplify reassembly place a spacer between the brake pads — a suitable piece of clean wood or preferably a piece of plastic tubing would be ideal. Remove the four cross-headed screws securing the master cylinder to the right switch cluster, hold the master cylinder but allow the switch cluster to hang on its leads. Pull back the plastic switch cover from the master cylinder and disconnect both Lucar terminals. Remove flexible hose and master cylinder unit, caliper and lower flexible hose to a safe, clean place; also bundy tube mid-connecting pipe, and lightly reassemble to protect from ingress of foreign matter — until refitted. Avoid dust and never use fluffy rags to cover or wipe components.

Support the motorcycle by using a box or block of wood beneath the lower frame rails and proceed as follows:

1. Remove the front wheel (see Section H5). Remove the instrument panel.

2. Unscrew and lift the fork tube large chrome top bolts and using two spanners as shown in *Fig.* G6 release the damper rod from each top bolt.

3. Lift clear the speedometer and tachometer in their cases and allow them to hang on their cables, and similarly remove the instrument panel.

4. Slacken the lower lug socket headed pinch screws (See Fig. G4).

The fork main tubes are a tapered fit into the upper yoke and require a shock to free them. The shock may be delivered by grasping the fork slider with both hands and snatching downwards several times. If this fails to break the taper, replace the chrome top bolt at least six threads without the instrument case and using a block of wood to protect the chrome finish (see *Fig.* G3) deliver several blows with a hammer. This will release the main tube from the upper yoke.

5. Remove the first fork leg, replacing the top bolt to prevent oil loss.

6. Repeat the operation for the second leg.

Note that the steering head bearings are of the sealed ball journal type which will not be disturbed by removal of the yokes and stem.

7. Remove the lower yoke. This is accomplished by releasing the tab washer and removing the large nut from the bottom of the fork stem. Support the headlamp and tap the lower yoke downwards clear of the stem.

Front Forks/Steering

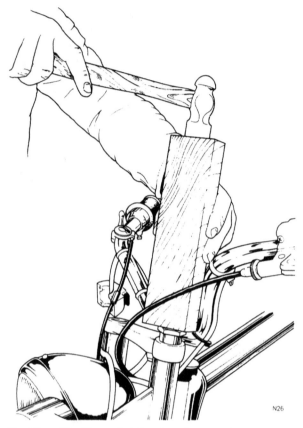

Fig. G3   *Shocking main tubes free of upper yoke*

SECTION G4

DISMANTLING FORK LEG

Removal of the fork leg assemblies is described in Section G3. Pour oil, from the fork leg to be dismantled, into a suitable receptacle and proceed as follows:

1   Secure the bottom of the slider in a plain jawed vice, with the leg vertical.

2   Lift the plastic gaiter up the main fork tube.

3   Remove the threaded collar by hand pressure only, or, if necessary, by the use of strap wrench 064622 which will not damage the finish.

4   Grasp the main fork tube in both hands and with a number of upward jerking movements, free the oil seal, paper washer and top collar.

5   Lift the main tube away from the slider.

6   Remove the damper tube anchor bolt (the various components are shown in *Fig.* G4) and collect the thick washer.

7   Lift the main spring and damper tube attached, clear of the slider.

8   Collect the bottom fibre washer from the damper tube for re-use.

9   Remove the slider from the vice, secure the damper tube *carefully* in the vice, taking care not to crush it.

10   Unscrew and lift away the alloy damper tube cap.

11   Withdraw the damper rod.

12   Grip the rod in a vice and remove the damper rod locknut, collecting the squared washer and damper valve.

13   The damper valve stop pin is free to be removed.

14   Removal of the square section circlip at the bottom of each fork tube permits removal of the steel bush.

8   Collect the two bottom and one top 'O' ring released by each headlamp bracket and top cover and allow the headlamp to hang down on its harness, with fork covers attached.

9   The upper yoke is now captive only by the tightness of the stem in the steering head bearings. Use a hide mallet or soft drift to drive the stem up through the bearings, allowing the upper yoke to be removed. Collect the dust cover and washer.

Note: The Mark III and all previous 850 models use a special pair of fork yokes identified by "ANG" stamped on lower surfaces of both yokes. These yokes must be used for 850's and must not, under any circumstances, be interchanged with earlier types.

Front Forks/Steering   G

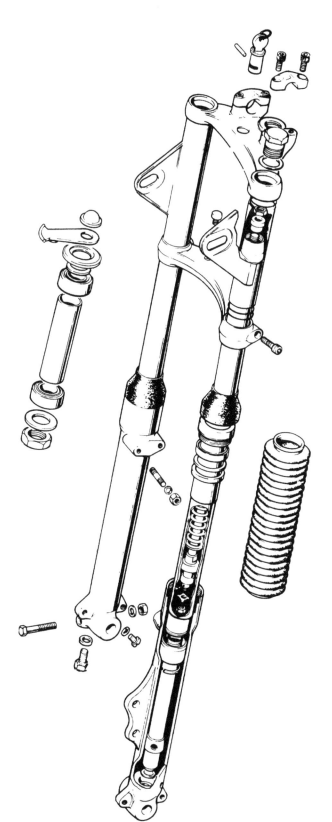

Fig. G4   Front fork exploded view

REASSEMBLING FORK LEG

Prior to reassembly, wash all parts very thoroughly in gasoline (petrol) and allow to dry. Examine for wear on the fork bushes and main tube. Check that the damper valve and stop pin are undamaged and that the damper rod is not bent. When all parts are sound, proceed to reassemble as follows:

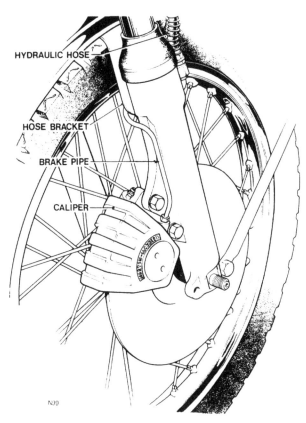

Fig. G5   Hydraulic system fittings to fork leg

1   If the lower bush on the main tube has been removed, fit a new bush and refit the circlip ensuring that it is bedded well all round.

2   Grip the damper rod in a vice and fit the damper valve stop pin. The order of assembly is shown in *Fig.* G4.

113

Front Forks/Steering **G**

3 At the peg end of the damper rod assemble the damper valve, lip end down (when in the vice) followed by the squared washer and nut which must be tightened securely.

4 Assemble the damper rod to the damper tube then fit and secure the damper tube alloy cap.

5 Place the spring over the damper rod and secure with the thick washer and nut.

6 Place the fibre washer over the end of the damper tube and offer the damper tube assembled, to the slider, securing with the thick washer and bolt.

7 Smear the main tube with clean oil then enter it into the slider.

8 Fit the top bush, paper washer and oil seal: the oil seal will need to be tapped home using a suitable tubular drift.

9 Fit the threaded collar and tighten down.

10 Refit the plastic gaiter.

The fork leg is now ready to refit as described in Section G8.

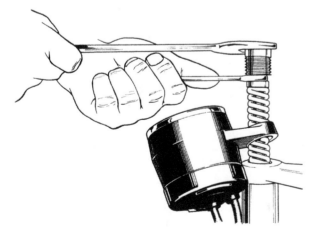

Fig. G6 Releasing damper rod from fork top bolts.

SECTION G6

RENEWING STEERING HEAD BEARINGS

850 Mark III Commando models utilise sealed non adjustable ball journal bearings with a spacer tube to prevent the bearings being forced into the frame head tube. After removal of the forks as in Section G3, the bearing spacer tube must be pushed to one side so that a drift can be applied to the inner race of the bottom bearing and the bearing driven out with care. The bearing spacer will be released at the same time. By using the drift from the other end of the steering tube the second bearing can then be driven out.

To replace the bearings, fit the bottom bearing fully home into the housing absolutely square. Use a shouldered drift through the bearing to hold it in line with the housing whilst abutting against the outer race. Place the spacer tube loosely in position and drive the top bearing in to abut to the spacer tube.

As the fork yokes are assembled the bearings will be pulled up to the spacer tube.

SECTION G7

STEERING HEAD ADJUSTMENT

On 850 Commando Mark III models – The steering head bearing arrangement, where the bearings abut to a centre spacer tube, is non-adjustable. The stem nut fitted from beneath the lower yoke has a tab washer to prevent slackening. See illustration *Fig.* G7.

Front Forks/Steering   **G**

REFITTING FRONT FORKS

Reassembly of the front forks is virtually a reversal of the dismantling procedure though for clarity, the full procedure is detailed below:

1   Place the top dust cover and washer over the top steering head bearing. Note that the washer fits below the cover.

2   Pass the stem of the upper yoke through the bearings. This will almost certainly require the use of a block of wood and a hammer to tap the stem fully home.

3   Lift the headlamp and top covers roughly into position, place the single 'O' ring in each side of the upper yoke to locate the tops of the fork covers Use heavy grease to hold the 'O' rings in place.

4   Place the lower yoke, with two 'O' rings to locate each fork cover, over the steering stem. Fit the tab washer and nut to the stem and commence to tighten. As the lower yoke is raised, locate the top covers, both top and bottom.

5   Tighten the nut sufficiently to pull the lower yoke into position, but do not secure fully yet.

6   Offer both fork legs through the lower and upper yoke and pull the main tube tapers into the upper yoke using the instrument cases and large chrome top bolts.

7   With the fork legs secured by the top bolts, snug the socket headed pinch screws.

8   Now tighten the fork securing points, viz: Chrome top bolts, main fork stem nut, lower yoke pinch screws. Note that the stem nut must not be over-tightened.

9   Tighten the stem nut to 15 lb/ft (207 kg/m) and tap over the stem nut tab washer.

10   Again lift the large chrome top bolts, firstly to add oil and secondly to connect the damper rods. Measure the required quantity of oil for each fork leg (150 cc of SAE 20). Pouring the oil into the leg will prove a long operation. To speed up the filling operation, pour in as much of the measured quantity as possible, place the hand firmly over the top of the main tube and extend the fork leg. Do this several times to speed up oil drainage into the slider. When the measured quantity has been added, and with the instrument case held in position, connect the damper rod to the chrome bolt as in *Fig.* G6. Using a socket wrench on the chrome bolts, tighten them down on to the fork tubes to 40 lbs/ft (5.83 kg/m).

11   Secure the master cylinder to the right switch cluster with the four long screws.

12   Bolt the caliper assembly to the left fork slider using two bolts and washers tightened to a torque setting of 25 ft/lbs (3·45 kg/m). Fit the hydraulic hose bracket over the studs on the left slider· Reassemble all the brake pipe unions and strictly observe the IMPORTANT procedure directed in Section H11 (Caliper Assembly) 11, 12, 13, 14, 15, 16 to complete the vitally important assembly of this brake "pressure-line". After carefully examining each union for leaks finally re-check the fluid level in the reservoir, topping up as necessary.

13   Fit the front fender, securing the four plain washers and nuts at the bridge stay and one bolt and plain washer at the fork end of the lower stay.

14   Refit the front wheel as in Section H6.

15   Feed the front brake stop switch leads through
      the stop switch cover one at a time and connect
      the Lucas terminals at the stop switch.

It is vital to "pump" the front brake lever several
times after the wheel has been removed to restore brake
pressure and settle the friction pads before the brake
is used.

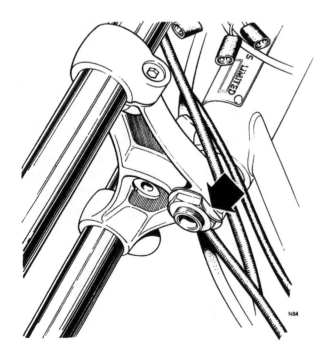

Fig. G7   Showing stem nut tab washer locked to nut

Brakes

Wheels

and

Tires

Brakes, Wheels and Tires H

REMOVAL OF REAR WHEEL

(Without disturbing sprocket or chain)

The Mark III Commando has a redesigned genuine quickly detachable rear wheel incorporating a "rubber in shear/compression" cush-drive and equipped with a powerful disc-brake, hydraulically operated.

The rear wheel can be removed by detaching it from the sprocket unit leaving the chain and sprocket undisturbed, in position on the swinging arm. The brake caliper can be lifted clear with hydraulic hose attached avoiding the need to drain the system. A hook is provided on the top loop to "stow" it.

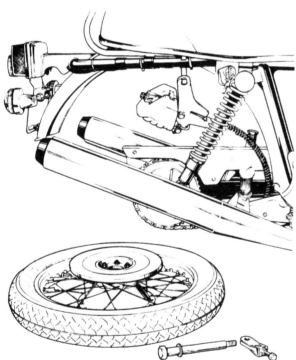

Fig. H1   Rear wheel removal

1   Support the machine firmly on the centre stand, extending the prop stand for additional support. It is advisable to tie the centre stand to the frame bottom cross-member beneath the power unit to prevent the machine from rolling forward off the stand.

2   Engage 1st or 2nd gear to simplify refitting the wheel.

3   Slacken the lower right hand suspension strut nut and withdraw it as far as the locating circlip.

4   Unscrew and remove the axle from the right hand side.

5   Ease the wheel over to the left and withdraw the right hand chain tensioner clevis.

6   Carefully lift the caliper and mounting plate upwards but make sure the friction pads still engage the disc.

7   Pinch the chain tensioner clevis together and wedge it between the friction pads, preventing them from falling out.

8   Lift and invert the caliper hanging the mounting plate on to the special attachment hook provided on the frame loop (on early despatches use string or wire).

9   Lean motor cycle to the left on its centre stand and extract the wheel, under the tail guard from the right rear.

10 Whilst the wheel is removed it is good practice to check the shock absorber for signs of "granulation" of the inserts.

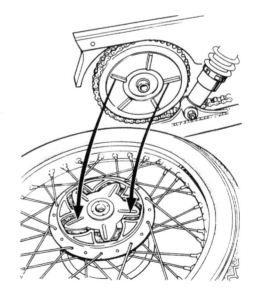

Fig. H1(a)   Quickly detachable Rear Wheel and Cush-Drive

Brakes, Wheels and Tires H

SECTION H2

REFITTING OF REAR WHEEL

1   Tilt the motorcycle to the left whilst inserting the wheel with the disc at the right side, between the swinging arm tubes.

2   Locate the wheel to the shock absorber paddles (illustration H1(a)

3   It may help to locate the axle loosely through the wheel whilst it is held to the left side and the paddles engaged.

4   With the axle loosely in position, unhook the mounting plate and move the caliper down (taking great care to "untwist" the hose), engaging the hole in the mounting plate to the bottom suspension bolt.

5   Holding the caliper in position, withdraw the axle bolt also the tensioner clevis used to wedge the friction pads.

6   Guide the caliper and pads carefully over the disc until the plate boss aligns between the wheel and swinging arm.

7   Open up the chain tensioner clevis, refit to the right side, lining up the holes – and insert the axle from the right.

8   Ensure the tensioner fits snugly to the swinging arm and tighten the wheel axle and suspension bolt nut.

9   Pump the brake pedal and apply heavy pressure to restore the friction pads to their correct relationship to the disc before the brake is used in service.

10 Remember to fold both stands before riding machine.

CAUTION:

If for any reason a pad should drop out, ensure that it is refitted correctly so that the friction material faces the disc. Position the caliper over the disc with the pads located correctly at each side of the disc and the pad

"ears" in the caliper slots. Locate the caliper plate slot on the suspension unit bottom bolt and line the boss up with the hub. Hold the chain tensioner in position then insert the wheel axle and thick washer and secure. Tighten the suspension unit bottom nut. It is essential to apply the brake several times to restore full pressure before the brake is returned to service.

SECTION H3

COMPLETE REAR WHEEL REMOVAL

In order to remove the wheel complete, support the motorcycle on the centre stand and proceed as follows:

1   Disconnect the rear chain at the split link.

2   Disconnect the speedometer cable from the drive box on the left hand side.

3   Slacken the lower right hand suspension strut nut and withdraw it as far as the locating circlip.

4   Unscrew and remove the axle from the right hand side.

5   Ease the wheel over to the left and withdraw the right hand chain tensioner clevis.

6   Carefully lift the caliper and mounting plate upwards but make sure the friction pads still engage the disc.

7   Pinch the chain tensioner clevis together and wedge it between the friction pads, preventing them from falling out.

8   Lift and invert the caliper hanging the mounting plate on to the special attachment hook provided on the frame loop (on early despatches use string or wire).

9   Remove the left side axle nut and thick washer.

10 Pull wheel over to the right so that the dummy axle clears the slot in the fork end.

11 The wheel can now be lifted clear.

Brakes, Wheels and Tires

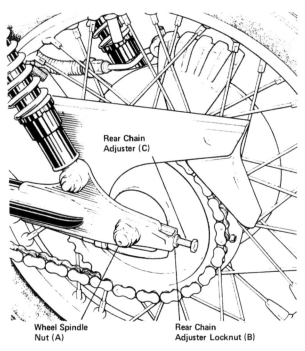

Rear Chain
Adjuster (C)

Wheel Spindle
Nut (A)

Rear Chain
Adjuster Locknut (B)

Fig. H2   Rear wheel features

SECTION H4

REAR HUB DISMANTLING

In order to change the wheel bearings, remove the wheel complete as described in Section H3 and lift off the washer, speedometer drive gearbox and internal distance collar from the sprocket side. With the wheel axle removed separate the sprocket from the wheel hub – the "paddles" on the sprocket are a pushfit in the machined slots in the spider. A double row ball journal bearing is fitted in the sprocket centre, pinched up on the dummy axle, with positive circlip location, and provided with its own oilseal. The bearing arrangement is clearly illustrated in the "exploded" drawing. *Fig. H3(a).*

To dismantle the rear hub proceed as follows:

1   First remove the five attachment nuts and spring washers and detach the disc, then starting with the shock absorber side of the wheel unscrew the LEFT HAND THREAD lockring using peg spanner tool 063965, and remove. (At this stage it is an advantage to warm the hub if possible to 100°C ONLY, if facilities are available. Boiling water "ladled" over the outside will help.)

2   Extraction of the lockring on the shock absorber side reveals the sealed ball journal bearing which provides positive lateral location of the rear wheel. Removal of the opposite side distance collar from the oilseal will expose the bearing spacer tube, and, using the wheel axle bolt as a drift, the spacer can be driven back into the hub with a hide mallet (or similar). ($\frac{5}{16}$" inward movement approximately will release the location bearing opposite – the tube stands $\frac{1}{2}$" proud of the disc side bearing and provides ample purchase.)

3   With the location bearing removed, the larger disc side bearing can now be driven out of the hub by knocking back the spacer tube with the axle inserted and any suitable distance collar to pack out the length. Take care to avoid burring the face of the spacer tube during the operation. The bearing will drive out the oilseal as it extracts.

4   Removal of the double-row bearing from the sprocket centre requires extraction of the locating circlip, using circlip pliers, and driving out the bearing from the seal side, leaving the oilseal to be pressed out with a suitably sized drift. Here again it will assist the operation to warm the sprocket if possible. Avoid bruising the speedo drive slots.

SECTION H5

REAR HUB REASSEMBLY

Prior to reassembly, clean and inspect the bearings and seals for roughness, wear, damage or corrosion and make replacements as necessary. Proceed as follows:

1   Pack bearings with the recommended grade of grease (see Section K1).

2   Reassembly is virtually a reversal of the dismantling procedure. Fit the larger single row bearing into the disc side of the hub, driving on the outer spool squarely (preferably under a press) until it stands under the disc-spigot approximately $\frac{5}{16}$" (7·94 mm). Pack grease over bearing cage and assemble oilseal flush with face of spigot (metal flange on outside).

3   Insert bearing spacer tube through bearing until shoulder touches inner spool.

Brakes, Wheels and Tires **H**

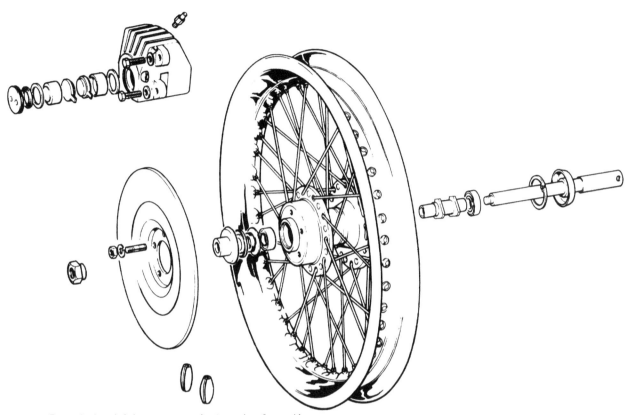

Fig. H3   Front wheel exploded arrangement, showing order of assembly

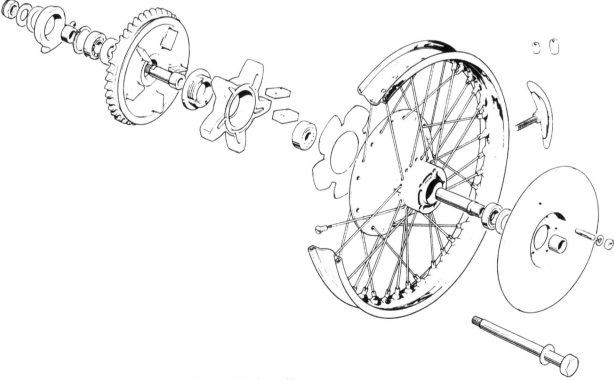

Fig. H3(a) Rear wheel exploded arrangement, showing order of assembly

Brakes, Wheels and Tires

4 Fit the smaller single row bearing into opposite side (sealed face outwards) after packing with grease.

5 Fit the locking ring and tighten. Remember that the lockring is LEFT HAND threaded. Tighten with peg spanner tool 063965 until bearing bottoms in its recess, this will also position the opposite side bearing if it was too deep in its housing.

6 The bright distance collar can now be inserted in the disc side oilseal over the protruding bearing spacer preventing loss of grease.

7 The brake disc can now be reassembled on the five studs and the spring washers installed and nuts tightened to 20 lbs/ft (2·76 kg/m).

8 Check that the shock absorber rubbers are free from granulation and the paddle slots and paddles are serviceable.

REASSEMBLY OF SPROCKET BEARING

1 Pack the bearing with the recommended grade of grease (see Section K1).

2 Using a suitable shouldered drift against the edge of the outer race, drive the double row bearing squarely into the sprocket centre housing.

3 Fit the bearing retainer circlip, sharp edge outwards, and ensure that it is bedded all the way round the groove. Failure to observe this precaution can permit free lateral movement of the sprocket and cause subsequent damage due to misalignment.

4 Fit the inner oilseal, squarely and flush with the face, metal flange outwards from the bearing.

5 The sprocket is now reassembled ready for accepting the dummy axle, distance collar, speedometer gearbox and facing washer. A small quantity of grease can be applied, to be retained by the speedo gearbox, as it seals off the centre boss when installed. The unit is now ready for fitting to the main wheel.

SECTION H6

REMOVING AND REFITTING FRONT WHEEL

Removal

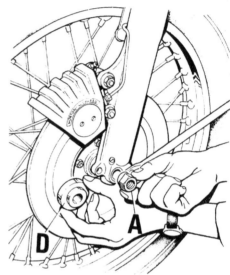

Fig. H4   Disc brake front wheel removal

The brake disc is removed with the wheel whilst the caliper remains fixed to the left fork leg. and it is not necessary to disturb the hydraulic system.

1 Support the motorcycle on the centre-stand with extra support beneath the crankcase to lift the front wheel clear of the ground.

2 Remove axle nut 'A' from the left (disc) fork leg. Slacken pinch bolt 'B' at the right fork leg.

3 Taking the weight of the front wheel in one hand withdraw the axle using a tommy bar. It will be found that the wheel can be removed most easily by withdrawing it forwards to disengage the disc from the pads.

4 To prevent the brake pads being ejected by unintentional application of the brake with the wheel removed, place a clean ¼" (6·7 mm) spacer of wood, metal or plastic between the pads.

5 Collect the wheel bearing dust covers 'C' and 'D' to prevent loss. Note that the left one 'D' has an additional spacing boss. (See *Fig.* H4).

Brakes, Wheels and Tires H

Refitting

6 Remove the brake pad wedge from the caliper. Offer the wheel in position from the front, and with care, guide the disc between the brake pads. Replace the wide bright plated spacer, and dust cover at the disc side and the other spacer and dust cover from the right side.

7 Grease and engage the wheel axle from the right side, fit the large axle nut (plain end inboard) and secure. There is no washer at this point. At this stage the motorcycle should be taken off the stand and, before tightening the fork end clamping nut the fork compressed a few times to centralise the fork leg on the axle.

8 Tighten the pinch nut at the bottom of the right hand fork slider to clamp it on to the axle. Do not over-tighten the nut as there is a danger of fracturing the lug.

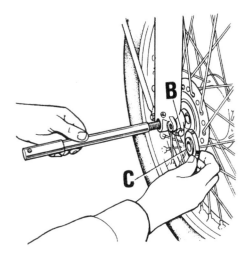

Fig. H5   Front wheel removal

9 If the fork action is stiff, slacken the axle nut and the fork end clamping nut and move the forks up and down to allow the fork tubes to take up alignment on the axle. Re-tighten the nuts.
   If stiffness still remains, release fender stay bolts and move forks up and down, finally retightening the stay bolts.

No adjustment to the brake operating mechanism is required. Apply the brake several times to refill the caliper, restore brake pressure, and settle the pads in correct relationship.

SECTION H7

DISMANTLING FRONT HUB

To gain access to the front wheel axle and bearings, remove the wheel as described in Section H6. It is not necessary to remove the brake disc. Proceed as follows :

1 Extract circlip from right hand end of hub releasing single-row bearing location.

2 Heat the alloy wheel hub with hot water *only* to a temperature of 100°C.

3 Insert a bar into the bearing spacer tube and force the spacer over fractionally. This will provide just sufficient room to allow a drift to abut on the inner race of the bearing to be removed.

4 Using a suitable drift to the bearing inner race start to drive the single row bearing out. Force the spacer tube over to the other side of the hub and tap on the inner race at the new point. Continue this operation until the bearing is driven out.

5 Lift out the bearing spacer tube. If this has been damaged and cannot be corrected, a new spacer should be obtained for reassembly.

6 Using a suitable sized drift through the hub towards the remaining bearing, drive it out of the hub, taking with it the washers and seal.

Brakes, Wheels and Tires

SECTION H8

FRONT HUB REASSEMBLY

Prior to reassembly, clean and inspect both bearings, and components for roughness, wear, damage or corrosion and replace as necessary. Proceed as follows:

IMPORTANT

The Mark III front hub has been redesigned and incorporates a single row, rubber sealed, single sided ball bearing at the right hand end of the hub, supplemented by a bright "flinger" on the distance collar shrouding the hub centre.

It is important to ensure that a correct type sealed bearing replacement is fitted with it's sealed side facing outwards.

1   To re-assemble, first pack the bearings with grease (se section K1) then proceed as follows:

2   Press the single row bearing into position at the right side of the hub, sealed end facing outwards

3   Fit the circlip, ensuring it is correctly bedded.

4   Insert the bearing spacer from the left, ensuring it that it is fully home against the single row bearing. Pack the space between the bearing spacer and hub with grease.

5   Enter the double row bearing squarely into the hub, passing the front axle through until it enters the

opposite bearing. Drive the end of the spindle until the double row bearing comes up against the distance tube and stops.

6   Fit the felt seal into the hub recess.

7   Insert the longer distance collar and brignt dust cover-"flinger" into felt seal.

8   The wheel is now ready for fitting.

SECTION H9

DISC BRAKES (FUNCTION)

Disc brakes function by the pressure of friction pads gripping a disc which is attached to the wheel hub. As the brake operating pedal or lever is applied, fluid from a master cylinder reservoir is forced through the hydraulic line to the "slave" cylinder in the caliper gripping the pads against the disc.

The brake requires no adjustment since wear on the pad is compensated by extra brake fluid passing from the master cylinder reservoir into the system.

CAUTION:

Replace the friction pads when lining material is worn to a minimum thickness of $\frac{1}{16}$" (1·5 mm). Should the brake become "spongy" in operation or acquire excessive pedal (lever) travel, the hydraulic system should be examined and rectified at once.

SECTION H10

NORTON LOCKHEED HYDRAULICALLY OPERATED DISC BRAKES

This brake is a very powerful and progressive unit. The servicing routine is straightforward but it is absolutely essential for the components of the hydraulic system to be handled with particular care, avoiding any

Brakes, Wheels and Tires

possible marking of the bores and pistons of the master cylinder and of the caliper since these are machined to unusually fine limits. Similarly it is vital to exclude even the finest particles of dirt and foreign matter from the hydraulic system and to avoid the use of any fluid or cleaning agent which could cause even the smallest degree of deterioration on the rubber seals. Throughout the following instructions, reference is made to the use of Lockheed Series 329 Hydraulic Fluid for Disc Brakes. This is the fluid used by the factory and recommended for use in the Commando disc brake hydraulic system in subsequent service, the fluid complying with the requirements of USA/Canada Safety Standard 116. The hydraulic system is sealed and the master cylinder and caliper with hose and pipe connected can be removed as an assembly if required from the rear brake arrangement without the loss of fluid and without the need for bleeding on reassembly. Providing the bellows seal is in situ in the master cylinder there will be no loss of fluid even from the breather hole in the cap.

The Mark III Front Brake Hose passes through the fork middle lug and requires disconnecting if the fork is dismantled.

IMPORTANT

After rework disturbing the hydraulic unions always inspect *after applying maximum load* and make certain all joints are again pressure tight. Any witness of seepage must be re-examined and rectified before the machine is used·

It is not necessary to remove the caliper assembly from the fork leg during renewal of the friction pads as described below:

Caliper Friction Pad Renewal

1   Remove the front wheel (see Section H6).

2   Rotate the friction pads slightly and remove.

3   Inspect the friction pads for excessive wear. uneven wear or scoring. If there is any doubt whatsoever on the condition of the pads, obtain new pads. It is important to replace the pads as a pair : never attempt to replace one pad only.

4   Clean the friction pad recesses and exposed ends of the pistons using only a small soft brush. **DO NOT** utilise any solvent or wire brush for the removal of dust, dirt or scale.

5   Smear lightly the piston faces and brake pad recesses with Disc Brake Lubricant.

6   Remove the master cylinder cap and bellows seal to observe the level which will rise during the next operation.

7   Press the pistons back into the caliper, observing the fluid level in the master cylinder to prevent overflowing. If necessary, excess fluid can be siphoned off.

If at this stage it is found that the pistons are locked or seized in position and not free to move, the caliper must be removed, drained and overhauled as described later in this section.

8   On motorcycles using the cast iron disc, a rust build-up may have occurred which prevents entry of the disc between the new friction pads. Remove any such rusting by the careful use of a fine flat file.

9   Ensure that the new friction pads are of the correct friction type to suit the cast iron disc. It is important to consult the replacement parts catalogue and thus obtain the correct pads.   Frictional and noise problems will arise if incorrect combinations of disc and pads are used. Any roughness or manufacturing flashes must be trimmed from the edges of the metal backing plate.

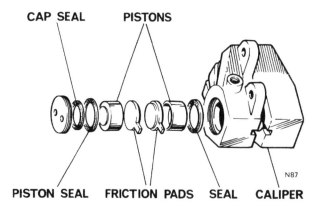

Fig. H6   Exploded view of caliper group

10   Avoiding the friction material, smear the edges of the pad backing plates with Disc Brake Lubricant and press fully home against the pistons.

Brakes, Wheels and Tires

11 Replace the front wheel as in Section H6, support the motorcycle so that the front wheel spins freely and apply the front brake lever at the handlebar several times to restore the fluid in the caliper and locate the pads correctly.

12 Restore the master cylinder level as in *Fig.* H7 using Lockheed Series 329 fluid and replace the bellows seal and cap.

CAUTION: It is dangerous to ride the motorcycle after pad and hydraulic system attention without first applying the brake a number of times to restore pressure and locate the pads to the disc. To avoid glazing of the friction surfaces, the brake must be applied gently if possible over the first 50 miles of use.

Caliper Overhaul

It is unnecessary to remove the front wheel but the hose support bracket must be released from the central fork mudguard bridge mounting studs and the hose to bracket clamp nut slackened to facilitate separation of the hose and pipe from the fork leg. Proceed as follows:

1 Prior to releasing the caliper from the fork leg, ease the fit of the caliper end plug which will be very tight. This will require the use of peg spanner tool 063965. *Do not* yet remove the plug.

2 Remove the two caliper bolts and washers and swing the caliper clear of the fork leg, taking the weight to avoid straining the brake hose.

3 Lift the two friction pads from the caliper.

4 Brush clean the exposed ends of the pistons and the outer surfaces of the caliper body, using methyl alcohol (methylated spirit) if required.

5 Lubricate the exposed ends of the pistons to ease their passage through the seals.

6 Place a clean receptacle below the caliper to receive displaced brake fluid and remove the inner piston. The outboard piston can be removed easily at a later stage if necessary. For this reason we recommend the use of a clamp to restrain the outboard piston. Apply the handlebar brake lever and the inner piston will be ejected into the friction pad cavity, and fluid released. Do not use any tool or airline to remove the piston nor use excessive pressure at the handlebar if the piston is seized.

NOTE THAT THE ONLY SATISFACTORY REMEDY FOR A SEIZED PISTON IS RENEWAL OF THE COMPLETE CALIPER ASSEMBLY.

7 Remove the clamp restraining the outer piston.

8 Slacken the lower brake pipe union nut and separate the pipe from the caliper.

9 Remove the caliper end plug, drain the remaining fluid into the receptacle.

10 Remove the piston from the caliper. If there is any difficulty, push the piston towards the centre of the caliper and clean carefully the outer working surfaces of the piston, removing any traces of dirt, dust or scale with methyl alcohol and/or metal polish before pressing the piston back into the caliper body and withdrawing through the end plug aperature.

11 Using a blunt nosed tool and taking the greatest possible care not to damage the seal grooves in any way whatsoever, remove the pressure seal from the outer bore.

12 Remove the inner piston through the outer cylinder bore then with the same care remove the pressure seal from the groove in the inner bore.

13 Pencil mark "Inner" and "Outer" on the friction material of the pads as applicable for future reference.

Caliper Component Inspection

Clean the pistons, caliper bores and seal grooves with ethyl alcohol or clean brake fluid.

Brakes, Wheels and Tires

1 Examine the pistons and renew if there are any signs of wear, damage or corrosion. No attempt must be made to rectify damage wear or "out of square" thrust faces by machining, filing or polishing. It is permissible only to restore pistons by the ultimate use of a fine metal polish.

2 Examine the caliper bores for abrasion, scratches and corrosion, or damage to the seal grooves. The caliper bores are not normally subject to premature failure or wear but irreparable damage can be caused during removal of damaged or corroded pistons or careless removal of seals with a sharp instrument.

After examination clean all the parts thoroughly in methyl alcohol or clean brake fluid.

Caliper Re-Assembly

1 Coat the new pressure seals with Lockheed Series 329 Hydraulic Fluid and ease the first pressure seal into the groove in the inner bore with the fingers, taking care to bed it correctly. It will be noted that the diameter of the seal is larger than that of the seal groove, in order to provide an interference fit. In addition, the seal groove and seal are different in section so that when bedded, the seal feels proud to the touch at the edge furthest from the bore. This is normal.

2 Coat the inner piston (the pistons are identical) with Lockheed Series 329 Fluid, insert it squarely right through the outer cylinder into the bore of the inner cylinder, closed end into the bore. Leave the piston protruding approximately $\frac{5}{16}$ in. (8 mm) from the mouth of the inner bore.

3 Fit a new pressure seal to the caliper outer bore groove, again bedding it correctly.

4 Coat the second piston with Lockheed Series 329 fluid and insert it open end first into the bore with the fingers. Avoid tilting the piston and continue inserting it gently through the bore until approximately $\frac{5}{16}$ in. (8 mm) of the open end protrudes from the inner mouth of the bore.

5 Replace the end plug using a new 'O' ring seal and tighten into position. For final tightening, the caliper must be secured to the fork leg.

6 Wipe the caliper clean, removing excess fluid which may subsequently contaminate the brake friction pads, taking care not to allow any rag particles to pass anywhere near the brake pipe feed union.

7 Fit the two friction pads and ensure that they seat correctly.

8 Assemble the caliper assembly over the wheel disc and offer the caliper to the fork leg, securing with two bolts and washers.

9 Tighten the caliper end plug using peg spanner tool to 26 lb./ft. torque.

10 Refit the fluid feed hose bracket to the mudguard bridge stud.

IMPORTANT

Before connecting the lower end of the brake pipe to the caliper, note that the pipe olive is specially formed to provide an effective high pressure oil seal against the caliper union seating. The olive is very susceptible to overtightening and if it is severely distorted by overtightening it may be impossible to remove thus rendering the caliper scrap.

11 Examine the union olive of the metal brake pipe for symptoms of previous overtightening such as distortion, damage and cracks and if necessary renew the pipe.

12 Offer the olive of the brake pipe to the caliper, hold the pipe in the required position and run the union screw fully down the thread until the pipe is just "nipped" on to its seating. Tighten the union nut with a spanner *one flat only,* i.e. 60°.

13 Slacken the bleed nipple one full turn and connect with a suitable bleed tube to a clean container (see *Fig. H8*).

14 Fill the master cylinder reservoir with Lockheed Series 329 brake fluid.

Brakes, Wheels and Tires

15 Operate the brake lever until fluid begins to flow through the bleed tube. During this operation, guard against the master cylinder fluid level becoming too low, otherwise air will be drawn into the system. The master cylinder bellows seal must be removed to observe the fluid level.

If replenishment is necessary during this operation, hold the lever to the handlebar whilst the reservoir is topped up. Similarly, when fluid free of bubbles flows from the bleed pipe, tighten the caliper bleed nipple, whilst the brake lever is held against the handlebar.

16 With the bleed nipple tightened up, remove the bleed hose, apply the brake lever a number of times to check for sponginess (indicating air still in the system and a need for further bleeding) and examine the system for leaks.

17 Finally recheck the fluid level in the master cylinder reservoir, topping up as necessary, then road test the motorcycle.

Master Cylinder Overhaul

Prior to commencing work on the master cylinder it is desirable to obtain a supply of new Lockheed Series 329 Fluid in a sealed container. Where supplies are unobtainable and the fluid may have to be re-used, it is suggested that fluid is collected in a clean jar or receptacle by means of a short length of clean rubber tubing from

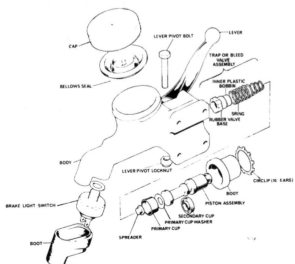

Fig. H7 Master Cylinder—Exploded view

the bleed screw to the collecting jar. Release the caliper bleed screw one full turn and operate the hand brake lever a number of times until the master cylinder reservoir is empty. Close the bleed screw and detach the drain tube. Store the collecting jar safely and cover carefully to prevent dirt ingress.

Master Cylinder Removal

1 Disconnect the brake stop light pressure switch spade terminals and lift away the plastic switch cover exposing the hose union into the master cylinder.

2 Detach the hose from the master cylinder.

3 Remove the four switch casting screws and lift away the master cylinder complete.

Master Cylinder Dismantling – See *Fig.* H7

1 Remove the reservoir cap and bellows seal.

2 Remove the brake light pressure switch.

3 Remove the pivot bolt locknut and withdraw the pivot bolt and lever.

4 Carefully prise the boot circlip from the lower end of the master cylinder. This can be achieved if care is taken to lift three or four adjacent segments progressively, a little at a time until the circlip is tipped sufficiently to clear the mouth of the cylinder bore.

5 The boot is located into the piston and is best removed with the piston. Lift the piston out complete with boot and secondary cup.

6 Remove the primary cup washer, primary cup spreader, spring and bleed (or trap) valve assembly. To dislodge these items it may be necessary either to bump the casting on a block of clean soft wood to dislodge them or alternatively to apply *gentle* air pressure at the hose union bore and blow the parts free.

Brakes, Wheels and Tires

Inspection of Master Cylinder and Components

Discard the primary and secondary cups, the trap valve and boot. Clean the master cylinder and piston in brake fluid or methyl alcohol – do not use abrasive materials or solvent fluids.

Inspect the master cylinder body for wear in the piston bore. Normally, if the seals have been operating satisfactorily no wear need be expected, but if seal failure has occurred, the piston may have destroyed the bore finish. If there is any doubt whatsoever, the cylinder must be replaced.

If the cylinder is found to be fit for further service, ensure the two cylinder ports into the reservoir chamber are perfectly clear and clean. Inspect the hose union and switch threads for clean and satisfactory condition, and the lever pivot bolt bore for wear or cracks, or fractures. Replace the master cylinder if any doubt exists.

Check the brake lever for pivot bore wear and possible wear on the piston thrust face. Replace the lever if necessary. Next examine the piston for signs of scuffing on the ground outer diameters, and any wear on the lever thrust face.

Do not attempt to polish or grind the piston in any way, using abrasive compounds, as the slightest residual trace of such materials, even after intensive cleansing will damage master cylinder and caliper working parts beyond repair, and can result in premature brake failure.

Inspect the brake hose for cuts, signs of leakage or deterioration. Replace if the slightest doubt exists.

Master Cylinder Reassembly

After inspecting and cleaning the master cylinder, clean the piston, spring, spreader and cup washer in clean hydraulic fluid, and place in order of assembly on a perfectly clean working surface, in a dust free room or workshop.

DO NOT USE A FLUFFY RAG TO WIPE THE COMPONENTS. ALLOW TO DRAIN.

Soak the new primary and secondary cups in hydraulic fluid for fifteen minutes, kneading occasionally to encourage the special rubber cups to gain their maximum supple state prior to assembly. Ensure the three relief holes in the "crown" of the piston are clear and clean.

1 Take the "hollow" secondary cup and place it non lipped side against the ground "crown" diameter of the piston. Work the cup over the "crown" by hand, then down the piston body, over the shoulder into its groove adjacent to the main body ground diameter.

CAUTION – Do not use any form of tool to ease assembly of the cup to the piston for fear of damage to the lip.

2 Fit the boot over the piston open end towards the piston crown and ensure the upper end is fitted squarely and snugly in the piston groove. The piston is now ready for assembly.

3 Assemble the trap valve to the spring, ensuring the inner plastic bobbin is accurately seated in the rubber valve base, and that the small diameter bleed hole in the bobbin base is clear and free. Ensure the plastic spreader is securely and firmly pressed home on the other smaller diameter end of the spring.

4 Offer the spring/trap valve assembly into the master cylinder, valve end first, keeping the master cylinder bore upright. It is permissible to hold the nose of the casting securely in a soft jawed vice, provided it is in no way overtightened.

5 Assemble the primary cup washer into the bore, open end of the cup facing into the bore, followed by the primary cup washer. Ensure only *one* cup washer is employed at this point. Place this dished primary cup washer, "hump" upwards, towards the open end of the cylinder bore. (The effect of the dished cup washer is to close the primary cup during the return stroke, allow oiling to by-pass the cup and replenish the pressure cylinder).

6 Offer the piston crown first into the cylinder. Place the 10 eared boot circlip over the top of the boot, the slight set on the ears facing away from the cylinder. Ensure fluid is smeared onto the secondary cup and into the mouth of the cylinder bore.

Brakes, Wheels and Tires

The next series of operations, to locate the piston, boot and circlip by means of the brake lever and pivot bolt can be difficult without the aid of special tools, and the assistance of a second operator. However, if care is taken, assembly can be completed without such help, the difficulty being to locate the base of the boot into the cylinder counterbore and finally locate and snug home the circlip whilst holding the piston assembly within the bore of the master cylinder, against the trap valve spring, long enough (and with sufficient piston thrust pad clearance) to be enabled to fit the hand lever and to locate it with the pivot bolt. The method of assembling these parts is detailed below:

7 Take the master cylinder assembly in the left hand (having assembled up to the point as described above) supporting the casting with the first and second fingers under the switch boss (hose and pressure switch threaded bores pointing downwards) and left thumb on the top of the casting close to the piston thrust "pad." Apply a gentle rotary action with the right hand to the piston thrust pad, at the same time maintaining downward thrust pressure against the trap valve spring assembly – ensuring the lip of the secondary cup enters the cylinder bore freely and without damage to the lip. When the piston has entered the bore, move the left thumb over to maintain the piston within the bore, at the same time using a blunt prod to snug the lower boot shoulder into the cylinder counter bore. Once this is seen to be achieved, and still maintaining pressure on the piston thrust pad, work the boot retaining circlip down to locate and restrain the boot in position. Still maintaining pressure on the piston thrust pad with the left thumb, slide the brake lever into position at the fulcrum slot, engaging the thrust pad close to the operator's left thumb. By holding the lever knob against the chest, alignment of the holes can be achieved, and the pivot bolt slid into position, and located with the locknut.

Master Cylinder Refitting

Refitting the master cylinder is the exact reverse procedure of the dismantling sequence described above. Refit the master cylinder to the handlebar, the oil pressure switch and brake hose. Slide the plastic switch cover over the hose, hold in a convenient location whilst the brake light wires are connected to the brake switch terminals and slide the cover into final location. Enter the lower hose into the fork support bracket, locate in position with the locknut and tighten up the upper brake pipe union nut. Bleed the hydraulic system as described in the following text, after ensuring that the master cylinder is level on the handlebar.

Bleeding and flushing the Hydraulic Brake System

1 Purging of air from a hydraulic system, commonly known as "bleeding", should only be necessary when some part of the system has been disconnected, or after the fluid has been drained off and renewed. However, in normal service, should the presence of air in the system be indicated by a "spongy" brake effect, the cause should be traced and rectified.
   Remove the reservoir cap. Remember that brake fluid ruins paintwork and do not allow fluid to spill during filling.

WARNING:

Fill the master cylinder supply tank using only brake fluid to USA DOT 3 specification (Lockheed Series 329 brake fluid Norton Part No. 063111), and keep topped up throughout the operation, otherwise air may be drawn into the system, necessitating a fresh start.

2 Attach a suitable length of clean rubber or plastic tubing to the bleeder screw of the hydraulic unit, and allow the other end of the tube to be submerged in a small quantity of new fluid contained in a glass jar. Open the bleeder screw half a complete turn (*Fig.* H8). The procedure is the same for both front and rear brakes.

Brakes, Wheels and Tires

Apply the brake slowly, allowing it to return unassisted. Repeat the pumping action, with a slight pause between each stroke. When stopping the pumping action such as for refilling the master cylinder or when clear fluid, free of air bubbles, emerges from the tube, tighten the bleeder screw whilst the brake lever is fully pulled to the handlebar or in the case of the rear brake, the pedal is fully depressed.

Verify that the master cylinder supply tank is replenished to the correct level. FLUID BLED FROM THE SYSTEM MUST BE DISCARDED· The above procedure applies equally to front and rear brakes.

3   Unscrew the bleed screw one full turn and start to pump slowly the handlebar lever allowing it to return unassisted. As fluid is forced to the caliper and through the bleed nipple, the master cylinder level will drop. Take care throughout the operation that the level does not drop sufficiently low to allow further air to be pumped into the system and top up where necessary.

Fig. H8   Bleeding disc brake hydraulic system

4   Continue pumping the lever until fluid free of air bubbles exits from the bleed tube into the fluid container then hold the brake lever "on" against the handlebar whilst the caliper bleed screw is tightened and the bleed tube removed.

5   Test the brake for "sponginess." If the action feels "spongy," then air remains in the system and further bleeding must be undertaken.

6   Ensure that the master cylinder reservoir is brought to the correct level then refit the bellows seal and cap.

USED FLUID BLED FROM THE SYSTEM MUST BE DISCARDED.

7   Finally check all unions for security and freedom from leaks.

FLUSHING PROCEDURE

Every eighteen months, or after every 24,000 miles, whichever occurs first, the fluid in the hydraulic system should be renewed with the Lockheed series 329 brake fluid, Norton part number 063111.

Brake fluid, particularly disc brake fluid, absorbs water from the atmosphere; accordingly, fluid must only be exposed during the time taken to fill the system. It is also important that the greatest care is taken to prevent dirt from entering the system during the filling operation.

Follow the "bleeding" procedure until new clean fluid emerges from the flexible tube, thus establishing complete renewal of the fluid.

If the fluid in the system is contaminated by mineral oil (engine oil) or other spurious fluid, the complete hydraulic system must be stripped. Hydraulic assemblies must be renewed or overhauled as detailed in the workshop manual, and flexible hoses replaced. Furthermore, ensure that all metal fluid pipes are cleaned thoroughly before reassembling.

REAR BRAKE

Above procedure applies to the rear brake in all respects.

SECTION H11

REAR BRAKE PEDAL ADJUSTMENT

Adjustment of pedal height is made on the rear master cylinder piston rod.

Brakes, Wheels and Tires

1   Slacken the locknut (A) and adjust as required using nuts B and C which are locked together during manufacture and which must not, under any circumstances, be turned in relation to each other. Disturbing this relationship will alter piston stroke and may render the brake inoperative. After adjustment retighten the locknut. See Fig. H9

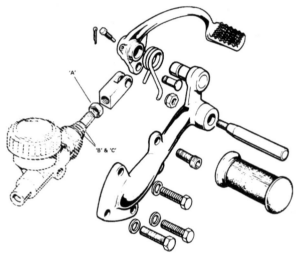

Fig. H9   *Rear brake pedal (exploded) Showing order of assembly and adjusting nuts.*

MOST IMPORTANT

In the event of a rider having the misfortune to "drop" the machine and damage or distort the brake operating mechanism (either front or rear) it is *imperative he checks* the freedom and correct functioning of the affected lever or pedal. The rear brake, in particular, must be inspected and the 'eye' and clevis and piston rod examined before attempting to ride away. Make sure the cylinder is delivering full pressure and that the pedal returns freely and unassisted to its correct height in "repose". *Fig.* H9 shows an exploded layout of the rear brake pedal mechanism and gives a pictorial definition of the assembly order.

SECTION H12

TIRES

Tire changing is largely a matter of technique and what to the layman may seem a difficult task is perfectly straightforward when the correct technique is followed. To change either tire, the wheel must be removed. See Sections H6&8 for front wheel removal and Section H1 for

rear wheel removal. The same basic principles apply for all types of tire – lubricate the beadings such as with soapy water, to allow the beadings to slip easily over the rim, use heel pressure wherever possible in preference to tire levers for easing the tire on to the rim and minimise the risk of damage by "nipping" and ensure that the opposite side of the tire is pressed well into the rim well to provide maximum freedom where the beading is being slid over the wheel rim. *Note:* that the rear tire only has one security bolt to prevent tire "creep" such as under hard acceleration. No security bolt is fitted to the front tire. For this reason separate routines are given for front and rear tires. The full technique is as follows:

Removing Front Tire (No security bolt)

1   Remove the dust cap from the valve and using a suitable notched type of cap or removal tool, unscrew the valve core to deflate the tire completely.

2   Remove the knurled ring securing the valve at the rim. Store the cap, core and knurled ring clean for re-use.

3   Lay the wheel down, if possible on a clean surface to avoid scratching and, also to prevent damage to the front axle. Leave the disc uppermost or place with disc inside a large 5 gallon drum or bin. This is common practice in many workshops and protects disc from damage or distortion. If it is found that the disc causes obstruction, remove it.

4   Tread the tire beading away from the rim – after a great deal of service the tire beading has a tendency to stick

Brakes, Wheels and Tires

Fig. H10   *Levering close to valve whilst pressing opposite bead down into rim*

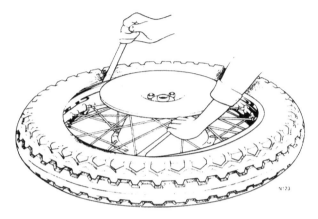

Fig. H11   *Two tire levers in use to remove first bead of tire*

5   Brush a lubricant such as soapy water onto the tire beading and rim and also dip the tire levers (two short ones are recommended) in the solution before each leverage.

6   Insert the first lever between the tire valve and rim at the valve position, press the opposite side of the tire down into the rim well and apply leverage (see *Fig.* H10).

7   Insert the second lever approximately 4 in.   (100 mm) from the first and lever the tire beading over the rim.
It is possible, and some advantage, to hook one lever under the disc whilst operating with a second or third lever – thereby using, as it were, a "third hand".

8   Remove the first lever and re-insert at the next stage, continuing round the rim a little at a time (see *Fig.* H11) until the beading can be pulled clear of the rim.

9   Push the valve out of the rim and withdraw the inner tube.

10   If it is required to remove the tire from the rim, hold the wheel upright and apply pressure to a lever inserted between the second beading and wheel rim.

Before fitting note that new Avon tires have red and Dunlop tires white paint dots at the lightest point. Note also that the latest Dunlop tires have directional arrows on the sidewalls. It is most important to fit the tires with the tread correctly located by the direction arrow.

Brakes, Wheels and Tires

Refitting Front Tire (No security bolt)

1   If the tire has been removed completely, ensure that the rubber rim tape is fitted properly, rough side towards and central in the spoke nipple area of the rim.

2   Replace the valve core and inflate just sufficiently to "round" the tube and minimise the risk of "nipping" at a later stage. Dust the tube with French chalk and place the tube inside the tire, aligning the paint dots on the tire with the valve stem.

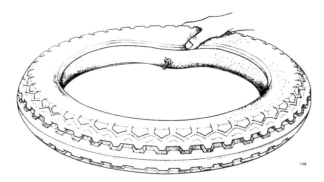

Fig. H12   Tube within cover squeezing cover to hold valve protruding

3   Lay tire and tube over rim ensuring that "front wheel rotation" arrow (if any) points in direction of wheel rotation.

4   Lubricate the beadings with soapy water.

5   Squeeze the beadings together with the hand, permitting the edge of the tube to protrude for approximately 2 in. (50·8 mm) at each side of the valve. Offer the tire and tube to the rim, feeding the valve through the rim tape and rim holes.

6   Pressing this side of the tire into the rim well, and working from the valve, press the first beading over the rim by hand pressure and lever the last few inches into position as in *Fig.* H14. Take special care that the inner tube is not nipped during this operation.

7   Press the second beading into the rim well, starting opposite the valve then use the heel to press the bead into position as far round as possible.

8   As shown in *Fig.* H15, taking care to avoid "nipping", lever the last portion of the beading over the rim, finishing at the valve.

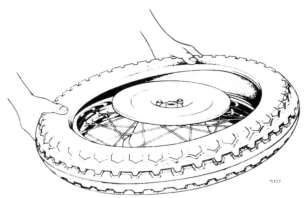

Fig. H13   Refitting tire to wheel with valve engaged in rim hole

9   Push the valve inwards to the rim to ensure that the tube near the valve is not trapped between the beading and rim then pull the valve back and inflate to pressure.

10 To ensure that the tire is true on the rim, check the tire moulded fitting line in relation to the rim. The position can be corrected by "bouncing" the side of the tire on the ground at any point where the fitting line is too near the rim.

11 When the tire is fitted correctly, fit the knurled valve securing rim and replace the valve dust cap.

Removing Rear Tire (Security bolt fitted).

The routine for removing and refitting a tire with security bolt is basically the same as for a tire without security bolt but it is important to deal with this item in the correct sequence. The full procedure is therefore detailed as follows:

1   Remove the dust cap from the valve and using a suitable notched type of cap or removal tool, unscrew the valve core to deflate the tire completely.

Brakes, Wheels and Tires **H**

2   Remove the knurled ring securing the valve at the rim. Store the cap, core and knurled ring clean for re-use.

3   Unscrew the security bolt nut and push the bolt inside the cover.

4   Lay the wheel down, if possible on a clean surface to avoid scratching.

5   Tread the tire bead away from the rim – after a great deal of service the tire beading has a tendency to stick.

10 Remove the security bolt from the rim.

11 Push the valve out of the rim and withdraw the inner tube.

12 If it is required to remove the tire from the rim, hold the wheel upright and apply pressure to a lever inserted between the second bead and wheel rim.

Fig. H14   First bead being levered into the rim

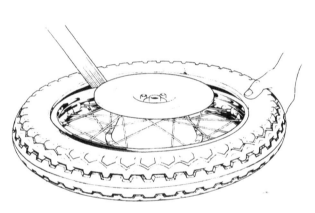

Fig. H15   Careful levering of second bead over wheel rim

6   Brush a lubricant such as soapy water onto the tire bead and rim and also dip the tire levers (two short ones are recommended) in the solution before each leverage.

7   Insert the first lever between the tire valve and rim at the valve position, press the opposite side of the tire down into the rim well and apply leverage (see *Fig. H10*).

8   Insert the second lever approximately 4 in. (100 mm) from the first and lever the tire bead over the rim.

9   Remove the first lever and re-insert at the next stage, continuing round the rim a little at a time (see *Fig. H11*) until the bead can be pulled clear of the rim.

Refitting Rear Tire (Security bolt fitted)

1   If the tire has been removed completely, ensure that the rubber rim tape is fitted properly, rough side towards and central in the spoke nipple well of the rim.

2   Ensure "rear wheel direction" arrow (if any), is pointing in direction of wheel rotation and fit the first tire beading over the rim without the inner tube, ensuring that the paint dots align with the security bolt hole.

Brakes, Wheels and Tires   H

3   Lift the free side wall as in *Fig. H16* and insert the security bolt less nut. Loosely fit the leather washer and nut.

4   Replace the valve core and inflate just sufficiently to "round" the tube and minimise the risk of "nipping" at a later stage. Dust the tube with French chalk and place the tube inside the tire, feeding the valve through the rim tape and rim holes.

5   Lubricate the bead with soapy water.

Fig. H16   Lifting cover and engaging security bolt to rim

9   Push the valve inwards to the rim to ensure that the tube near the valve is not trapped between the bead and rim then pull the valve back and inflate to pressure.

10   To ensure that the tire is true on the rim, check the tire moulded fitting line in relation to the rim. The position can be corrected by "bouncing" the side of the tire on the ground at any point where the fitting line is too near the rim.

11   Bounce the tire several times in the centre of the bead where the security bolt is fitted then tighten the securing nut. Recheck that the fitting line is still equidistant to the rim.

12   When the tire is fitted correctly, fit the knurled valve securing nut and replace the valve dust cap.

6   Pressing this side of the tire into the rim well, and working from the valve, press the first bead over the rim by hand pressure and lever the last few inches into position as in *Fig. H14*. Take special care that the inner tube is not nipped during this operation.

7   Press the second bead into the rim well whilst keeping the security bolt pressed back into the tire as in *Fig. H17* starting opposite the valve then use the heel to press the bead as far round as possible into position.

8   As shown in *Fig. H,17* taking care to avoid "nipping", lever the last portion of the bead over the rim, finishing at the valve.

Fig. H17   Pressing security bolt back through rim whilst levering second bead into position

Electrical

Electrical

J

SECTION J1

DESCRIPTION

The Commando electrical system is grouped into four areas for the purpose of this manual. The areas are:

Sections J2 to J8: Those parts connected with the charging system.

Sections J9 to J14: Those parts connected with the ignition system.

Sections J15 to J19: Those parts connected with the lighting system.

Sections J20 to J28: Other electrical equipment, including the electric starter.

IMPORTANT

Before starting any electrical test procedures, isolate the warning light unit whichever type is fitted (see Section J8 for details) by disconnecting the green/yellow lead to the unit at the alternator green/yellow lead double snap connector.

The Commando electrical system is positive earth (ground).

SECTION J2

CHARGING SYSTEM

The charging system comprises an alternator with the 6 charging coils connected permanently (fitted in the primary chaincase and driven by the engine crankshaft). This supplies alternating (A.C.) current to the rectifier where it is converted to half-wave direct (D.C.) current. The D.C. current is fed to the lead/acid battery in parallel to the Zener diodes which are mounted on the left and right support plates for the silencer and footrests, one each side of the machine.

The function of the Zener diodes is to regulate the flow of D.C. current and thus prevent overcharging of the battery. Surplus current is directed to the heatsinks (in this case, the light alloy support plates for the silencers and footrests) where it is dissipated as heat.

The increased output of the RM23 alternator (now producing 15 amps at 6,000 r.p.m.) has prompted the use of two regulating Zener diodes in the charging system.

The rectification still follows a basic push-pull "bridge connected" layout but the two earthed diodes are replaced by Zener diodes, moved apart and earthed separately.

When the system voltage is below approximately 13 volts, the Zener diodes operate as ordinary semi-conductors and the full output from the alternator is supplied to the battery and loads.

As the system voltage rises the Zeners by-pass the excess current having become conductive in the reverse direction. See Section J15. In this operating condition, during part of one half cycle, one Zener operates in the reverse direction, the other in the forward direction.

The opposite occurs in the next half cycle. As a consequence of the above it is unnecessary to match the Zener diodes, any combination within commercial tolerances will be satisfactory.

The high output of the RM23 is thus shared between two Zeners and two heatsinks, the system is working within moderate limits at all times, giving improved reliability and increased component-life to the equipment.

IGNITION SYSTEM

The Commando Mk III is equipped with a 12-volt electrical system but uses 6-volt ignition coils, protected behind a ballast resistor, ensuring an adequate spark intensity even under adverse conditions.

Should the battery fail completely the electrolytic capacitor will provide starting, ignition and direct lighting (parking lights excepted).

Below are detailed the components of the charging system with applicable test procedures:

Electrical

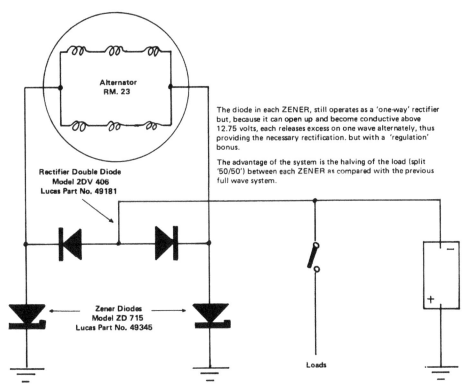

The diode in each ZENER, still operates as a 'one-way' rectifier but, because it can open up and become conductive above 12.75 volts, each releases excess on one wave alternately, thus providing the necessary rectification. but with a 'regulation' bonus.

The advantage of the system is the halving of the load (split '50/50') between each ZENER as compared with the previous full wave system.

Fig. J1.   Mark III Commando Simplified Diagram of Half Wave Rectifier and Twin-Zener System

SECTION J3

ALTERNATOR – LUCAS TYPE RM23

The alternator produces an alternating current (A.C.) by means of a six-pole permanent-magnet rotor which rotates within a stationary six-pole laminated-iron stator assembly.

The rotor is attached to the engine crankshaft, which revolves at engine speed. The stator sub-assembly, comprising the windings and laminations, is mounted on an outrigger plate (which also provides a bearing for the new electric starter gear train) and supported on four studs which clamp the inner primary cover to the drive side crankcase.

Maintenance

The alternator and associated equipment requires no maintenance except for an occasional check to ensure that all the external cable connections are clean and tight. The rectifier mounting is no longer in essential electrical contact. If it should be necessary to remove the alternator rotor from the engine crankshaft, the use

of magnetic keepers is not necessary, but keep the rotor away from magnetically-attracted metal foreign matter.

Mk III Commando – Electrical System Loads

The following table lists the electrical loads on the Mk III Commando:

		Amp
1	Ignition (running) – approximate	2·5
2	Main beam (60W Q-H+45W)	5·0 or 3·8
3	Dip beam (55W Q-H+40W)	4·6 or 3·3
4	Pilot bulb (5W)	0·4
5	Tail bulb (5W)	0·4
6	Speedometer bulb (3W)	0·3
7	Tachometer bulb (3W)	0·3
8	Ignition warning light bulb+circuit	0·1
9	Main beam warning light bulb ($\frac{1}{4}$W)	—
10	Direction indicator warning light bulb ($\frac{1}{4}$W)	—
11	Direction indicator bulb pair (21W each)	3·5
12	Stop lamp bulb (21W)	1·8
13	Horn – typical value	3·5
14	Neutral indicator bulb ($\frac{1}{4}$W)	—
15	Electric start solenoid (approximate)	3·0
16	Electric starter	up to 250A peak
	(dependent upon engine state and temperature)	

Electrical

J

Testing the alternator in situ

(a) Disconnect the alternator leads at the snap connectors.

(b) Connect an A.C. voltmeter (with 1 ohm resistor in parallel) as detailed in the table below. See Section J25 for instructions on making a 1 ohm resistor.

(c) Start engine and run at approx. 3,000 rev./min. noting voltmeter readings.

VOLTMETER AND RESISTOR ACROSS	MINIMUM VOLTAGE READINGS
	Stator: Two lead
	Type: RM23
White/Green. Green/Yellow	9
Any one lead and stator earth (ground)	NO READING

CONCLUSIONS:

If the reading is low, check the rotor by substitution. Zero reading indicates open-circuited coil(s).

Testing the D.C. input to battery

(a) Connect a D.C. ammeter in main battery lead (between battery negative terminal and battery cable), red lead to cable, black lead to battery terminal.

(b) Ensure Zener Diodes are connected normally.

(c) Start engine and run as shown in table.

The following reading will be obtained if the battery and charging systems are in good condition.

Switch Position	Minimum Current Reading	Engine r.p.m.
Ignition and Lights (Main Beam) Filament Bulb	0·5 Amp	3,000
Ignition and Lights (Main Beam) Q.H. Bulb	0·5 Amp	3,500

CONCLUSIONS:

If the readings obtained are higher than the figures quoted, the system is satisfactory. If the readings are lower, proceed to test the alternator itself as in the preceding text.

SECTION J4

RECTIFIER TYPE 2DV.406

The rectifier, which is of the silicon crystal bridge-connected half-wave type, requires no maintenance beyond a periodic check on the cleanliness and security of the terminals. If for any reason the rectifier is removed, DO NOT twist the plates in relation to one another since this will break internal connections and render the rectifier unfit for further service. The centre bolt must be held with a spanner whilst the fixing nut is

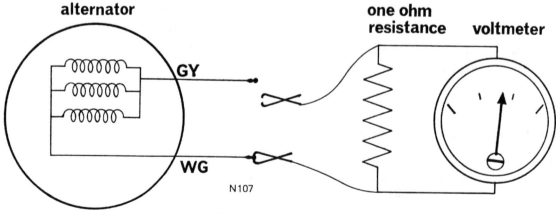

Fig. J2   Alternator test

Electrical

J

turned. This bolt is now insulated from the circuit and no longer needs to make electrical contact with the frame. Never disturb the nut clamping the plates together; these are pre-loaded by the manufacturer to give correct performance. The rectifier is accessible when the seat is lifted.

Testing the rectifier

Testing the rectifier in circuit is no longer a straight-forward procedure as the Zener diodes form part of the rectification function.

However, a bench test is feasible and quite satis-factory for confirming a faulty unit.

The method is as follows:

Bench testing the rectifier

Connect a 12 volt, 45–50 watt bulb and 12 volt battery

across terminals 2 and 1 (for a period not exceeding 30 seconds). See *Fig*. J3.

Repeat test with reversed battery polarity.

Carry out similar tests on terminals: 2 (*center terminal*) and 1, 2 (*center terminal*) and 3, repeating with *opposite polarity*, *i.e.* reverse the connections.

The test lamp should illuminate fully in *one* direction only for each of the connections made.

CONCLUSIONS:

Rectifier must be replaced if:

(a) Bulb shows sign of illumination in both direction
(b) Bulb shows no sign of illumination in either direction

for each connection made.

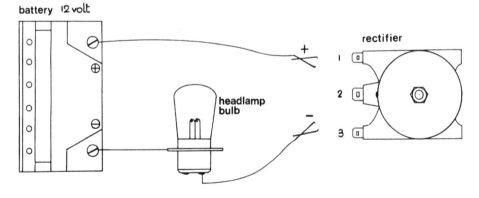

Fig J3   Bench testing rectifier

SECTION J5
Zener Diode

The Zener Diode is a semi-conductor device that becomes conductive in the reverse direction at a critical but predetermined voltage.

Assuming the battery is in a low state of charge, its terminal voltage (the same voltage is across the diode) will also be low, therefore the maximum charging current will flow into the battery from the alternator. At first none of the current is by-passed by the diode, the

latter being non-conductive due to the low battery terminal volts. However, as the battery voltage is restored, the system voltage rises until, at approximately 14 volts, the Zener diode becomes partially conductive, thereby providing an alternative path for a small part of the charging current. Small increases in battery voltage result in large increases in Zener conductivity until, at approximately 15 volts, about 5 amperes of the alternator output is by-passing the battery. The battery will con-tinue to receive only a portion of the alternator output as long as the system voltage is relatively high.

Electrical

J

Depression of the system voltage, due to the use of headlamp or other lighting equipment, causes the Zener diode current to decrease and the balance to be diverted and consumed by the component in use. If the electrical loading is sufficient to cause the system voltage to fall below approx. 14 volts, the Zener diode will revert to its high resistance state of virtual non-conductivity and the full generated output will go to meet the demands of the system.

In the event of one Zener failing open circuit – i.e. if it is continuously conductive, it produces a *short circuit*. If the system is to be run in daytime (no lights) leave the shorted Zener diode *connected* until replaced. The reduced output which is still regulated by the other Zener diode would be adequate for daytime loads.

For night-time running (with battery) the shorted Zener diode should be *disconnected* thus obtaining a greater but unregulated output.

When operating without a battery the diode *must not* be disconnected as the system voltage could rise excessively with serious consequences, "blowing" bulbs, etc.

A rough guide to a failed Zener diode is provided by the heatsinks. Correct balance is shown by approximately equal temperatures at the heatsinks.

When refitting a Zener diode (or if either unit is disturbed) the contact between the diode and the heatsink must be clean and free from corrosion. The tightening torque for the retaining nut is 24–28 lb./ins. (3·32–3·87 kg/m). In addition the seating face must be true and free from burrs. It is most important that the earth lead is not fitted between the face of the Zener diode and the footrest plate.

Bench testing a Zener Diode

Using any convenient D.C. current source with variable control, *e.g.* two 12-volt batteries, fully charged, connected in series, feeding via a suitable rheostat. See Fig. *J4*.

1   Connect a D.C. ammeter (0–5 amps min.) in series between the Lucar terminal of the Zener diode and feed cable. (Red lead to Zener, Black lead to cable.)

2   Connect a D.C. voltmeter (0–18 volts min.) between the Lucer terminal of the Zener diode and earth (ground) on the heatsink, which is earthed to the batteries. Red lead to earth, Black to the Zener lucar blade.

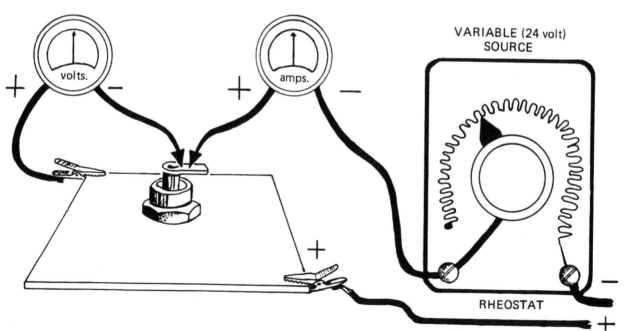

Fig. J4   Bench testing a Zener Diode. Showing ammeter and voltmeter connections for test purposes

Electrical

J

3 Gradually increase the current feed via the Rheostat, whilst observing both meters:

(a) The series connected ammeter must indicate zero amps, up to 12·75 volts which will be indicated on the shunt connected voltmeter as current is increased.

(b) Increase current still further until lower current indicated is 2·0 amps. At this value the Zener voltage should be within 13·5 volts to 15·3 volts.

TEST CONCLUSIONS

If the ammeter in test (a) registers any current at all *before* the voltmeter indicates 12·75 volts, then a replacement Zener diode must be fitted.

If test (a) is satisfactory but in test (b) a higher voltage than that stated is registered on the voltmeter *before* the ammeter indicates 2·0 amps, then a replacement Zener diode must be fitted.

SECTION J6

BATTERY – ELECTRICAL

A single, compact, 12-volt, high-efficiency lead acid battery with ultra-high discharge rate, is now fitted to the Mk III Electric-start Commando.

The makers of the YUASA YB14L have developed a uniquely thin separator using a specially treated, micro porous, plastic membrane; permitting nine plates per cell to be accommodated in this remarkably compact unit.

The battery acid is visible through the casing and the electrolyte level is clearly marked on the case. A breather vent is fitted. The vent is totally sealed during transportation and pre-service storage, to avoid deterioration of the plates, but must now *be opened to atmosphere* before filling the cells with electrolyte.

Table 1   Maker's Data: Battery Capacity

Battery Type	YB.14.L
Voltage	12 volts
Capacity (at 10 hour rate)	13 amp/hour
Normal Charging Current	1·3 amps
Total Volume of Electrolyte	0·81 liters
Specific Gravity at 20°C (68°F) – Tropical	1·240
Specific Gravity at 20°C (68°F) – Temperate	1·280

Initial Charging

With the introduction of electric starting the demand on the battery has increased the need for careful initial servicing, and to ensure maximum performance and life the recommended routine should be strictly observed, as follows:

1 Remove sealing plugs and vent seal from elbow. Fit vent pipe securely to elbow.

2 Fill each cell to "UPPER LEVEL" as marked on the case. Use dilute sulphuric acid. Make sure its temperature is below 30°C/86°F and the specific gravity (strength) is correct as follows:
REQUIRED SPECIFIC GRAVITY AT 20°C/68°F
Tropical climates normally above
25°C/75°F   1·240
Temperate climates normally below
25°C/75°F   1·280

3 Leave battery to stand for 12 hours (previous instructions have stated minimum half hour). For optimum battery performance, the factory has now recommended this increased soak-period.

4 "Top-up" as required with above strength electrolyte.

5 CHARGING TIME:
The charging time needed by a new battery is determined by the number of months that have elapsed since manufacture. The date of manufacture is printed on the tape enclosed with the vent plugs. The following table confirms recommended charging times relative to age since manufacture.

Electrical

Table 2

Months after manufacture	Within 6	Within 9	Within 12	Over 12
Necessary Charging Hours	20	30	40	60

6 Charge continuously at 1·3 amps for the recommended time. As the charge "comes up" the voltage and specific gravity of the electrolyte attain their correct level and become constant, but still continue the charge for about 3 more hours with the same current after they have stabilised.

7 Near the end of the charging period, adjust the specific gravity of the electrolyte to the value shown in Table 1. After charging is completed top up to UPPER LEVEL with DISTILLED WATER.

8 Replace vent plugs. Wash off acid spillage with water. Dry off the battery.

Battery Mounting

For access to the battery, remove the left side cover by giving one half turn on the slotted fastener at the bottom of the left side cover using a coin or similar object, lifting the seat on its hinge then removing the panel up and forwards clear of the locating pegs.

To remove the battery, pull down on the battery strap buckle to disengage it from the battery carrier hook. Disconnect the heavy duty starter lead and red lead from the "+" terminal and the brown/blue lead from the "—" terminal on the battery. Slide the vent pipe clear. Lift out the battery, taking care not to spill acid.

When refitting, turn the battery so that the terminals are towards the rear of the motorcycle. If the tension on the battery strap is insufficient, the strap can be tightened through the buckle before the buckle is hooked on to the battery tray. The electrolyte level can be seen embossed on the battery casing without removal.

Battery Maintenance

Due to continual evaporation and gassing during charging, a two-weekly inspection must be made on the electrolyte level. Since the level will normally rise whilst the battery is being charged, the level must only be checked during off-charge periods. Any loss of electrolyte should be made good by the addition of distilled water until the level mark is reached. The level should not exceed this mark, for spillage may occur with subsequent damage to surrounding parts.

It is important to keep the battery connections clean and tight with the positive lead + always connected to ground (earth). Dirt and moisture must be wiped away from the battery top periodically.

If the motorcycle is stored for a period, the battery should be removed and maintained in a good state of charge every two weeks, with a short refreshing charge at 1 ampere.

CAUTION:

Do not use a naked light when inspecting the battery during charging. Because the gases given off are of an explosive nature. Always ensure the breather pipe is clear of the frame and not trapped, and connected to the battery.

Never use tap-water to top up as this may contain salts harmful to the battery.

The battery terminals must never be reversed otherwise the equipment will be damaged. Red must be earth/ground: Brown/Blue live wire.

Service Life

When material falling from the grids almost fills the sediment space below the plates the service life is over.

If the battery is left in discharged condition and plates have become white, it will no longer be serviceable.

Electrical

J

Checking the state of charge

A very small capacity hydrometer is required for this check (each cell contains 133 cc of electrolyte only). The specific gravity should be checked for each cell and the results checked with the table below:

Table 3

	SPECIFIC GRAVITY (Corrected to 15°C (60°F))	
	Climates normally below 25°C (77°F)	Climates normally above 25°C (77°F)
Fully Charged	1·270 – 1·290	1·230 – 1·250
70% Charged	1·230 – 1·250	1·190 – 1·210
Discharged	1·110 – 1·130	1·070 – 1·090

Electrolyte temperature correction:

For every 10°C (18°F) below 15°C (60°F) subtract 0·007.

For every 10°C (18°F) above 15°C (60°F) add 0·007.

A variation of more than 40 points (0·040) between any cells indicates that the battery is suspect and should be thoroughly checked by the battery manufacturer's agent.

High rate discharge check

(Battery must be at least 70% charged).

Connect voltmeter and high rate discharge resistance (0·5 ohm) across battery terminals for 15 seconds.

Directly after 15 seconds the reading should remain steady.

A lower or rapidly falling voltage indicates the battery requires charging or has a faulty cell.

BATTERY VOLTAGE	VOLTMETER READING
12	9·4

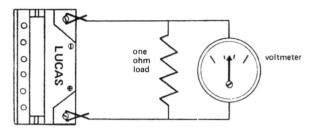

Fig. J5   High rate discharge test

Running with battery disconnected

Before running with the battery disconnected always insulate the negative (brown/blue) live lead to prevent shorting to earth on any part of the machine.

SECTION J7

WIRING

Cable Harness

The cable harness requires no maintenance beyond checking that there are no signs of chafing along its length, especially around the steering head where the harness is continually flexing. The harness must not be stretched at any point and the terminals must be clean and tight.

Fused Battery Lead

A fuse is fitted in an in-line fuse holder incorporated in the battery live (negative) lead close to the battery terminal. The fuse is of the cartridge type, in a nylon holder. If this fuse fails, it indicates a fault in the electrical system (such as a short-circuit). The cause of failure should therefore be ascertained before fitting a replacement fuse.

Access to the fuse is gained by pushing the fuse-holder body halves together and twisting. At no time must the value of 35 amps be exceeded.

Electrical

J

The correct rating of the fuse is 35A. This rating must not be exceeded, neither must the fuse holder be by-passed to overcome fuse failure.

NOTE: When refitting the battery, ensure that the fused lead is not stretched to reach the battery terminal, as this may cause an open circuit at the fuse holder.

SECTION J8

WARNING LIGHT UNIT
Early Mk III Models

Should the warning light fail to light when the ignition is switched on and with the engine stationary, disconnect the White/Brown lead from the "W L" terminal of the control unit and temporarily reconnect to the "E" terminal; if the bulb lights, this indicates that the control unit is faulty, but should the light still fail, then the bulb, connections, and associated wiring should be checked.

Warning Light Unit: Current Models (except Canada)

The former electro mechanical Lucas 3AW (Warning Light Simulator fitted on early electric starter Mk III models) has now been replaced on all models (except Canada) by a solid-state encapsulated Warning Light Control 06-6393.

When the ignition is switched on the warning light is illuminated and as engine revolutions increase the light goes out, confirming the system is working.

Automatic "Lights-on" (when running) Canada:

Canadian legislation now requires (on all machines manufactured after 1st January 1975 and imported into Canada) that the headlamps must be illuminated WHENEVER THE ENGINE IS RUNNING.

To meet these requirements a fully encapsulated device is now fitted which overrides the main switch and automatically illuminates the head and tail lamps even though the switch is in the "ignition only" position.

In addition a new Lucas master switch No. 30825 (Norton No. 06-6625) is introduced, replacing Lucas No. S149A and incorporating a revised connection in the OFF position. This does however switch on the pilot lights in the IGN position before starting the engine, but presents no problem in practice, as the pilot lights illuminate automatically immediately the engine starts.

See *Fig*. J6 for switch modes and functions.

Do not attempt to utilise the original switch in conjunction with this circuit.

Re-connect the new switch exactly as previously. Failure to do this will create incorrect external switching problems.

As the engine starts the red warning light dims and remains a warning "glow", reminding the rider that in this position of the switch his lights are "on" but are receiving *direct alternator current only*. This is acceptable for daylight running but when the engine revolutions drop – *e.g.* at traffic lights or when going slow – it is undesirable in darkness.

When the warning light is glowing, especially after dark, we strongly advise always moving the switch to "head" to feed in the main D.C. (battery) lighting circuit and maintain full brightness (especially of the tail lamp), in slow traffic or when halted and idling in darkness.

"Lights-on" Conversion Mk III Commando

Where it is necessary to convert an early Mk III model, the following action should be taken:

Remove battery cover, battery and fuel tank. On early electric starter Mk III models, remove the Lucas type 3AW part number 38717 ignition warning light simulator complete with spring from the rear frame gusset plate. On later models, remove the encapsulated ignition warning light control device, part number 06-6393 from the battery tray (taking care not to drop the bolt), and replace unit with the new headlamp warning unit, part number 06-6392.

Electrical

J

Ignition W/L Control Unit Simulator
original connections

Harness Wire	Code	Terminal	Connection
White	W	IGN	Ignition Switch
*Green/Yellow	GY	AL	Rectifier
*White/Green	WG	AL	Rectifier
White/Brown	WN	WL	Warning Light
Red	R	E	Earth (ground)

H/L Warning Unit connections

Harness Wire	Code	Terminal	Connection
Brown/Green	NG	TL	Tail Light
Green/Yellow	GY	AL	Rectifier
*White/Green	WG	AL	Rectifier
*White/Brown	WN	WL	Warning Light
Blue	U	HL	Head Light

Redundant wires (IGN and earth (ground) must be carefully insulated and securely taped back to the harness for protection). The required conversion wires will be found in the harness on later Mk III models.

*On early models, where ignition warning light simulator (Lucas part number 38717) was fitted, the rectifier leads are not included in the wiring harness. To fit the headlamp warning unit, the additional connecting wires will have to be made up and adapted.

To complete the conversion a new master switch No. 30825, Norton No. 06-6625 should be fitted and reconnected on identical contacts.

SECTION J9

MASTER SWITCH

The four-position, key operated switch, with waterproof cover, is located in the warning light console. The switch controls ignition and also energises the lighting system. The switch is a sealed unit requiring no attention other than a routine check on connections. The four switch positions are shown below in *Fig.* J6.

The four Switch Positions are:

1. **Parking Lights Only** (Ignition off)
   The key may be removed in this position enabling the machine to be parked safely at night.

2. **Off Position**
   Again the key may be removed leaving all circuits isolated. (Lights and Ignition off.)

3. **Ignition Only**: Ignition and Parking Lights engine stopped: (Canadian models): Ignition and Main lights: engine running (Canadian models).

   The key cannot be removed. This position is used during normal daytime running, not at night. See "Lights-on" electrical equipment. (Appendix to Section J8.)

4. **Ignition and Lights** (All Markets)
   Again the key may not be removed. This position is used for night riding.

The lock with keys is captive in the switch body. If for any reason the lock needs to be replaced, it can be removed from the switch body to which it is held captive by a spring operated plunger. A sharp pointed implement such as a ground-down spoke would be ideal for depressing the plunger through the hole in the side of the switch body. Whilst depressing the plunger the switch body should be shaken and the lock ejected.

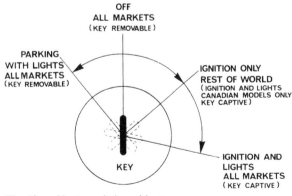

Fig. J6   Master switch positions

Electrical

CANADIAN MASTER SWITCH: Modes and Functions
Mk III Commando for Canada with Master Switch 06-6625 and Headlamp Warning Unit 06-6392

Switch Position	Connecting Contact Points – Wiring Diagram J00	Current Source	Function
1 Park	1–3	Battery	Pilot lights and instruments - ON
2 Off	None	—	OFF. All electrical circuits disconnected.
*3 Ign.	1–2–3	Direct from Alternator	Pilot lights, instruments, warning lights and ignition – ON. *Headlamp when engine runs. +Brightness varies with speed. Ignition warning light varies inversely with speed.
*4 Ign. & Lights	1–2–3–4	Battery	(a) Handlebar light switch on PILOT, function as 3. (b) Handlebar switch on HEAD. Head, tail, instruments and warning lights ON. Headlamp brightness constant. Ignition Warning Light ceases to function. When engine stops, Headlamp remains on, Ignition Warning Light remains off.

*Headlamp Dip Switch functions normally on **3** and **4**.
+Indicating need to switch to position **4** (HEAD).

SECTION J10

TESTING IGNITION SYSTEM

Testing Sequence for Ignition System

Engine; will not start – difficult to start – misfires.

(a) Check battery.

(b) Check main fuse

(c) Check for spark at both spark plugs.

(d) Ensure timing, contact breaker and spark plug gaps are satisfactory.

(e) Check capacitor by substitution.

(f) Check wiring for loose connections.

(g) Test Zener Diode and ignition system.

(h) Check ballast resistor for short circuting, when hot.

(j) *N.B.* Engine fires but will not run. Check position of "kill button". It may be in the off position.

Ignition System Tests

(a) Connect D.C. voltmeter Black lead to C.B. terminal of contact breaker and Red lead to earth.

(b) Ensure contact points are open.

(c) Switch on ignition. Voltmeter should indicate battery volts.

(d) Ignition still on, close contact points. Voltmeter reading should fall to zero.

Note: Repeat the test for each coil with its appropriate contact set.

CONCLUSION:

No reading for test (c) may indicate faulty ignition switch, open circuit primary winding, broken lead, short circuit to earth on C.B. lead, faulty capacitor or blown main fuse.

Low reading indicates high resistance in the primary circuit or across ignition switch contacts. A reading for test (d) indicates voltage drop across the contact points (dirty) or poor distributor earth.

Electrical

J

SECTION J11

IGNITION COILS

The ignition coils consist of primary and secondary windings wound concentrically about a laminated soft iron core, the secondary windings being next to the core.

The primary winding usually consists of some 300 turns of enamel covered wire and the secondary some 17,000 – 26,000 turns of much finer wire – also enamel covered. Each layer is paper insulated from the next in both primary and secondary windings.

When the contact breaker opens, causing a sudden cut-off of current flow in the primary windings, H.T. current is induced in the secondary windings and a spark occurs at the spark plug.

Note: The coils are of the oil filled type and must be protected from mechanical damage which will cause leakage.

IGNITION COILS LUCAS TYPE 17M6 (6 VOLT)

Six volt ignition coils are used in conjunction with a ballast resistor to allow their use in an otherwise 12 volt electrical system. This system has been adopted to ensure an adequate spark with the battery in a heavily discharged state. The ignition coils are sealed units, requiring only a periodic check on connections.

TESTING AN IGNITION COIL

An electrical test set is necessary for full testing of the ignition coil and though a similar set-up can be

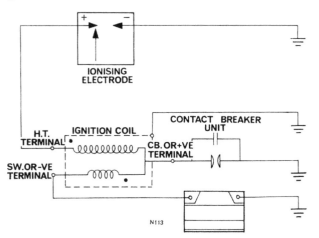

Fig. J7   *Ignition coil testing arrangements incorporating 3 point test*

produced as shown in *Fig.* J7 provision will have to be made for a contact breaker which can be motored at 100 r.p.m. Use a 6 volt battery for this test.

Before commencing the main test, check the condition of the primary windings. This is done by connecting an ohmeter across the low tension terminals. At 20°C the minimum resistance should be 1·7 ohms and maximum resistance, 1·9 ohms for 17M6 (6 volt) coils.

Set the adjustable gap to 8 mm for the 6 volt coil and connect up as in *Fig.* J7. If the coil is in good condition, sparking should occur regularly with no more than 5% missing per 15 seconds.

SECTION J12

BALLAST RESISTOR
(With 6 volt coils)

The ballast resistor is fitted across the front of the coil mounting and permits the use of 6 volt coils in an otherwise 12 volt system. The two coils are wired in parallel with the resistor in series. When the battery voltage has dropped due to the heavy current taken such as by the use of an electric starter, the ignition coils are fed direct, by-passing the resistor and thus enabling the coils to work at their approximate potential. The ballast resistor can only be tested against its resistance value of 1·8–2 ohms, and requires no maintenance except an occasional check on the security and cleanliness of the terminals.

CONTACT BREAKER ASSEMBLY – LUCAS TYPE 10CA

The contact breaker and auto advance mechanism are covered fully in Section C39 & C40 adjacent to engine ignition timing details.

SECTION J13

CONDENSER (CAPACITOR) PACK TESTING

The two condensers (capacitors) are mounted in a "tandem" pack (LUCAS RCP) behind the ballast resistor on the coil cluster bracket. The rubber cover

Electrical

J

is easily removed to gain access to the individual capacitors. The capacitors can be tested in situ. To test, turn on the ignition and take voltage readings across each set of contacts when open. If no reading is gained, the capacitor is unserviceable due to a breakdown of the internal insulation. If a reading is gained but the capacitor has reduced capacity, evidenced by excessive arcing and severe burning of the contact points, a new capacitor should be substituted on the affected cylinder.

CHANGING A CONDENSER (CAPACITOR) PACK

Remove the complete coil cluster (see Section C1). Release the capacitor pack (2 screws and nuts). Remove the rubber cover: the individual capacitors are retained to the base plate by single nuts.

Reassembly is a direct reversal of the foregoing. Take care to reconnect the wiring correctly. If necessary consult the wiring diagram at the end of this section.

EMERGENCY START CAPACITOR
(Batteryless running)
ELECTROLYTIC CAPACITOR 2MC (Fig. J8)

The capacitor is an electrolytic polarised type, spring mounted to the rear of the battery. This unit will be damaged beyond repair if it is connected incorrectly. The small ($\frac{3}{16}$ in.) terminal is the Positive ground (earth) terminal with a red spot on the terminal rivet. The double terminal is the Negative connection. The capacitor should only be fitted with the terminals pointing downwards. The battery may be removed altogether or be completely discharged whilst the 2MC capacitor permits normal starting and running. With the capacitor in use, the lights may be used whilst the engine is running though there is no parking facility.

Periodically the capacitor should be tested by disconnecting the battery terminals – the negative terminal should be insulated to prevent a possible short circuit. Start and run the engine – full lighting should be available. If the engine fails to start and run, test as follows:

(a) Disconnect capacitor.

(b) Connect capacitor direct to 12 volt battery for 5 seconds (see polarity note).

(c) Disconnect battery and let charged capacitor stand for 5 minutes.

(d) Connect D.C. voltmeter across the terminals (see polarity note) and note the steady reading* which should not be less than 9v for a serviceable unit.

*Some meters may show immediate needle overswing which should be ignored.

Polarity note: 2MC capacitors are polarity conscious and correct battery connection must be made. The smaller Lucar terminal blade (rivet marked red), is positive and the larger double Lucar connector forms the negative terminal.

Conclusions:

If meter reading is less than 9v, capacitor is leaking (inefficient) and must be replaced.

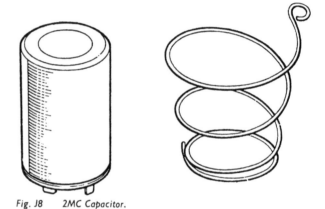

Fig. J8   2MC Capacitor.

SECTION J14

SPARK PLUGS – CHAMPION N7Y

Protruding nose self-cleaning spark plugs are fitted. It is most important to use the correct heat grade since a spark plug of too low heat grade can cause preignition and subsequent damage to the engine.

To avoid damage to the insulator, use the plug spanner provided in the tool kit to remove and refit the spark plugs. The spark plugs should be tightened firmly (not excessively) to ensure a gas tight joint.

When adjusting the gap to the recommended setting of ·028 in. (·59/·72 mm), only the side contact must be adjusted. Under no circumstances attempt to bend the centre electrode to adjust the gap.

SECTION J15

LIGHTING SYSTEM

The lighting system operates on direct current drawn from the battery (or from the rectifier where the 2MC capacitor replaces the battery) and controlled by the 4 position master switch (described in Section J10). As the master switch is turned to the "lights on" position, the tail lamp, instrument lights and pilot lamp illuminate. Selection of headlamp illumination is controlled by the

Electrical

J

switch in the warning light console. Headlamp high beam or dip beam are selected by the two position switch included in the handlebar left switch cluster.

When high beam is selected, a warning blue light in the instrument console illuminates.

All Canadian machines manufactured after 1st Jan. 1975 require lights-on when engine is running - See Section J8.

SECTION J16

HEADLAMP (SS700P or MCH66)
TO CHANGE THE HEADLAMP AND PILOT BULBS

Release the screw on top of the headlamp shell adjacent to the rim. The rim with light unit can then be lifted out from the top first. Press down the main bulbholder towards the reflector and rotate counter clockwise. The holder will lift away and the bulb can be removed. On quartz-halogen and Continental headlamps pull the adaptor free of the bulb and release the retaining clip to remove the bulb.

The pilot bulbholder complete with pilot bulb should be pulled away from the light unit. The bulb is a bayonet fitting into the bulbholder.

Note: Do not touch a quartz halogen bulb envelope with the fingers. Accidental marks can be removed with alcohol.

BULBS

Conventional filament bulbs:

U.K., U.S.A., Canada	Type 370
Continental (not France)	Type 410
France only	Type 411

Quartz Halogen type bulbs:

U.K., U.S.A., Canada	Type 463
Continental	Type 472

Parking Light bulb (Pilot bulb):

Lucas 12 volt 6 watt	No. 989

SECTION J17

TO CHANGE THE TAIL/STOPLAMP BULB

The lens is secured by two bright plated screws. Release these and lift away the lens and thin gasket. The bulb is a bayonet fitting into the bulbholder. Note that the bulb has offset pins and will only fit the correct way into the bulbholder on reassembly. Take care not to crack the lens by over-tightening the screws.

Stop/tail lamp bulb:

Lucas 12 volt 6/21 watts	No. 380

Indicator Repeater Light
Ignition Warning Light
H-beam Warning Light
Neutral Indicator Light

Each warning light has integral bulb unit which is not intended to be renewed separately. If a warning light should fail, fit a new coloured unit complete with bulb. Access can be gained simply from beneath the console. To replace, detach the two spade terminals and prise the holding clip free of the light body. When fitting the new light, ensure the clip is fitted to the body so that it is a tight fit to the console and can not rattle.

Speedometer Bulb

12 volt 2·2 watts	No. 643

After pulling down the PVC instrument case bottom cover, the bulb holder is merely a push-in fit to the bottom of the instrument and the bulb a bayonet fitting into the holder.

Tachometer Bulb

12 volt 2·2 watts	No. 643

Bulb removal is similar to that for the speedometer.

Direction Indicator Bulb

Lucas 12 volt 21 watts

Care must be taken when refitting the lenses that the screws are not over-tightened, resulting in splitting.

Electrical

J

SECTION J18

BRAKE STOP LIGHT SWITCHES, NEUTRAL INDICATOR SWITCH

Front Brake Stop Switch

A sealed, non-adjustable Lucas compression switch is incorporated in the hydraulic master cylinder. This unit cannot be serviced though a check should be made periodically on the cleanliness and security of the lead terminals.

Rear Brake Stop Switch

The rear stop switch is a sealed non-adjustable "pressure switch" fitted in the hydraulic system at the "T" piece in the pressure line and operated by fluid pressure.

The unit cannot be serviced but should be periodically checked for cleanliness and security of the lead terminals.

NEUTRAL INDICATOR SWITCH

The neutral indicator switch (new on the Mk III) is fitted in the gearbox-shell beneath the rear cross-shaft and is a sealed pressure switch, actuated by a plunger, contacting a button on the gear shift camplate in neutral only. The device is pre-set on assembly and should not be readjusted. Maintenance consists of cleaning and ensuring good electrical connections.

Current is supplied by the *white* wire to the green lamp in the warning light console, via the slate-grey wire to the connector, onward to the switch via the green cable and thence by a red wire to earth.

The unit is energised in master switch positions 3 (IGN) and 4 (IGN & LIGHTS) only.

SECTION J19

HANDLEBAR SWITCH CLUSTERS

The switch clusters are accommodated in light alloy castings. Whilst the switches are not sealed units, the method of assembly renders reassembly by an owner or dealer extremely difficult, if not impossible, and we must recommend against attempts at dismantling.

SWITCH CLUSTER: RIGHT HAND

Light Selection Switch
Engine Stop-switch: cut-out or "kill" button
Electric Starter Button

These controls are mounted in the console on the right handlebar. The lighting switch selects the "head" position by an upward movement; "pilot" position by a downward movement. (Models for CANADA only are equipped with an automatic over-riding control which illuminates head and tail lamps whenever engine is started.) See Section J8 for details.

The engine "stop" switch or kill-button is a 3 position emergency switch – move to left or right to stop engine and return (manually) to the central position before attempting to re-start.

N.B. The engine *will fire* if the starter is operated with the kill-button at "STOP" but will not continue to run!

This can be confusing, especially in the dark, and should be remembered if the engine fails to run when apparently firing. Always check that the stop button has been returned to "center" before starting.

Normally use the ignition switch to stop the engine.

STARTER BUTTON

The button is pressed in bursts to operate the electric starter. On contact the button energises the solenoid which connects the high discharge circuit to the starter motor.

SWITCH CLUSTER: LEFT HAND

Dip Switch
Direction Indicator
Horn Button and Flash

These controls are mounted in the console on the left handlebar and are marked to indicate their function.

The dip switch moves to "HI" for main (high) beam, to "LO" for dip or low beam.

The direction indicator moves horizontally, "L" for left or "R" for right.

The horn is operated by pressing the bottom button, lifting the horn button operates the headlamp flash facility.

Electrical

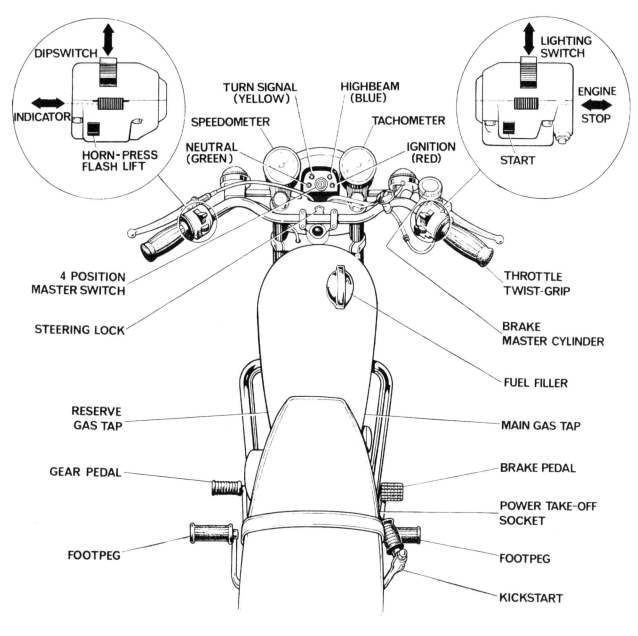

Fig. J9   Controls - Showing Handlebar switches

Switch modes and circuits

1   The starter button is fed by the white wire which contacts the red/black wire (via the starter button) to the solenoid. When operated this closes the contacts on the high-discharge circuit, feeding via the heavy-duty, black cable to the starter motor. Keep connections clean and tight, checking frequently. The white (low tension) wire to the starter button is energised in positions 3 (IGN) and 4 (IGN and LIGHTS) of the master switch; not in "PARK" or "OFF".

2   The Head/Pilot lighting switch receives its current via the blue/yellow wire with master-switch in position 4 (IGN and LIGHTS). With the button moved to the "down" position the right-hand switch isolates the blue/yellow feed from the blue wire to the dip switch in the left-hand cluster. In the "up" position the blue/yellow connects with

Electrical

the blue wire illuminating the head lamp via the left-hand dip switch, feeding either filament as directed by the "dipper".

3 **Stop-switch, "Cut-out" or "Kill-button"**
This is normally "closed". Move horizontally left or right to open switch which makes contact between the white and white/yellow wire which feeds back to the ballast resistor, onward to the ignition coils as white/purple in the ignition circuit.
The circuit is broken when the button is moved either to left or right.

4 The **dip-switch** is energised by the blue wire feeding across from the right-hand light selection switch when the button is in head position (UP). In "Hi-beam" position the switch connects the blue/white wire and illuminates the main (high) filament of the head bulb. In "LO" beam position the switch connects the blue-red, lighting the dip or low beam filament in the bulb.
The blue wire is only live in position 4 (IGN and LIGHTS) of the master switch with the selector on "head" (up).

5 The **direction indicator** (now fitted on all models as market requirement or at customer's option) are fed by the light green/brown wire from the flasher unit (Lucas type 8FL) – which in turn receives its current via the white wire as controlled by the master switch. The flasher is a sealed unit requiring no maintenance.
Sideways movement to the *right* switches in the green/white wire to the right-hand indicators.
Horizontal movement to the *left* connects the green/red of the left-hand indicators.
The direction indicators are energised in positions 3 (IGN) or 4 (IGN and LIGHTS) of the master switch.

6 The **horn button** is fed by the white wire and when pressed makes contact with the purple/black wire which connects with the horn thence via the red wire to earth. The horn push operates in position 3 (IGN) and 4 (IGN and LIGHTS).

7 The **headlamp flash** switch connects the white (horn) wire with the blue and white "main-filament wire". When the horn button is lifted up, the flash facility operates only in positions 3 (IGN) and 4 (IGN and LIGHTS).

SECTION J20

POWER TAKE-OFF SOCKET

This is located on the right side of the machine, and provides a power source for any accessory selected by the owner, providing the battery capacity is borne in mind. With the battery in good condition and fully charged it provides 12 volts at a maximum of $17\frac{1}{2}$ amps for accessories, such as a radio or shaver; an auxiliary lamp, etc. We recommend that the engine is run up as soon as possible after the power take-off socket has been used to restore the battery to a good state of charge.

Caution must be exercised not to discharge the battery completely. The same power socket is used for charging the battery from an outside source.

When appropriate, ensure that the plug is connected with the correct polarity. On this machine the positive – (indicated by a red wire) – is earthed (ground).

SECTION J21

FLASHING DIRECTION INDICATORS
Bulb replacement

To replace the bulb, unfasten the screws retaining the lens and carefully remove the lens. The bulb is then removed by pushing inwards and rotating anticlockwise. When replacing the lens, ensure that the lens body locates into the sealing gasket, before the retaining screws are tightened.

Electrical

J

Checking for faulty operation

If a fault occurs in the system, the following procedure should be adopted.

1 Check that the bulb filaments are not broken.

2 Check that all flasher circuit connections are clean and tight.

3 Switch on ignition and check with a voltmeter that the flasher terminal "B" is at battery voltage.

4 Connect together flasher unit terminals "B" and "L" and operate the indicator switch. If the flasher lamps on the respective side now light without flashing, the flasher unit is faulty and should be replaced with the same type of unit as the original.

If a flasher lamp stalk is replaced

On reassembly, take care not to damage the green lead when passing through the screw thread of the lamp shell. Final adjustment of the lamp position *must* be made by tightening of the locknut and not by straining the flasher unit.

Important

When tightening the stanchion locknut against the body of the flasher lamp, ensure that the torque loading figure of 35–45 lbs./ins. is not exceeded.

Flasher Unit Lucas Type 8FL

The unit is mounted inside the headlamps, clipped into the mounting bracket and if for any reason the bracket is to be removed, the unit must first be withdrawn from the clip.

SECTION J22

ALTERNATING HORN SET INTERPOL ONLY TYPE HC3

SPECIAL NOTE: This equipment is not available in U.S.A.

The alternating horn set comprises an alternating horn control, special 9H horns, two 6Ra relays, a switch and suitable connectors. Details of the individual units are as follows:

HC 3 Alternating Horn Control

This is a transistorised multivibrator, designed to pulse two 6Ra continuously rated relays alternately. The frequency of the unit is set during manufacture and cannot readily be altered. Hence the risk of faulty setting due to tampering is eliminated. The unit must be mounted so that its temperature does not exceed 50°C. Connection polarity must be observed. The alternating horn wiring is shown in *Fig.* J10.

Horns

These are type 9H and have been reset after a "running-in" period to ensure maximum life. They must be rigidly mounted on a solid member of the vehicle with no loosely mounted components in the vicinity otherwise the tone will be adversely affected. It is recommended that the horns are mounted facing forward. The flares should be tilted slightly downwards to allow any water entering the horn trumpets to drain out.

Relays

Standard 6Ra continuously rated relays are used. These should be so positioned that the cables carrying the horn current are as short as possible.

Electrical

J

Technical Data

Frequency of Notes	438–495 Hz
Ratio of Notes	8 : 9
Sound Intensity	90 dB at 50 ft. (15·24 m)
Cycle of Signal	1–1·2 Hz
Power Consumption	60 watts

Testing Procedure

If the horns do not sound when the switch is operated, check the voltage at the HC 3 control as follows:

1   Connect a voltmeter, red lead to the cable removed from the +ve terminal, black lead to the cable removed from the —ve terminal. Operate switch, voltmeter should read the nominal voltage of the system.

If the voltage is satisfactory at the control unit proceed to check the individual horns and relays separate from the control unit as follows:

1   Remove leads from one "R" terminal and the +ve terminal on the control unit and join together. Operate switch, the relay should be energised and the associated horn should sound, if satisfactory.

2   Repeat above operation by joining together the leads removed from the other "R" terminal and the +ve terminal.

3   If both horns and relays operate normally, the fault is in the HC 3 control unit. Replace unit.

4   If either horn does not sound, check further by earthing leads connected to "C1" in the relay. If horn now operates satisfactorily, the fault is in the relay. Replace unit.

Other faults, i.e.: continuously sounding horns, incorrect cycle of operation, etc., can be attributed to a faulty control unit, which should be replaced.

Retuning the 9H Alternating Horns

After horns have been in use for a long period there will probably be a deterioration in performance due to normal wear of the contact breaker mechanism. If the rest of the system is in order, proceed to reset the horn contacts as follows:

Contact Adjustment on Motorcycle

1   Connect a voltmeter across the terminals of the horn, to check the voltage as the adjustment is being made.

2   Connect an ammeter (range 0–25A) between terminals "C1" and "C2" of the relay which supplies the horn to be tuned.

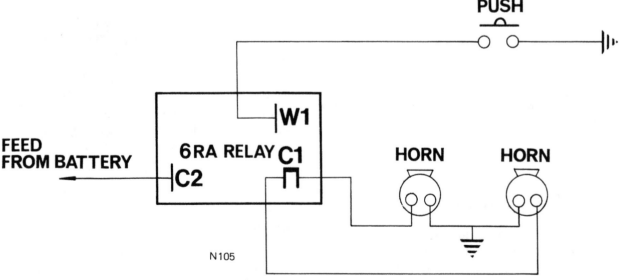

Fig. J10   Alternating horn circuit

Electrical

J

3 The adjustment screw should be tuned while operating the horn until the ammeter indicates the appropriate current consumption (see below)· Turn the screw clockwise to reduce the ammeter reading.

NOTE:

1 Do not under any circumstances disturb the centre core slotted screw and locknut.

2 It is essential, when adjusting on the vehicle, that the wiring is not overloaded. This could be caused by attempting to sound the horn, while the contacts are out of adjustment, and hence do not open. If the horn supply is fused, the fuse should be shorted out until adjustment has been completed.

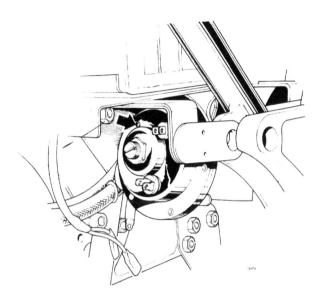

Fig. J11   Horn in position – note cross headed adjuster screw for horn contact breaker (arrowed)

Contacts Setting Data

High Note Horn

	Setting Current	Setting Voltage
12 volt	3·0 – 3·5A	13 volts

Special Low Note Horn

	Setting Current	Setting Voltage
12 volt	3·0 – 4·0A	13 volts

Horns should be checked for a good clear note over the following voltage range.

12 volt	11–12–15 volts

SECTION J23

HORN ADJUSTMENT (SINGLE STANDARD HORN)

The horn is shown in *Fig.* J11 with the adjustment screw arrowed. Adjustment will take up wear on the moving parts which, if not attended to, will cause roughness and a loss of performance.

To adjust the horn, operate the horn button and slowly turn the adjustment screw anti-clockwise until the horn just fails to sound. Release the horn button and turn the adjustment screw clockwise one notch at a time until the original performance is regained. The amount of adjustment may be expected to vary between a quarter and three-quarters of a turn. Note that if original performance is not restored, the horn must receive attention by the electrical manufacturer.

Electrical

J

SECTION J24

FITTING A LUCAR CONNECTOR

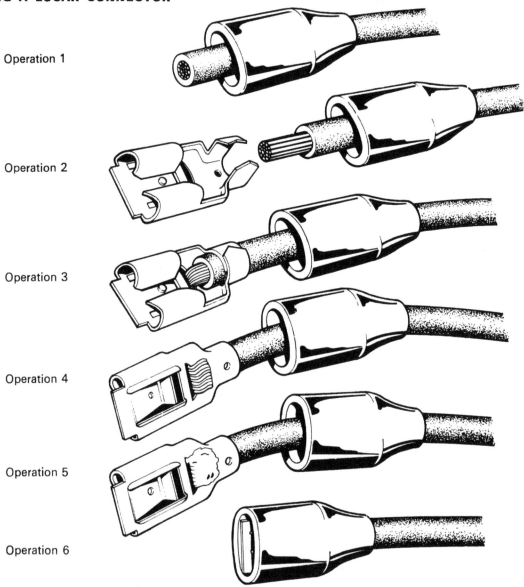

Operation 1

Operation 2

Operation 3

Operation 4

Operation 5

Operation 6

Fig. JI2 Fitting instructions for Lucar connectors

Operation 1
Thread the insulating cover over the cable.
Operation 2
strip the insulation neatly from the conductor.
Operation 3
Feed the conductors through the aperture and grip the cable firmly in the tags.
Operation 4
Splay conductors back towards the cable and spread flat.

Operation 5
Solder securely and neatly to the connector. Do not allow solder to run through the aperture.
Operation 6
Allow the joint to cool. Slide the cover over the connectors.

It is essential that the Lucar connector is fitted in accordance with the above instructions to ensure the efficient operation of the associated equipment.

Electrical

J

SECTION J25

HOW TO MAKE UP A ONE OHM RESISTOR

The 1 ohm resistor must be accurate otherwise correct voltage (or current) values will not be obtained.

A suitable resistor can be made from 4 yards 18 S.W.G. (·048 in. dia.) NICHROME wire together with two flexible leads and suitable crocodile clips, see *Fig*. J13.

To Calibrate

Bend the wire into two equal parts.

(a) Fix a heavy gauge flexible lead to centre bend of the wire, and connect this lead to the positive terminal of a 6-volt battery.

(b) Connect a voltmeter across the battery terminals.

(c) Connect an ammeter to the battery negative post.

(d) Take a lead from the other terminal of the ammeter, connect a crocodile clip to it, and connect to the free ends of the wire (which should be twisted together).

(e) Move the clip along the wire, making contact with both wires until the discharge reading on the ammeter exactly equals the number of volts shown on the voltmeter. The resistance is then 1 ohm.

(f) Cut the wire at this point, twist the two ends together and fix a second heavy gauge flexible lead.

(g) Wind the wire on to a hollow asbestos former 2 in. dia. (approximately).

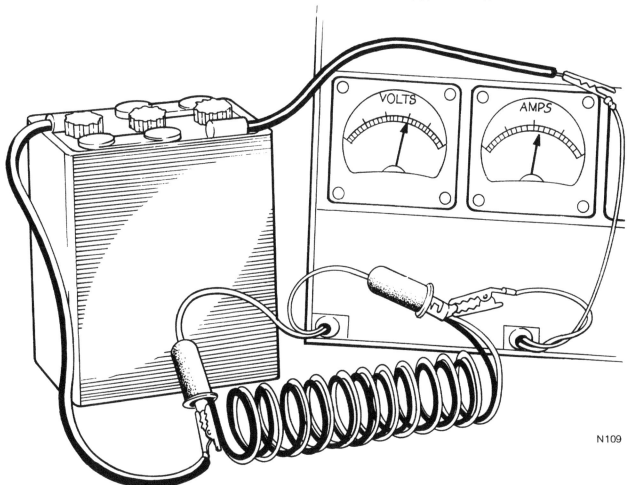

N109

Fig. J13   Construction of a one ohm resistor

Electrical

J

SECTION J26

ELECTRIC STARTER MOTOR

The Prestolite Starter Motor is an earth (ground) return machine, with series connected field coils.

Operation of the starter switch on the right-hand handlebar cluster, energises a solenoid causing its contacts to close and transmit high-discharge current (by-passing the main line fuse) via a heavy duty cable to the feed terminal on the starter, which will then operate.

MAINTENANCE/OPERATION

Ensure that the battery starter and solenoid connections are clean and always tight. If the connections become dirty clean the contact surfaces and smear with petroleum jelly, replacing the protective rubber boot on the starter terminal. No lubrication of the armature bearings is necessary between major engine overhauls when the unit should preferably be examined by an expert.

Occasionally check the mounting screws in the primary cover to ensure the motor is firmly fixed.

On cold-starting it is recommended that the initial load is reduced by always freeing the clutch with the kick-starter pedal and starting in *neutral gear* with the *clutch disengaged*. An efficient, well charged battery, is the best guarantee of reliable electric starting.

OVERHAULING STARTER MOTOR

Although the starter motor is unlikely to need attention before a very extended mileage the following information is given to users wishing to service their own unit, and using the parts-packs available.

DISMANTLING

1   Remove the rubber boot and disconnect the main-feed terminal from the starter body.

2   Unscrew the three posidrive screws from the primary cover mounting-flange, and detach the motor from its spigot collecting the large 'O'-ring

sealing the joint. The unit will withdraw complete with its driving pinion which is integral with the armature shaft. An outrigger bearing previously used at this end is no longer "bushed" since Engine No. 325689.

3   Mount the motor carcase horizontally in a vice (using protective jaws). (*Note marks on* both end covers to ensure re-assembly in the original (radial) relationship to the body.

4   Using a close-fitting ⅜" A/F ring spanner (an open wrench will invariably slip) slacken the two hexagon headed through-bolts. Considerable initial torque will be needed to "crack" the locking compound on these very secure bolts. The threads should disengage at about ¾" withdrawal length. Remove the two bolts.

5   Tap the end of the armature with wood to protect the shaft and loosen the "blind" end-cover. Stop when the cover has moved ⅛". Grasp the gear end of the shaft to prevent it moving and ease the cover off releasing the brush mounting plate which is sandwiched between the cap and body. Resistance to removal is usually due to the blind bush in the cap. It will be necessary to withdraw the cap firmly, maintaining good axial alignment with the armature which has the commutator and spring-loaded brushes at this end. The brushes are captive in closed-ended holders.

6   Now tap the commutator end of the shaft (still using the wood) and ease off the drive end-cover. Examine the bush and oil seal and determine need for replacement. Removal is straightforward as the bush is open ended and will drive out, preferably with a shouldered drift and warming the cover.

As the commutator withdraws from under the brushes they will spring out of their holders (from below). Note the method of assembly and the run of the tail-wires. The armature will now withdraw through the carcase and the commutator be examined for scouring. It is unlikely that the diameter will need truing (skimming) as the working life is not arduous, and operation only intermittent.

Electrical

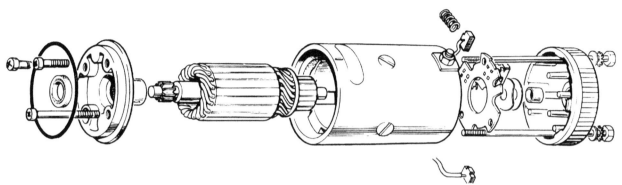

Fig. J14   Electric starter motor: Exploded arrangement: Showing order of assembly

8   Collect the thrust washer and spring-shim from the commutator end, observing the order of assembly for re-building; spring-shim next to commutator. See *Fig.* J14.

9   Withdraw the nylon terminal block from the mortice in the carcase releasing the main input brush with its tail-wire soldered to the contact. The tail can be detached with a torch or a hot iron if a replacement is needed.

10 The second brush is attached to the field windings and crimped or swaged to its terminal. The tail can be sheared off neatly (avoid dropping "bits" into the windings) and the new tail soldered to the terminal without overheating the field insulation. Make a clean neat joint using a high melting point solder, as the starter temperature can rise under extreme conditions.

11 The bush in the blind end cap will need extracting with a tap and bolt—a "hot-plate" will ease the fit if available to warm the casting.

12 With both end caps re-bushed and a replacement oil seal in the drive-cover, using the pre-sized components available as a service pack (see spares list) – the new brushes soldered to their respective contacts and tail-wires correctly insulated, proceed with re-assembly as follows.

13 Lightly smear each bush with "2% molybdenum disulphide grease", also the thrust washer and spring shim—don't over-do the quantity of grease.

14 Assemble brush-springs and brushes into their respective holders, fixing the nylon terminal block back into its mortice, position the brush plate in situ, on the carcase and, holding back the brushes against their springs, feed the armature through the field windings and insert the commutator under the brushes—which are now "Captive" again, and must be free in their holders.

15 With the thrust washer and spring shim positioned as dismantled on the commutator end, locate the brush plate squarely in place, line up the armature journal in the bush and press on the cap.

16 Assemble the drive-end cap over the gear (locating as marked before dismantling) insert the two set-screws through from the blind-cap applying a small amount of thread locking compound, and tighten up to 8 lb/ft. (1.10 Kgm). Check that the armature runs freely (as permitted by the brushes) and remember the large "O" ring seal when installing back on the cover.

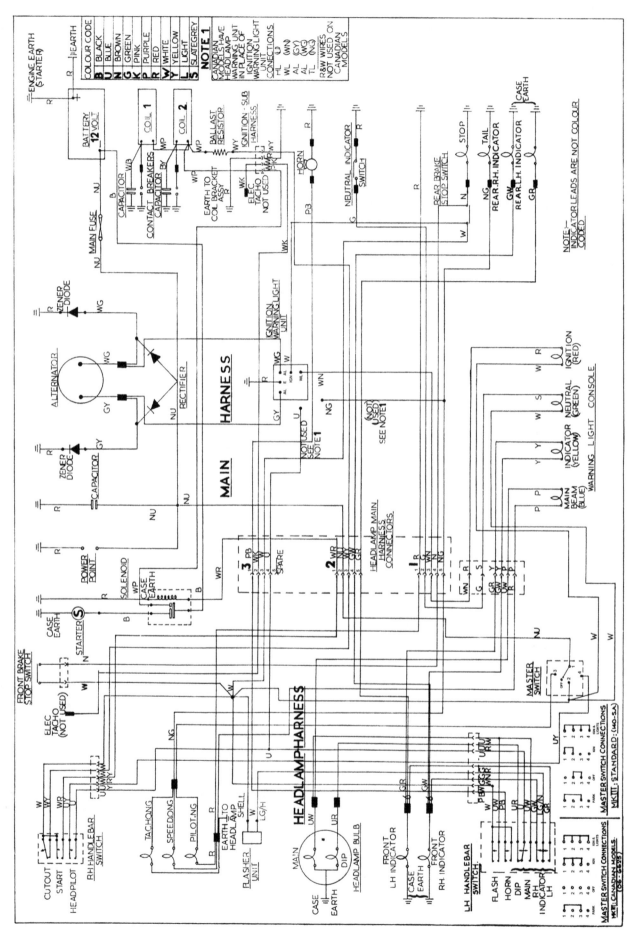

Routine Maintenance

Routine

Maintenance

Routine Maintenance

Lubrication chart

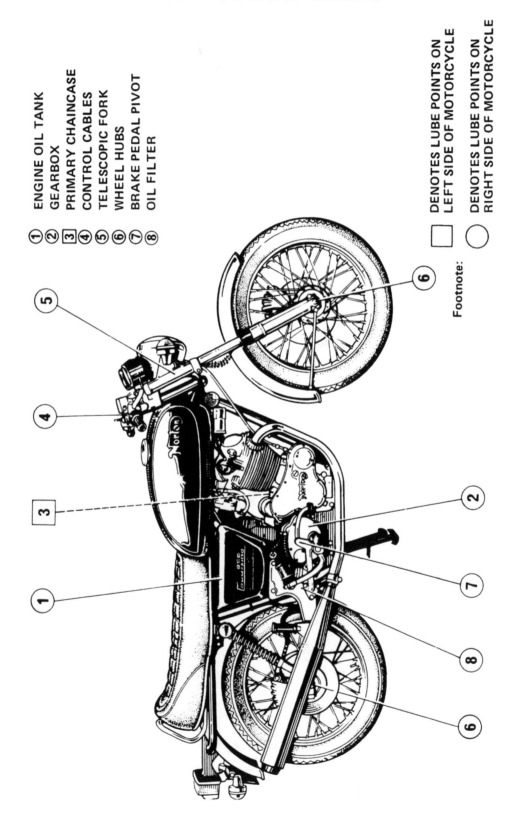

1. ENGINE OIL TANK
2. GEARBOX
3. PRIMARY CHAINCASE
4. CONTROL CABLES
5. TELESCOPIC FORK
6. WHEEL HUBS
7. BRAKE PEDAL PIVOT
8. OIL FILTER

☐ DENOTES LUBE POINTS ON LEFT SIDE OF MOTORCYCLE

○ DENOTES LUBE POINTS ON RIGHT SIDE OF MOTORCYCLE

Footnote:

Efficient lubrication is of vital importance and it is false economy to use cheap grades of oil. When buying oils or grease it is advisable to specify the brand as well as the grade and, as an additional precaution, to buy from sealed containers.

UNIT	ENGINE	PRIMARY CHAINCASE	GEARBOX	SWINGING ARM BUSHES	HUBS AND FRAME PARTS	FRONT FORKS	REAR CHAIN	EASING RUSTED PARTS
Castrol	Castrol HD40 or Castrol GTX	Castrol GTX	Castrol Hypoy	Castrol Hi-Press	Castrol LM Grease	Castrolite 10W/30	Castrol Graphited Grease	Castrol Penetrating Oil
Mobil	Mobiloil 40 or Mobiloil Super Mobiloil 20W/50	Mobiloil Super or Mobiloil 20W/50	Mobilube HD90	Mobilube HD140 or C140	Mobilgrease MP or Mobilgrease Super	Mobiloil Super	Mobilgrease MP or Mobilgrease Super	Mobil Spring Oil or Mobil Handy Oil
Esso	Uniflo or Esso Extra Motor Oil 20W/50	Esso Uniflo	Esso Gear Oil GX90/140	Esso Gear Oil GX90/140	Esso Multipurpose Grease H	Esso Uniflo	Esso MP Grease Moly	Esso Penetrating Oil
Texaco	Havoline SAE40 or Havoline 20W/50	Havoline Motor Oil 20W/50	Multigear Lubricant EP90	Multigear Lubricant EP140	Marfak All-Purpose Grease	Havoline Motor Oil 10w/30	Marfak All-Purpose Grease	Graphited Penetrating Oil
Duckhams	Flectol HDX40 or Duckhams Q20/50	Duckhams Q20/50	Duckhams Hypoid 90	Duckhams Hypoid 140	Duckhams LB10 Grease	Duckhams Q5500	Duckhams "Chainguard"	Duckhams Adpenol Penetrating Oil
Sun Oil	Sunlube 2800-C SAE50 or Sunoco Special Motor Oil	Sunoco Special Motor Oil	Sunep 1070	Sunep 140	Sunep 1130	Sunoco Special Motor Oil 20W/50	Sunoco MD2 Moly	Sunoco Penetrating Oil
Filtrate	Filtrate Racing 40 or Filtrate Super 20W/50	Filtrate Super 20W/50	Filtrate EP90	Filtrate Gear 140	Filtrate Super Lithium Grease	Filtrate AT Fluid F	Filtrate Linklyfe	Filtrate PDQ
Gulf	Gulf Formula G40 or Gulf Multi-G 20W/50	Gulf Multi-G 20W/50	Gulf Multi-purpose Gear Lubricant 90	Gulf Multi-purpose Gear Lubricant 140	Gulfcrown Grease No. 2 or Gulflex A	Gulf Multi-G 10W/30	Gulflex Moly	Gulf Penetrating Oil
BP	* BP Super Visco-Static 20W/50	BP Super Visco-Static 20W/50	BP Gear Oil SAE 90 EP	BP Gear Oil SAE 90 EP	BP Energrease L2	BP Super Visco-Static 10W/40	BP Energrease A0	BP Penetrating Oil
Shell	* Shell Super Motor Oil	Shell Super Motor Oil	Shell Spirax 90 EP	Shell Spirax 90 EP	Shell Retinax A or CD	Shell Super Motor Oil	Shell Retinax A or CD	Shell Easing Oil

LUBRICANTS RECOMMENDED

The engine lubricants recommended above are suitable for all operating temperatures above 0°C (32°F). For ambient temperatures above 32°C (90°F) HD50 monograde engine oils are recommended.

Approval is given to companies other than those listed, provided they have similar grade characteristics and meet API service SD/SE performance.

* **NO SUITABLE MONOGRADE AVAILABLE**

Routine Maintenance

SECTION K1

BREAKING IN

In the process of manufacture the best possible materials are used and all machined parts are finished to a very high standard but it is still necessary to allow the moving parts to "bed in" before subjecting the engine to maximum stresses. The future performance and reliability of the engine depends on the care and restraint exercised during its early life.

For the first 500 miles, throttle openings should be limited to about one-third of twist grip movement and the cruising speed should be varied as much as possible within this limit. Provided the engine is not allowed to labour, the actual road speed is relatively unimportant but throttle control should be smooth and the gearbox used to the full to enable the engine to cope with the prevailing conditions without undue stress. This will also assist in "break-in" of the gearbox components. At all times avoid violent acceleration.

After the 500 miles service the amount of throttle opening can be increased progressively but the cruising speed should still be varied. Full throttle should not be used until the machine has covered at least 1,000 miles and even then only for short bursts until 1,500 miles has been covered, whereupon maximum performance may be sought whenever desired.

During the "break-in" period, a certain amount of adjustment will be necessary as the components bed in. Attention should be given to valve rocker adjustment, chain tension. contact breaker points gap and brakes, all of which tend to settle down.

Do not allow the oil tank level to fall too low as with the reduced amount in circulation the oil will become unduly hot.

It is most essential to avoid glazing of the friction surfaces during the first few miles of use. During the first 50 miles only it is necessary to apply the disc brake gently to mate the friction surfaces. After 50 miles of use, the brake will be fully bedded down and ready for maximum application.

The following information is in accordance with the requirements of the U.S. National Highway Traffic Safety Administration, Department of Transportation. Part 575 Consumer Information.

Brakes should be bedded in progressively during the first 300 miles. This is achieved by gradually increasing brake lever pressure during the period, and braking from progressively increasing speeds.

For guidance refer to the table below. The deceleration in ft/sec^2 is converted to the equivalent braking time/distance.

Stage	1	2	3
Speed of commencement of stage (m.p.h.)	30	50	70
Speed at end of stage (m.p.h.)	0	30	30
Deceleration (ft/s^2)	12·5	12·5	12·5
Distance travelled (ft)	77	135	344
Time taken (sec)	3·5	2·3	4·7

Stage 1

A minimum of 20 stops using the front and rear brakes together. Decelerate from 30 m.p.h. to rest using the distance travelled or time taken to obtain the required deceleration.

Stage 2

A minimum of 50 decelerations from 50 to 30 m.p.h. using front and rear brakes together.

Stage 3

A minimum of 30 decelerations from 70 to 30 m.p.h. using front and rear brakes together.

Routine Maintenance

The distance between brake applications should not be less than $\frac{1}{4}$ mile in each case. Disengage the clutch when carrying out the procedure to ensure that the brakes receive the full braking load. The use of the above procedure, subject to traffic conditions will ensure that any high spots on the brake linings are not hardened, resulting in reduced brake efficiency. Correct burnishing will give an approximate minimum lining contact area of 50% which qualifies the published brake performance figures.

Fuels

This motorcycle (Mk III Commando) is designed to operate on fuels of at least 94 octane rating (U.K. 3-Star or U.S.A. premium).

Always ensure that the fuel used is clean and free from water. Do not allow foreign matter or water to enter the fuel tank at any time.

Any engine that shows a tendency to overheat or detonate (ping) under hard use when ignition system and carburetors are in proper order may be cured by switching brands of fuel or using fuel of a higher octane rating.

FREE SERVICE CHECK

All owners of new Commando motorcycles are entitled to a FREE SERVICE CHECK at 500 miles (800 km) or, at latest, three months after taking delivery.

This service should preferably be undertaken by the supplying dealer but can be undertaken by any Norton franchised dealer.

1   Check and adjust, if necessary:

(a)   Valve clearances.

(b)   Contact breaker. Set gap.

(c)   Ignition timing. Strobe each cylinder.

(d)   Spark plugs. Check heat range and gap.

(e)   Clutch operation and cable adjustment.

(f)   Check fluid level for both brakes.

(g)   Adjust and inspect rear chain.

(h)   Wheels. Check for freedom of rotation, bearing looseness, and spoke tension.

(i)   Wheel alignment. Check and adjust rear wheel if necessary.

(j)   Check tire pressures.

(k)   Isolastic mountings. Check for clearance and adjust.

2   Drain oil tank and sump, clean gauze strainer and tank, and replace cartridge oil filter and refill with correct grade of oil.

3   Drain and refill primary chaincase.

4   Top up gearbox.

5   Top up battery.

6   Check all electrical equipment.

7   Drain and clean carburetors.

8   Adjust and oil all control cables.

9   Grease rear brake pedal nipple.

10   Tighten all external nuts and bolts. Retorque cylinder head and base nuts.

11   Drain and refill front forks.

12   Start the engine and check for:

(a)   Oil leaks.

(b)   Oil return to tank and feed to rockers.

(c)   Alternator charging battery.

13   Road test the machine. If no other rectification is necessary; set carburetor idling adjustment. While engine is hot, tighten exhaust lockrings fully. Check for any signs of oil or fuel leakage.

The owner must pay for all replacement materials but labor and time are free of charge.

It is essential for the FREE SERVICE card to be completed, detached from inside the front cover of this manual and handed to the dealer who has carried out this service for return by him to the main distributor.

The warranty applies only to the first owner. There is no transfer of warranty under any circumstances.

Routine Maintenance

K

SECTION K2

**ROUTINE MAINTENANCE
INTRODUCTION**

This section tables the maintenance periods for various operations, co-relates these operations to other sections of this manual and details those operations not falling within the normal scope of the overhaul sections.

To obtain the best possible service from your Commando, a regular sequence of maintenance is essential. This is divided into simple checks by the rider at frequent intervals, supplemeneted by dealer serivces at set mileages. Full details of such services are given both as follows and in the service voucher booklet which you will receive automatically.

**Regular check procedures by the owner
Weekly**
Check tire pressure and wheel alignment. Use Chain-spray to lubricate rear chain.

Every two weeks
Check battery electrolyte level.

Every 250 miles (400 Km)
Check engine oil tank level.

Every 500 miles (800 Km)
Check, adjust and spray lubricate rear chain.

Every 1,000 miles (1,600 Km)
Check primary chaincase oil level.
Oil all control cables.
Check disc brake fluid levels, front and rear. Examine front and rear disc brake pads for wear.

**Service voucher chargeable by franchised
Norton dealer**

Mileage (Km)	Type of service
3,000 (5,000)	A
6,000 (10,000)	B
9,000 (15,000)	A
12,000 (20,000)	C
15,000 (25,000)	A
18,000 (30,000)	B
21,000 (35,000)	A
24,000 (40,000)	C
27,000 (45,000)	A
30,000 (50,000)	B
33,000 (55,000)	A
36,000 (60,000)	C
39,000 (65,000)	A
42,000 (70,000)	B
45,000 (75,000)	A
48,000 (80,000)	C

Service A

Check spark timing and adjust contact breaker points.

Clean spark plugs and set gaps.

Change primary chaincase oil.

Check clutch adjustment.

Change engine oil and cartridge filters.

Relubricate and adjust rear chain.

Check transmission (gearbox) oil level.

Grease rear brake pedal pivot.

Check front and rear Isolastic mountings for excessive free play.

Check and adjust valve rocker clearances.

Clean and re-oil air filter element.

Service B

Includes "A" Service – plus the following:

Change transmission (gearbox) oil.

Change oil in forks.

Check and adjust camshaft chain.

Clean contact breaker points.

Lubricate contact breaker cam felt and auto advance unit.

Clean and re-oil air filter element.

Check swinging arm bushes for wear.

Check loose or unequal spoke tension – front and rear wheels.

Rebalance wheels where necessary.

Check front and rear wheel spindle clamp nut tightness.

Check on front and rear tire tread condition and wear pattern. Rebalance wheels where necessary.

Examine and if necessary replace the rear wheel shock absorbing rubbers.

Routine Maintenance

Service C

Includes "B" Service – plus the following:

Repack wheel bearings with grease.

Dismantle and clean both carburetors and check for wear.

Adjust rear chain.

Check steering head bearings.

Check head steady and head steady mounting rubbers. Also suspensory spring. Check and tighten all front and rear engine mounting bolts.

Check swinging arm spindle.

Change hydraulic brake fluid, check flexible pipes, unions, seals.

SECTION K3

MAINTENANCE TABLE

The following table lists the normal servicing operations, the section numbers affected and the servicing intervals. The service carried out after the motorcycle has completed its first 500 miles is deliberately omitted, being outside the scope of normal routine maintenance and being covered in detail elsewhere.

		Section
Weekly	Check tire pressures and wheel alignment	K15
	Use chainspray to lubricate rear chain	K17
Every two weeks	Check battery electrolyte level	K13
Every 250 miles (400 Km)	Check engine oil tank level	K4
Every 500 miles (800 Km)	Check, adjust and spray lubricate rear chain	C42
Every 1,000 miles (1600 Km)	Check primary chaincase oil level	K8
	Oil all control cables	—
	Check disc brake fluid levels front and rear	K12
	Examine front and rear disc brake pads for wear	H9/10

Every 3,000 miles (5000 Km)	Check timing and adjust contact breaker points	C39
	Clean spark plugs and set gaps	K14
	Change primary chaincase oil	K9
	Check clutch adjustment	C35
	Change engine oil	K5
	Relubricate and adjust rear chain	C42
	Check gearbox oil level	K6
	Grease rear brake pedal pivot	H11
	Check Isolastic mounting for free play	F13/14
	Check and adjust valve rocker clearances	C10

Every 6,000 miles (10000 Km)	Change gearbox oil	K7
	Change oil in forks	K11
	Check and adjust camshaft chain	K20
	Clean contact breaker points	C39
	Lubricate contact breaker cam felt and auto advance unit	C39 & C40
	Fit new air filter element	E10
	Check loose or unequal spoke tension – front and rear wheels	
	Check front and rear wheel spindle clamp and nut tightness	
	Check front and rear tire tread and wear pattern.	
	Rebalance wheels where necessary	

Every 12,000 miles (20000 Km)	Re-pack wheel bearings (including the rear wheel sprocket bearing) with grease	H4 & H7
	Dismantle and clean both carburetors and check for wear	E3/4
	Check rear chain for wear and adjust	C42
	Check steering head bearings	
	Check head steady and head steady mounting rubbers	
	Check and tighten all front mounting and rear engine bolts	
	Check swinging arm spindle	

Routine Maintenance

SECTION K4

ENGINE OIL TANK LEVEL

The oil tank content is indicated on a dip stick incorporated in the tank filler cap which is removed by pressing and turning the cap anti-clockwise.

Access to the tank filler cap is made by releasing the seat lock, slacken right seat knob and lift the seat on its hinge.

Before filling fresh oil, run the engine for three to four minutes to return excess oil from the crankcase, observing the oil circulating through the oil tank filler orifice.

Allow the oil to settle in the tank, then fill sufficient oil of a recommended grade until the correct oil level is shown on the dipstick. The oil level should not exceed the "H" mark or fall below the "L" on the dipstick. It is most important not to exceed the "H" to prevent oil overflowing into the air filter, causing high oil consumption.

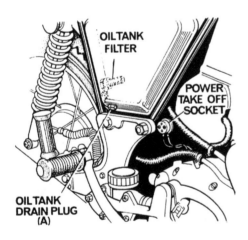

Fig. K2   Oil tank filter and drain plug

SECTION K5

ENGINE OIL CHANGING

Release the seat lock and lift the seat on its hinges. Take out the two right side cover top fixing bolts, and lift the cover clear at the bottom rubber mounting. Drain the oil from the tank by removing the oil tank drain plug. This should be carried out when the oil is

warm so that it flows more freely from the tank. (See Fig. K2, item A) The crankcase drain plug (see Fig. K3, item A) should be removed and the small amount of oil in the sump allowed to drain off.

Clean the filter and remove and clean the adjacent magnetic plug.

The filter can be dismantled for cleaning as shown in Fig. K4.

Replace the oil tank and crankcase drain plug. Fill the tank to the dip stick level with fresh oil and run the engine at a steady speed to check the oil circulation. The oil level should not exceed the "H" mark or fall below the "L" on the dipstick.

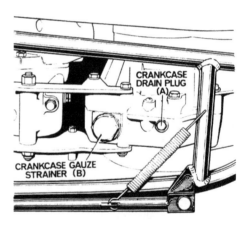

Fig. K3   Crankcase strainer and drain plug with magnetic core.

As the oil in the sump has been drained off, a moment or two will elapse before the scavenge side of the pump begins to return the oil to the tank. Run the engine for three minutes, then stop the engine and allow the oil to settle in the tank for a further two minutes. Recheck the oil level and top up as required. Finally, refit the side panel (where applicable).

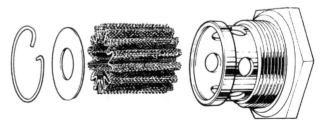

Fig. K4   Crankcase gauze strainer

Routine Maintenance

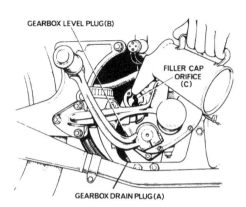

Fig. K5   Gearbox drain and level plugs

OIL TANK FILTER

A coarse mesh metal filter is incorporated with the oil feed pipe fixing bolt. This should be cleaned at 3,000 miles intervals – and when the oil is changed.

See *Fig.* K2.

CARTRIDGE TYPE OIL FILTER
(*Fig.* K6)

After the first 500 mile service, this filter must be changed at every 3,000 miles interval. The filter (shaded area) is located behind the gearbox, between the Isolastic mounting plates. To change, remove screw clamp, place oil drip-tray under filter and unscrew. Remove filter and old sealing ring. Moisten new sealing ring with oil and install new filter hand-tight only. Replace screw clamp.

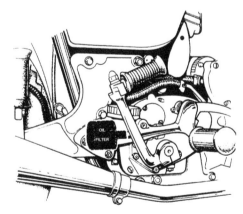

Fig. K6   Cartridge filter

OIL SEPARATOR

See Section K10 for details.
The oil separator (seen in *Fig.* K10) is fitted to the rear left side of the airbox and requires no routine attention other than a periodic check that the connection to the airbox is not disengaged. Only after considerable mileages have been covered need the separator be cleaned to prevent blockage, unless the motorcycle is continually used on very short trips where "sludging" may occur (especially in cold humid weather) requiring attention to clear the pipes more often.

SECTION K6

GEARBOX OIL LEVEL

An oil level plug is fitted in the gearbox cover (see *Fig.* K5).

To check level, remove plug (see *Fig.* K5, item B) whereupon oil should seep gently out if level is correct. If topping up is necessary, remove the filler cap (see *Fig.* K5, item C) and replenish with correct grade of oil until the oil begins to seep from the level plug orifice. Replace the filler cap and the level plug.

SECTION K7

GEARBOX OIL CHANGING

The gearbox oil should be changed after a run so that the warm oil flows more freely (see *Fig.* K5). Remove the filler cap and drain plug (A) and drain the oil into a suitable container. Replace the drain plug and fill the gearbox through the filler cap orifice (C). Allow time for oil to pass through the inner cover into the shell. When the level plug is removed, oil should run from the level plug hole (B). Allow the surplus oil to drain off and replace the level plug and filler cap. If this method is not followed a false level indication will be gained.

SECTION K8

PRIMARY CHAINCASE LEVEL

An oil level plug is fitted in the primary chaincase outer cover. (See *Fig.* K7). To check level, remove plug (see *Fig.* K7, item B) whereupon oil should seep gently out if correct. If topping up is necessary, remove the filler cap (see *Fig.* K7, item A) and replenish with correct grade of oil until the oil begins to seep from the level plug orifice. Replace the filler cap and the level plug.

Note: under no circumstances allow more than 7fl. oz. (200 cc) of oil in primary case.

SECTION K9

PRIMARY CHAINCASE OIL CHANGING

Remove the drain plug in bottom of alternator housing (preferably whilst machine is warm after a run) collecting used oil in a suitable container placed beneath the chaincase. Remove the filler cap, and level plug (B).

Routine Maintenance

Pour fresh oil into the filler cap orifice (A) until it begins to run from the level plug hole. Allow the surplus to drain off and refit the level plug and filler cap. Do not overfill.

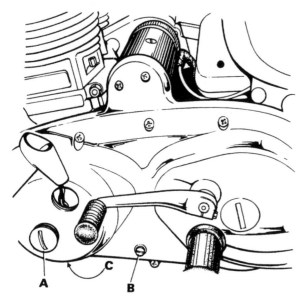

Fig. K7   Primary chaincase plugs

SECTION K10

SWINGING ARM PIVOT LUBRICATION

The Mk III swinging arm pivot is a pre-lubricated bearing, employing felt wicks, thoroughly impregnated with SAE 140 oil. (The factory use EP.140 with 2% molybdenum disulphide additive.)

The wicks feed oil to the bushes which are thus lubricated and sealed for life.

The king-pin is now rigidly cottered to its mounting on the Mk III. No routine maintenance is required.

SECTION K11

FRONT FORK OIL CHANGING

Under normal conditions the front forks will require no servicing other than an occasional change of oil. Should the oil level become low it will be indicated by excess movement of the forks, but only after considerable mileage.

Each fork leg is provided with a drain screw (see *Fig. G4*) and each leg should be treated separately. Remove the drain screw, take care not to lose the small fibre sealing washer. Take the machine off the stand, apply the front brake and move the forks up and down to expel the oil. Allow a few minutes for draining and repeat the operation with the other leg. Whilst draining the right fork leg, the forks should be turned on full right lock, and conversely for draining the left fork leg.

Refit the drain screws, place the machine on the centre stand. Remove handlebars to improve accessibility.

Unscrew the large filler plug at the top of each leg, remove the speedometer and tachometer and lift the front wheel to expose the springs.

Support the wheel with a block of wood to hold the springs clear. Using two spanners, unscrew the filler plugs from the damper rods.

Remove the wooden block and allow the forks to extend fully. Pour in a measured 150 cc (5 fl. oz.) of oil into each leg (see *Fig. K8*). Because of the springs inside the main tubes the oil will be slow to run down. Cover the top of the tube with the hand and "pump" the fork up and down to assist filling.

Expose the springs again and before refitting the filler plugs to the damper rods ensure that their locknuts are screwed down to the bottom end of the thread on the rod. Lock the filler plugs and locknuts together then screw in and tighten the filler plugs.

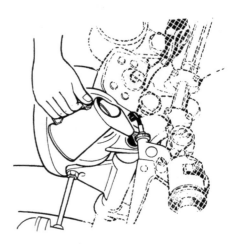

Fig. K8   Refilling fork leg with cap bolt removed

Routine Maintenance

K

SECTION K12

DISC BRAKES: FRONT AND REAR
CHECKING HYDRAULIC BRAKE FLUID LEVEL

The following instructions relate to both brakes which have common hydraulic "features".

The disc brakes are hydraulically operated. Before taking the motorcycle on the road for the first time ensure that the master cylinder reservoirs contain the correct amount of fluid.

Each master cylinder contains a flexible diaphragm seal which fits into the reservoir **over** the fluid. DO NOT FILL THIS. Lift the bellows out (*Fig.* K9) and lay on the upturned cap so that dirt does not adhere. Check that the fluid is to a level of ½ in. from the top of the reservoir and if necessary, correct the level using the recommended hydraulic fluid. Where the plain wall type of seal illustrated is fitted, collapse the diaphragm seal as shown (*Fig.* K9), replace the seal closed end downwards then refit the cap tightly. Where the seal is of the "bellows" configuration it is unnecessary to collapse this when fitting but the cap must still be refitted tightly.

Hydraulic brake fluid absorbs moisture and it is most important to keep the cap on tight and also to store the fluid only in sealed containers. The breather hole in the cap must be kept clear and no dirt or foreign matter must be allowed to enter the system.

Important

Hydraulic brake fluid must be handled with care as it will attack paintwork, certain types of rubber, and plastic.

When "topping up" or refilling the master cylinder reservoirs, use only fluid to U.S. DOT 3 specification, such as Lockheed Series 329 Fluid for Disc Brakes, obtainable under Norton part number 063111.

See Section H11 for disc brake maintenance and friction pad replacement.

SECTION K13

CHECKING BATTERY ELECTROLYTE LEVEL

For access to the battery, remove the left side cover by giving one half turn on the slotted fastener at the bottom of the left side cover using a coin or similar object, lifting the seat on its hinge then removing the panel up and forwards clear of the locating pegs.

To remove the battery, pull down on the battery strap buckle to disengage it from the battery carrier hook. (*Fig.* K10). Disconnect the heavy duty starter lead and red lead from the "+" terminal and the brown/blue lead from the "—" terminal on the battery. Slide the vent pipe clear. Lift out the battery, taking care not to spill acid.

When refitting, turn the battery so that the terminals are towards the rear of the motorcycle. If the tension on the battery strap is insufficient, the strap can be tightened through the buckle before the buckle is hooked on to the battery tray. At two weeks intervals, more frequently in hot climates, the level of the electrolyte should be checked. If necessary, add distilled water to maintain the level indicated on the side of the transparent battery case. Do not use tap water as this may contain impurities harmful to the battery. Never use a naked light when examining the cells.

If the machine is to be out of use for a lengthy period, have the battery fully charged and give it a short refreshing charge at 1 ampere about every two weeks. This will suffice to keep the battery in serviceable condition. When the battery is fully charged, the specific gravity of the electrolyte should be 1·270/1·290 at 60°F (16°C).

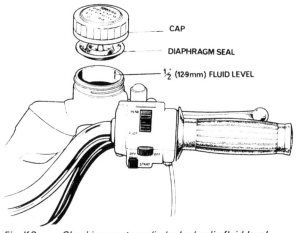

CAP

DIAPHRAGM SEAL

½ (12·9mm) FLUID LEVEL

Fig. K8   Checking master cylinder hydraulic fluid level

Routine Maintenance

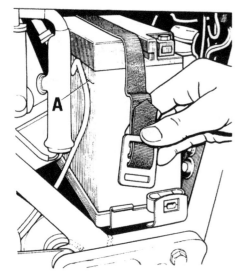

Fig. F10   Battery removal and electrolyte level checking

SECTION K14

SPARK PLUGS

It is most important to use the correct grade of spark plug, as a spark plug with a low heat factor can cause pre-ignition and subsequent damage to the engine.

The Champion N7Y is recommended for Commando engines.

To avoid damage to the insulator, use the plug spanner provided in the tool kit to remove and refit the spark plug, which should be firmly tightened to ensure a gas tight joint.

To adjust or reset the spark plug gap, this is affected by bending the earth, or side wire, which is ductile. Do not attempt to bend the centre electrode. The correct plug gap is 0·023 in. to 0·028 in. (0·59 mm to 0·72 mm).

Before refitting the plugs, see that the sealing washers are sound, and clean the threads of the spark plug body.

A smear of graphite grease applied to the threads of the plug will assist in subsequent removal.

SECTION K15

TIRE PRESSURES

Two different types of tyres, Dunlop K.81 (TT100) and Avon "GP" tyres, are used, in pairs, on Commando models. Although these tyres differ in detail, both require that tyre pressures be varied to cope with changes in the loading of the motorcycle.

The following chart lists approved tyre pressures corresponding to loads.

			lb/sq.in.	Kg/sq.cm.
Commando with one 168 lb. (76·2 Kg) rider:		Front	24	1·7
		Rear	26	1·8
Commando with two 168 lb. (76·2 Kg) riders:		Front	26	1·8
		Rear	28	1·969
Commando with two 168 lb. (76·2 Kg) riders and pannier luggage up to 100 lb. (45·36 Kg):		Front	28	1·969
		Rear	32	2·250

It is important to maintain correct tire pressure at no more than 3 p.s.i. pressure variation from above recommendation.

NOTE: Do not fit tires other than the recommended types and sizes or the handling of the machine may be adversely affected.

Larger section tires may also foul the mudguards (fenders) and stays.

Always ensure that tires are fitted in accordance with recommendation, that direction arrow points in direction of wheel rotation (when indicated on tire).

Routine Maintenance

SECTION K16

REAR CHAIN LUBRICATION

No chain oiler is fitted to the Commando. Instead, an aerosol can of "Chainspray" is provided in the toolkit. To use, support the motorcycle to allow rotation of the rear wheel. Using the extended spray tube of the can, apply lubricant to the exposed areas of the chain, rotating the wheel to gain access to all parts of the chain. The Chainspray should be used at least every week or each 500 mile interval to maintain adequate lubrication. Always protect disc to avoid spray depositing on braking surfaces.

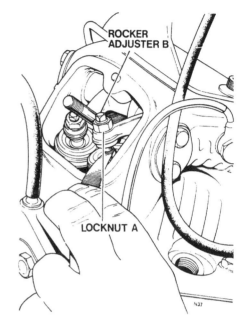

Fig. K11   Rocker adjustment

ENGINE AND IGNITION SYSTEM: ADJUSTMENTS

SECTION K17

Rocker Clearances

The rocker clearances are measured by feeler gauges inserted between the end of the valve stem and the rocker adjusting screw.

To gain access for adjustment, release the right side seat knob and seat lock and raise the seat on its hinge. Remove the fuel tank. This is attached to the frame by two nuts at the front and two bolts and a cross strap at the rear. The fuel pipe must be disconnected from both taps.

Remove the spark plugs and the three rocker covers on the cylinder head.

By means of the kick-starter pedal, rotate the engine until the left side inlet valve is fully open. With a 0·006 in. (0·15 mm) feeler gauge, check the rocker clearance of the right side inlet valve. If adjustment is necessary, slacken the right side rocker adjusting screw locknut (A) and screw the adjuster (B) out a couple of turns. Place the feeler gauge between the adjuster and the end of the valve stem and screw the adjuster in until it just nips the feeler gauge. Tighten the locknut and withdraw the gauge. It should not be tightly gripped but should slide easily through the gap.

Rotate the engine until the right side inlet valve is fully open and adjust the left side inlet valve in the same way.

Adjust the exhaust valve rocker clearances in the same sequence but using a 0·008 in. (0·2 mm) feeler gauge.

For further details refer to Engine Section C10.

SECTION K18

IGNITION TIMING/CONTACT BREAKER POINTS

See Engine Section C39 for full details of Ignition with Static and Stroboscope Methods of adjustment.

See Engine Section C40 for details of Contact Breaker adjustment and maintenance.

Routine Maintenance

SECTION K19

AUTO ADVANCE UNIT

See Engine Section C38 for full details of access, attention, etc.

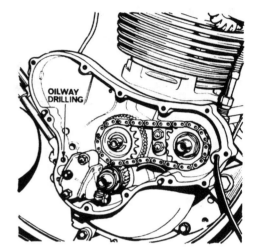

Fig. K12   Camshaft Chain / Blanking off Oil-way.

SECTION K20

ENGINE CAMSHAFT CHAIN

Engine Camshaft Chain Tension

To check tension an inspection plug is provided in the timing cover. The permissible amount of free up and down movement at the center run of the chain must not exceed $\frac{3}{16}$ in. If play is excessive, adjust as described in the following section.

Engine Camshaft Chain Adjustment

Have available timing cover gasket 06.1092.

To adjust camshaft chain, the timing cover must be removed by:

Disconnect oil union for rocker box oil pipe from timing cover.

Remove cap covering contact breaker cover (two screws).

Remove contact breaker base plate – with wires attached (two hexagon bolts).

Remove auto advance unit – use extractor bolt 06.4298.

Remove 12 screws securing cover. Tap lightly the joint face to break seal, withdraw the cover.

When the cover is removed oil will seep from drilling in crankcase. Blank off drilling. (*Fig.* K12).

The camshaft chain (*Fig.* K13) is provided with a slipper tensioning device (A). To adjust the chain, release the two nuts (B) securing the slipper, and move as required. The permissible amount of free up and down movement measured in the centre run of this chain is $\frac{3}{16}$ in.

Check chain tension in more than one position.

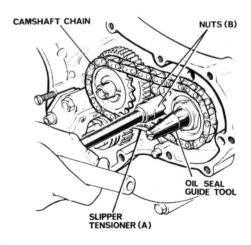

Fig. K13   Adjustment, Camshaft chain.

Retighten the two tensioner nuts when the correct adjustment has been made.

Routine Maintenance

Refitting the Timing Cover
(*Fig.* K12)

Use a new gasket to guard against oil leakage. Screw oil seal guide (supplied in tool kit) into camshaft. Put back the timing cover, firmly tighten the 12 screws.

Remove inspection cap on primary chaincase to expose indicator plate.

Position the engine on the drive side cylinder with the piston at top dead center on the firing stroke (both valves closed) until the machined mark on the rotor registers with 28° on indicator plate.

Insert the auto unit with the rivets for the bob weights in line with the two screw holes for the contact breaker cover – the slot in the cam face should be at approximately 9 o'clock.

Fit the contact breaker base plate – yellow and black lead is for the drive side cylinder.

Reset ignition timing as described in Section C39. Ensure the oilway is unplugged before refitting cover.

When the timing cover has been refitted, pour a little oil into the timing case, through the inspection plug thus providing initial lubrication for the timing gear until oil accumulates normally when running.

SECTION K21

CHAIN ADJUSTMENT

Primary Chain

The primary chain is equipped with a fully automatic oleomatic tensioner which maintains correct tension and requires no maintenance.

Rear Chain

See Engine/Primary Transmission C42 and Chains for full particulars and recommendations.

SECTION K22

CARBURETOR ADJUSTMENT

See Carburetor Section E9 for Synchronising and adjustments, cleaning, etc.

SECTION K23

AIR FILTER MAINTENANCE/CLEANING

See Section E10 for full details.

SECTION K24

CLUTCH ADJUSTMENT

The clutch control cable should be adjusted when necessary to give $\frac{3}{16}$ in. to $\frac{1}{4}$ in. (4·76 to 6·35 mm) free movement between the outer casing and the adjuster. The clutch lever inside the gearbox cover should display slight movement to confirm correct adjustment of the rod.

See Section C35 for full particulars.

SECTION K25

STEERING HEAD BEARING

The Mk III steering head uses sealed non-adjustable ball journal bearings requiring no routine maintenance. Should a bearing display malfunction it must be replaced.

See Section G6 for full details of Steering.

SECTION K26

DISC BRAKES – ADJUSTMENT

The hydraulic brakes require no adjustment except to position the lever or pedal for best rider-convenience.

See Section H11 for full particulars of Disc Brake maintenance, Pedal adjustment, Pad replacement.

Routine Maintenance

SECTION K27

ISOLASTIC ADJUSTMENT

The Mk III now incorporates "instant" screw thread adjusters front and rear. See Section F12/13 and Tech. Data for details of method and clearances.

N.B. Always remember to support the machine on a box or similar under the frame cradle or leave it on its wheels – not off the centrestand as this will exert stress on the mountings.

SECTION K28

SUSPENSORY SPRING ADJUSTMENT

Particulars of this supplementary spring device now added to the Mk III head-steady unit is dealt with in Section C1, which also shows an illustration and gives recommended limits of adjustment.

N.B. Always remember to support the machine on a box or similar, cradle, or leave it on its wheels to avoid stress in the mountings when adjusting.

Avoid tampering with the adjustment without cause. Factory settings have been checked and passed before despatch.

SECTION K29

DISC BRAKE MAINTENANCE

Major disc brake components used on front and rear installations are substantially common and particulars of the hydraulic brake apply in general to both applications.

Section H10 gives detailed instructions and information on construction.

ADJUSTMENT

The brake requires no adjustment. Wear is compensated by extra fluid passing from the master reservoir into the slave (caliper) cylinder as the pad reduces in thickness.

CAUTION

Replace the friction pads when the lining material is worn to a minimum thickness of $\frac{1}{16}$ in. (1·5 mm).

Should the brake become "spongy" in operation or have excessive lever travel, the brake hydraulic system should be examined and rectified by a Norton dealer.

SECTION K30

TRACING TROUBLE

Engine fails to start, or is difficult to start, may be due to:

Ignition not switched on.
Electrical short.
Water on high-tension coils or contact breaker.
Moisture on spark plugs.
Oiled up, or fouled, spark plugs.
Throttle opening too large.
Carburetor pilot jet choked.
Air lever in open position or bad air leak at carburetor joints.
Lack of fuel because of insufficient flooding.
Lack of fuel because pipe, or tap, obstructed.
Excessive flooding of carburetor (with hot engine only).
Valve not seating properly.
Contacts points dirty.
Incorrect contact point gap.
Kill switch at "off" position.
Electric starter disconnected (use kickstart).
Solenoid disconnected or defective (use kickstart).

Engine misfire may be due to:

Defective or oiled spark plugs.
Defective engine-to-frame earth wire.
Defective spark plug wire.
Incorrect contact point gap.
Contact breaker points loose.
Oil on contact breaker points.
Rocker adjustment incorrect.
Water in carburetor.
Air filter clogged.
Broken wire shorting on frame.
Partially obstructed petrol supply.
Disconnected carburetor balance pipe.

Routine Maintenance

Loss of power may be due to:

Faulty spark plugs.
Lack of oil in tank.
No rocker clearance, or too much clearance.
Weak or broken valve spring.
Sticky valve system.
Valve not seating properly.
Brakes adjusted too closely.
Badly fitting or broken piston rings.
Punctured carburetor float.
Engine carbonised.
Retarded ignition.
Clogged air filter.
Unsuitable fuel.

Engine overheats may be due to:

Lack of proper lubrication. (Quality or quantity of oil.)
Faulty spark plugs.
Air control to carburetor out of order.
Punctured carburetor float.
Engine carbonised.
Weak valve springs.
Pitted valve seats.
Worn piston rings.
Ignition setting incorrect.
Automatic timing control faulty.
Low octane fuel.

Engine stops suddenly may be due to:

Water on high tension coils or spark plugs.
Loose coil connections.
No petrol in tank, or choked petrol supply. Vent hole in petrol tank filler cap choked.
Choked main jet.
Water in carburetor float chamber.
Oiled up or fouled spark plugs.

Electric starter does not function may be due to:

Badly discharged battery.
Bad electrical connections.
Excessive engine oil viscosity.

Excessive petrol consumption

Excessive petrol consumption may be due to:
Leaks in the petrol feed system.
(Damaged fibre washers, loose union nuts on piping, defective float needle action).
Incorrect ignition settings. (Ignition not advanced sufficiently).

Steering unsatisfactory

Wheels out of alignment.
Front and/or rear tire tread not correctly manipulated to run true with wheel (causes handlebar oscillation at low road speed).
Tire treads worn flat.
Excessive luggage mounted too high or too far back.
Wheels out of balance.
Loose front or rear wheel spindle or wheel bearings.
Slackness of steering head bearings and swing arm spindle bushes.
Unequal suspension action caused by incorrect quantity or grade of oil in fork or dissimilar rear suspension unit settings.
Loose spokes — front and rear wheels.
Loose engine bolts.
Loose or broken engine head steady.
Isolastic mounting clearances in excess of 0·010 in. (0·254 mm).

Disc brake "spongy"

Air in brake hydraulic system.
Brake requires bleeding.

Abnormal tire wear

Abnormal tire wear may be due to:

Incorrect tire pressure.
Wheels not in alignment.
Harsh driving methods. (Misuse of acceleration and braking).

VELOCEPRESS MANUALS - MOTORCYCLE

1930'S BRITISH MOTORCYCLE CARBS & ELEC COMPONENTS (BOOK OF)
1930'S BRITISH MOTORCYCLE ENGINES (OVERHAUL & MAINTENANCE)
1930'S BRITISH MOTORCYCLE GEARBOXES & CLUTCHES (BOOK OF)
AJS 1932-1948 SINGLES & TWINS 250cc THRU 1000cc (BOOK OF)
AJS 1945-1960 SINGLES 350cc & 500cc MODELS 16 & 18 (BOOK OF)
AJS 1955-1965 SINGLES 350cc & 500cc (BOOK OF)
ARIEL UP TO 1932 (BOOK OF)
ARIEL 1932-1939 PREWAR MODELS (BOOK OF)
ARIEL 1933-1951 (WORKSHOP MANUAL)
ARIEL 1939-1960 4 STROKE SINGLES (BOOK OF)
ARIEL 1958-1964 LEADER & ARROW (BOOK OF)
BMW R26 R27 (1956-1967) FACTORY WORKSHOP MANUAL
BMW R50 R50S R60 R69S (1955-1969) FACTORY WORKSHOP MANUAL
BRIDGESTONE 90 SERIES FACTORY WSM & PARTS CATALOGUE
BRIDGESTONE 175 SERIES FACTORY WSM & PARTS CATALOGUE
BRIDGESTONE 350 SERIES FACTORY WSM & PARTS CATALOGUES
BSA BANTAM ALL MODELS FROM 1948 ONWARDS (BOOK OF)
BSA SINGLES & V-TWINS UP TO 1927 (BOOK OF)
BSA SINGLES & V-TWINS UP TO 1930 (BOOK OF)
BSA SINGLES & V-TWINS UP TO 1935 (BOOK OF)
BSA SINGLES & V-TWINS 1936-1939 (BOOK OF)
BSA OHV & SV SINGLES 250-600cc 1945-1959 (BOOK OF)
BSA OHV & SV SINGLES 250cc (ONLY) 1954-1970 (BOOK OF)
BSA OHV SINGLES 350 & 500cc 1955-1967 (BOOK OF)
BSA TWINS 1948-1962 (BOOK OF)
BSA TWINS 1962-1969 (SECOND BOOK OF)
CYCLEMOTOR (BOOK OF)
DOUGLAS 1929-1939 PREWAR ALL MODELS (BOOK OF)
DOUGLAS 1948-1957 POSTWAR ALL MODELS FACTORY SHOP MANUAL
DUCATI 160cc, 250cc & 350cc OHC MODELS FACTORY SHOP MANUAL
HONDA 50 ALL MODELS UP TO 1970 INC MONKEY & TRAIL (BOOK OF)
HONDA 90 ALL MODELS UP TO 1966 (BOOK OF)
HONDA 125-150cc TWINS C/CS/CB/CA FACTORY WORKSHOP MANUAL
HONDA 250-305 TWINS C/CS/CB FACTORY WORKSHOP MANUAL
HONDA 450 CB/CL 1965-1974 K0 TO K7 WORKSHOP MANUAL
HONDA C100 SUPER CUB FACTORY WORKSHOP MANUAL
HONDA C110 SPORT CUB 1962-1969 FACTORY WORKSHOP MANUAL
HONDA TWINS & SINGLES 50cc THRU 305cc 1960-1966 (BOOK OF)
HONDA TWINS ALL MODELS 125cc THRU 450cc UP TO 1968 (BOOK OF)
INDIAN PONYBIKE, BOY RACER & PAPOOSE ILL PARTS LIST & SALES LIT
J.A.P. ENGINES 1927-1952 & MOTORCYCLES 1934-1952 (BOOK OF)
LAMBRETTA 1947-1957 ALL 125 & 150cc MODELS (BOOK OF)
LAMBRETTA 1957-1970 LI & TV MODELS (SECOND BOOK OF)
MATCHLESS 1931-1939 ALL MODELS 250cc THRU 990cc (BOOK OF)
MATCHLESS 1945-1956 350 & 500cc SINGLES (BOOK OF)
MATCHLESS 1955-1966 350 & 500cc SINGLES (BOOK OF)
NEW IMPERIAL ALL SV & OHV FROM 1935 ONWARDS (BOOK OF)
NORTON 1932-1939 PREWAR MODELS (BOOK OF)
NORTON 1932-1947 (BOOK OF)
NORTON 1938-1956 (BOOK OF)
NORTON 1955-1963 MODELS 19, 50 & ES2 (BOOK OF)
NORTON 1955-1965 DOMINATOR TWINS (BOOK OF)
NORTON 1960-1970 TWIN CYLINDER FACTORY WORKSHOP MANUAL
NORTON 1970-1975 COMMANDO FACTORY WORKSHOP MANUAL
NORTON 1975-1978 MK 3 COMMANDO FACTORY WORKSHOP MANUAL
NSU PRIMA 1956-1964 ALL MODELS (BOOK OF)
NSU QUICKLY 1953-1963 ALL MODELS (BOOK OF)
PANTHER 1932-1958 LIGHTWEIGHT MODELS 250 & 350cc (BOOK OF)
PANTHER 1938-1966 HEAVYWEIGHT MODELS 600 & 650cc (BOOK OF)
RALEIGH MOPEDS 1960-1969 (BOOK OF)
RALEIGH MOTORCYCLES 1919-1933 (BOOK OF)
ROYAL ENFIELD 1934-1946 SINGLES & V TWINS (BOOK OF)
ROYAL ENFIELD 1937-1953 SINGLES & V TWINS (BOOK OF)
ROYAL ENFIELD 1946-1962 SINGLES (BOOK OF)
ROYAL ENFIELD 1958-1966 250cc & 350cc SINGLES (SECOND BOOK OF)
ROYAL ENFIELD 736cc INTERCEPTOR FACTORY WORKSHOP MANUAL
RUDGE 1933-1939 (BOOK OF)
SUNBEAM 1928-1939 (BOOK OF)
SUNBEAM 1946-1957 S7 & S8 (BOOK OF)
SUZUKI 50cc & 80cc UP TO 1966 (BOOK OF)
SUZUKI T10 1963-1967 FACTORY WORKSHOP MANUAL
SUZUKI T20 & T200 1965-1969 FACTORY WORKSHOP MANUAL
SUZUKI TWINS 1962 ONWARDS 125-500cc WORKSHOP MANUAL
TRIUMPH 1935-1939 PREWAR MODELS (BOOK OF)
TRIUMPH 1935-1949 (BOOK OF)
TRIUMPH 1937-1951 (WORKSHOP MANUAL)
TRIUMPH 1945-1955 FACTORY WORKSHOP MANUAL
TRIUMPH 1945-1958 TWINS (BOOK OF)
TRIUMPH 1956-1969 TWINS (BOOK OF)
VELOCETTE 1925-1970 ALL SINGLES & TWINS (BOOK OF)
VESPA 1951-1961 (BOOK OF)
VESPA 1955-1963 125 & 150cc & GS MODELS (SECOND BOOK OF)
VESPA 1955-1968 GS & SS (BOOK OF)
VESPA 1963-1972 90, 125 & 150cc (THIRD BOOK OF)
VILLIERS ENGINE UP TO 1959 INC. 3 WHEELERS (BOOK OF)
VILLIERS ENGINE UP TO 1969 (BOOK OF)
VINCENT 1935-1955 (WORKSHOP MANUAL)
YAMAHA 1961-1967 YA5 & YA6 (WORKSHOP MANUAL & ILL PARTS LIST)
YAMAHA 1971-1972 JT1& JT2 (WORKSHOP MANUAL & ILL PARTS LIST)

VELOCEPRESS TECHNICAL BOOKS – MOTORCYCLE

CATALOG OF BRITISH MOTORCYCLES (1951 MODELS)
LUCAS ELECTRONICS BRITISH M/CYCLES REPAIR & PARTS (1950-1977)
MOTORCYCLE ENGINEERING (P.E. Irving)
MOTORCYCLE ROAD TESTS 1949-1953 (Motor Cycle Magazine UK)
SPEED AND HOW TO OBTAIN IT (Motor Cycle Magazine UK)
TUNING FOR SPEED (P.E. Irving)

VELOCEPRESS MANUALS - THREE WHEELER'S

BSA THREE WHEELER (BOOK OF)
VINTAGE MORGAN THREE WHEELER (BOOK OF)

VELOCEPRESS MANUALS - AUTOMOBILE

ALFA ROMEO GIULIA WORKSHOP MANUAL 1300 TO 2000cc 1962-1975
ALFA ROMEO GIULIA TECH MANUAL CARBURETED CARS FROM 1962
ALFA ROMEO GIULIA TECH MANUAL FUEL INJECTED CARS FROM 1969
ALFA ROMEO GIULIETTA & GIULIA 750 & 101 SERIES 1955-1965 WSM
AUSTIN-HEALEY SPRITE & MG MIDGET WORKSHOP MANUAL 1958-1971
BMW 600 LIMOUSINE FACTORY WORKSHOP MANUAL
BMW 600 LIMOUSINE OWNERS HAND BOOK & SERVICE MANUAL
BMW 2000 & 2002 1966-1976 WORKSHOP MANUAL
BMW ISETTA FACTORY WORKSHOP MANUAL
CORVAIR 1960-1969 WORKSHOP MANUAL
CORVETTE V8 1955-1962 WORKSHOP MANUAL
FIAT 500 FACTORY WORKSHOP MANUAL 1957-1973
FIAT 600, 600D & MULTIPLA FACTORY WORKSHOP MANUAL 1955-1969
JAGUAR E-TYPE 3.8 & 4.2 SERIES 1 & 2 WORKSHOP MANUAL
JAGUAR MK 7, 8, 9 & XK120, 140, 150 WORKSHOP MANUAL 1948-1961
METROPOLITAN FACTORY WORKSHOP MANUAL
MGA & MGB OWNERS HANDBOOK & WORKSHOP MANUAL
MG MIDGET TC, TD, TF & TF1500 WORKSHOP MANUAL
PORSCHE 356 1948-1965 WORKSHOP MANUAL
PORSCHE 911 2.0, 2.2, 2.4 LITRE 1964-1973 WORKSHOP MANUAL
PORSCHE 911 2.7, 3.0, 3.2 LITRE 1973-1989 WORKSHOP MANUAL
PORSCHE 912 WORKSHOP MANUAL
TRIUMPH TR2, TR3, TR4 1953-1965 WORKSHOP MANUAL
VOLKSWAGEN TRANSPORTER, TRUCKS & WAGONS 1950-1979 WSM
VOLVO 1944-1968 ALL MODELS WORKSHOP MANUAL

VELOCEPRESS TECHNICAL BOOKS - AUTOMOBILE

FERRARI 250/GT SERVICE AND MAINTENANCE
FERRARI GUIDE TO PERFORMANCE
FERRARI OWNER'S HANDBOOK
FERRARI TUNING TIPS & MAINTENANCE TECHNIQUES
HOW TO BUILD A FIBERGLASS CAR
HOW TO BUILD A RACING CAR
HOW TO RESTORE THE MODEL 'A' FORD
MASERATI OWNER'S HANDBOOK
OBERT'S FIAT GUIDE
PERFORMANCE TUNING THE SUNBEAM TIGER
SOUPING THE VOLKSWAGEN
SOLEX CARBURETORS (EMPHASIS ON UK & EU AUTOMOBILES)
SU CARBURETORS (EMPHASIS ON UK AUTOMOBILES)
WEBER CARBURETORS (EMPHASIS ON ALFA & FIAT)

VELOCEPRESS BOOKS & GUIDES - AUTOMOBILE

ABARTH BUYERS GUIDE
COMPLETE CATALOG OF JAPANESE MOTOR VEHICLES
FERRARI 308 SERIES BUYER'S AND OWNER'S GUIDE
FERRARI BERLINETTA LUSSO
FERRARI BROCHURES AND SALES LITERATURE 1946-1967
FERRARI BROCHURES AND SALES LITERATURE 1968-1989
FERRARI OPP, MAINTENANCE & SERVICE H/BOOKS 1948-1963
FERRARI SERIAL NUMBERS PART I - ODD NUMBERS TO 21399
FERRARI SERIAL NUMBERS PART II - EVEN NUMBERS TO 1050
FERRARI SPYDER CALIFORNIA
HENRY'S FABULOUS MODEL "A" FORD
MASERATI BROCHURES AND SALES LITERATURE

VELOCEPRESS BOOKS – RACING

CARRERA PANAMERICANA - MEXICAN ROAD RACE (BOOK OF)
DIALED IN - THE JAN OPPERMAN STORY
IF HEMINGWAY HAD WRITTEN A RACING NOVEL
VEDA ORR'S NEW REVISED HOT ROD PICTORIAL

AUTOBOOKS WORKSHOP MANUALS & BROOKLANDS ROAD TEST PORTFOLIOS

FOR A COMPLETE LISTING OF THE AUTOBOOKS & BROOKLANDS TITLES THAT WE CURRENTLY HAVE AVAILABLE, PLEASE VISIT OUR WEBSITE.
www.VelocePress.com

Printed in the USA
CPSIA information can be obtained
at www.ICGtesting.com
LVHW070005210224
772409LV00011B/507